AIRLINE FINANCE

Airline Finance
Third Edition

PETER S. MORRELL
Cranfield University, UK

ASHGATE

Published by
Ashgate Publishing Limited
Wey Court East
Union Road
Farnham
Surrey GU9 7PT
England

Ashgate Publishing Company
Suite 420
101 Cherry Street
Burlington, VT 05401-4405
USA

Ashgate website: http://www.ashgate.com

British Library Cataloguing in Publication Data
Morrell, Peter S., 1946-
  Airline finance
  1. Airlines - Finance
  I. Title
  387.7'1

Library of Congress Cataloging-in-Publication Data
Morrell, Peter S., 1946-
 Airline finance / by Peter S. Morrell. -- [3rd ed.].
    p. cm.
 Includes bibliographical references and index.
 ISBN 978-0-7546-7000-1
 1. Airlines--Finance. I. Title.

 HE9782.M67 2007
 387.7'1--dc21

2006034812

ISBN 13: 978 0 7546 7000 1 (Hbk)
ISBN 13: 978 0 7546 7134 3 (Pbk)

Reprinted 2007, 2008, 2009

Mixed Sources
Product group from well-managed
forests and other controlled sources
www.fsc.org Cert no. SA-COC-1565
© 1996 Forest Stewardship Council
FSC

Printed and bound in Great Britain by
MPG Books Ltd, Bodmin, Cornwall.

Contents

List of Figures

List of Tables

Preface

The purpose of the book is to provide, as far as possible, a broad understanding of all areas of airline finance. To do this, it has been necessary to sacrifice some detail, but sometimes accountants and industry specialists will be directed to other texts to explore more complex topics further. In many cases, however, these other texts do not exist, at least in an air transport industry context. This significant gap, at least at the level of the non-specialist, is the main reason for this book. While there are obviously numerous financial management, corporate finance and related texts available, none of these provide explanations, as this book does, for some of the quirks of the airline industry (for example, the accounting treatment of frequent flyer programmes or the various aircraft leasing options available). Furthermore, none of them provide worked examples based solely on the air transport industry.

It is hoped that each area of airline financial management will be discussed in sufficient depth to satisfy both those in the industry without any financial background, and newcomers to the industry perhaps with some knowledge of finance. No prior knowledge is required of, for example, accounting, economics or statistics to gain considerable benefit from the book. In a few cases, notably in the chapters on investment appraisal and aircraft leasing, mathematical formulae have been used, but in such cases they are based on relatively simple compound interest concepts, and generally confined to a separate appendix at the end of the chapter.

The opening chapter describes the financial trends for the airline industry as a whole, with developments for the major regions and airlines also contrasted. This is followed by a step by step analysis of an airline's financial statements. British Airways has been chosen as an example because of the way it presents its published financial statements with sufficient clarity and detail for the reader to obtain a good understanding. Other airlines' accounts are also introduced to contrast different approaches, especially the AMR Corporation (the parent of American Airlines) and in the following chapter to compare financial performance and ratios.

The valuation of an airline as a whole, its route rights and airport take-off and landing slots are dealt with next, covering the techniques applied both in equity IPOs (Chapter 6) and airline privatisation (Chapter 7). First sources of finance are discussed and the institutions that specialise in airline financing. This is followed by a new chapter on equity finance that looks at way start-up airlines are financed. The application of some the key techniques in financial analysis are then explained and applied to the airline industry, supported by practical examples faced by airline planners. The role played by hedging and derivatives in the airline industry is introduced in the next chapter, again supported by actual airline examples. Fuel price hedging has been expanded in this third edition, both because of its close relationship with currency hedging, also because of its more widespread use by airlines and greater relevance. Leasing is examined in some detail, and aircraft securitisation is explained, as well as a new chapter on airline bankruptcy before concluding with an evaluation of the financial prospects of the industry. Wherever possible, the links between the various elements of airline finance will be highlighted, although the textbook nature of the book will ensure that each chapter and topic could be consulted separately.

Finally, it would be impossible to mention all those who have contributed, knowingly or otherwise, to the book. Over the past years, MSc students of air transport management at Cranfield University have made numerous valuable comments, pointed out errors, and generally provided the motivation for the development of much of the material presented here. Over the same period, airline industry executives attending one week airline finance short courses at Cranfield University have done the same, albeit from a different perspective. Special thanks must also be extended to senior airline industry experts who have given up their precious time to contribute to those courses (and my understanding of the industry), in particular more recently: Ian Milne of British Airways; Alan Robinson of ALM; John Ludden and colleagues from GECAS; Kevin Jones of ECGD; Alan Meldrum and colleagues from KPMG, and Andrew Lobbenberg, a former colleague now with ABN Amro.

I am also grateful to all my colleagues in the Department of Air Transport at Cranfield's College of Aeronautics for their help in discussing both industry trends and the more specific concepts included in this book.

Chapter 1

Industry Financial Performance

1.1 World Airline Financial Results

The airline industry has over the years been buffeted by both economic cycles and threats from terrorism and epidemics. Following seven years of good profitability that stemmed from a relatively long world economic upswing between 1994 and 2000, it suffered a severe setback in the 2000s with the post 'year 2000' downturn and the aftermath of 9/11. Cumulative net losses of the world's scheduled airlines amounted to US$20.3 billion between 1990 and 1993, but this was followed by almost $40 billion in net profits between 1995 and 2000. This highlights the cyclical nature of the industry, and the need to treat with caution comments after the Gulf War recession and 9/11 about the continued ability of the industry to finance expansion.

Since the end of the early 1990s recession, the airlines' balance sheets have been considerably strengthened, even allowing for the replacement of large numbers of noisier aircraft that did not meet the current Chapter 3 standards. ICAO figures show the debt/equity ratio for the world's scheduled airlines declining from a high of 2.90:1 at the end of 1993 to 1.42:1 at the end of 1999. This had deteriorated to 2.46:1 in 2003, before improving somewhat to 2.41:1 in 2004.[1]

Clouds appeared on the horizon in 1999, with the price of jet fuel jumping from 40 cents per US gallon a barrel to 75 cents in January 2000. This led to a drop in operating profits, although net profits were maintained largely due to the sale of aircraft and non-core investments such as holdings in IT and communications companies. The dollar price of fuel in 2001 was still well below its high in 1981. At that time fuel expenses rose to just under 30 per cent of total airline operating expenses. In 2000, they were still only 12 per cent of the total, even after recent sharp increases. This has been helped by substantial advances in fuel efficiency. For example, British Airways has reduced its average fuel consumption in terms of grams per revenue tonne-km from around 440 in 1990/1991 to 345 in 1999/2000 (or by an average of 2.6 per cent a year), and is on track to meet its target of 306 g in 2010.[2]

As stated above, the fuel price started increasing alarmingly in early 1999; a further advance occurred at the end of summer 2000 to a high of 107 cents, before the price fell back to around 75 cents by the end of 2000.[3] The next period of instability was in 2004, when prices ranged from a low of 92 to a high of 157 cents per US

---

1 ICAO: Tables A–4 from Financial data.

2 British Airways, (2000), *Social and Environmental Report 2000*.

3 Lufthansa Cargo Website, (2001). Retrieved from www.lufthansa.com average of spot jet fuel prices for Rotterdam, Mediterranean, Far East Singapore, US Gulf and West Coast.

gallon. In the following year the range rocketed up to 119–223 cents, and the 2005 high of 223 cents was again reached in August 2006.

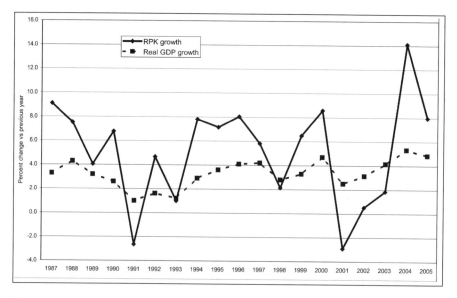

Figure 1.1   ICAO scheduled airline traffic growth *vs* world GDP growth

Some economists link any sudden and substantial rise in fuel prices to an economic recession about 18 months later. This appeared to be happening in 2001, as the downturn in the US economy began to have a serious effect on Asian exports, especially for countries such as Taiwan and Federation of Malaysia. The impact of declining GDP for the major world economies such as the US, EU and Japan has in the past led to a downturn in traffic (Figure 1.1). The first ever decline (as opposed to large reduction in growth rate) in world air traffic growth in 1991 was due to the combined effects of the Gulf War and the world economic recession, with a second in 2001.

Figure 1.2 shows the cyclical nature of past financial results for the world's scheduled airlines. As mentioned above, the impact of rising fuel prices on costs resulted in a deterioration in operating results for 1999 and 2000, and a slowing of the recovery in 2004/2005. Other cost items such as flight crew salaries also rose sharply for some airlines in 2000/2001, but this has been cushioned to some extent by lower distribution costs. The Asian financial crisis of 1997/1998 can be seen to have had little effect on the fortunes of the world's airlines, but a significant impact on a number of Asian carriers (see Figure 1.4). The SARS health threat of 2003 was more local, affecting carriers such as Cathay Pacific most severely.

The difference between the operating and net profit is caused by net interest paid, gains or losses on asset sales, taxes and subsidies, and provisions for restructuring. Interest paid is the largest of these items, and this has declined in the second half of the 1990s due to the combined effects of falling interest rates and lower debt outstanding. Profits from asset sales also make a good contribution in some years, generating over $2 billion in both 1998 and 2003.

Preliminary estimates for 2005 suggest that the recovery is continuing, and in 2006 even some of the ailing US legacy carriers reported profits. However, the cyclical pattern looks like recurring once higher oil prices start to affect consumer and business spending. Their impact on airlines in 2005–2006 could be mitigated by passing on some of fuel cost increases to consumers, against a background of strong demand. The danger is the combined impact of weak demand and continued high oil prices. The other difference this time is that more airlines are privately owned, and subsidies might be not be forthcoming. However, the re-nationalisation of Malaysian Airlines and Air New Zealand (see Chapter 7) suggests that air transport may still receive special treatment.

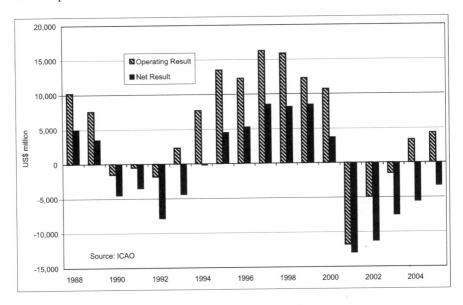

Figure 1.2   ICAO scheduled airline financial results

Subsidies approved by the European Commission for payment to just five European airlines (Olympic Airways, TAP Air Portugal, Iberia, Air France and Aer Lingus) between 1992 and 1997 totalled US$8.94 billion, or almost 17 per cent of the sum of the airlines' three previous years' revenues.[4] On the basis that they were paid in equal instalments over the 5 years, 1992–1997, this would have amounted to $1.8 billion a year. By 2006, two of these airlines had been successfully privatised, and a third radically transformed into a profitable airline expected to be privatised by 2007. The last two, TAP and Olympic, are still loss-making and defy efforts to privatisation.[5]

---

4   Cranfield University (1997), *Single Market Review, 1996: Impact on Services – Air Transport*, Kogan Page for the European Commission.

5   Unable to sell the airline, they both split off ground handling services with the intention of privatising that separately.

ICAO stress that published operating and net results are susceptible to 'substantial uncertainties'.[6] This is particularly the case with the net results, which are the small differences between estimates of large figures (revenues and expenses). Just under 15 per cent of revenues and expenses are estimated for non-reporting airlines.

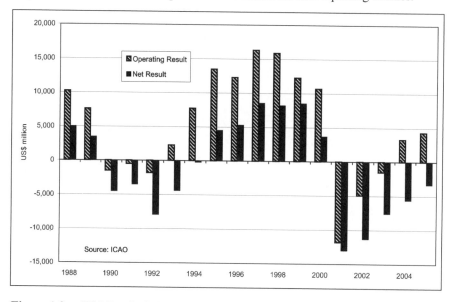

Figure 1.3   ICAO scheduled airline financial results as per cent revenues

The increased use of operating leases over the second part of the 1980s has tended to switch the emphasis of costs from non-operating interest on loans or finance leases to rentals, included in operating expenses. Thus, net interest paid would have increased further, had this trend not occurred. ICAO report that the share of aircraft rentals in operating expenses has increased from 5.3 per cent in 1994 to 7.4 per cent in 2004, despite the interest rate element of the rentals down sharply over this period.

The operating margin for the world's scheduled airlines only exceeded 5 per cent twice during the 1980s. This improved marginally to just three years in the 1990s (Figure 1.3) and none between 1998 and 2005. Smaller airlines would require higher margins to survive than larger, and two relatively small airlines, Gol of Brazil and Jet Airways of India, were amongst the top five world airlines in 2005 both with ratios of 22 per cent. Southwest, now a US major, achieved 18 per cent in 200 but was down to 10 per cent in 2005, and two Asian airlines, Singapore and Cathay Pacific, have traditionally been among the leaders of the larger world airlines.[7]

---

6   *ICAO Journal*, 18 (July/August 1996).

7   Financial Analysis: The Airline Rankings (2001), *Airline Business*, September, p. 62.

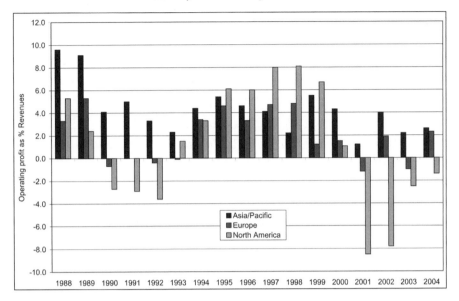

Figure 1.4   Operating result as per cent revenues by region of airline

Source: The World of Civil Aviation, ICAO

Figure 1.4 shows the financial margins for the world's airlines according to the region in which they are based. It shows that the North American airlines were hardest hit by the Gulf War recession, with a number going out of business, and the remainder surviving by obtaining new equity and debt finance. As mentioned above, some of the European airlines were more fortunate in obtaining government support. Asian based airlines were the least affected by the Gulf War recession, and experienced much better margins than airlines of other regions in the early 1990s. European airlines as a whole broke even, but the US airlines were mainly responsible for the large world airline operating losses of the early 1990s. The US airline problems in fact began before the Gulf War and early 1990s recession. Their unit costs and capacity both rose strongly in 1989 and 1990, resulting in a large loss in 1990.

A similar picture emerged after 9/11 with the North American airlines most badly affected. The European airlines recovered fairly quickly in 2002, but were hit in 2003 by the strength of the Euro, the Iraq War and SARS on Far Eastern routes.

The recovery of Asian economies, and the Asian airlines, from the region's 1997 financial crisis has been remarkable. The 18 members of the Association of Asia Pacific Airlines (AAPA) reported collective after-tax profits of US$1.88 billion for 1999/2000, a four-fold increase from the previous year. This contrasted with their combined loss of US$1.21 billion in 1997/1998, only two years previously.[8] This recovery stemmed principally from the bounce back of the economies of the region, but also from the success of implementing cost controls (apart from fuel costs which rose by 20.2 per cent) and a significant increase in staff productivity. Only two of

---

8   *Orient Aviation*, December 2000/January 2001, p. 16.

the 16 AAPA member airlines submitting data did not make an operating profit in 1999/2000: Malaysia Airlines and Royal Brunei Airlines.

In the USA, a Commission reported to the President and Congress in August 1993 on the state of the airline industry.[9] In addition to the accumulation of large amounts of debt, the Commission attributed some of the airlines' problems to the weak economy and government policies. The latter had imposed large tax increases on airlines at the beginning of the 1990s, as well as the costs of modernisation of airports and the air traffic control system. They recommended that the President should appoint an airline advisory committee, and that the Department of Transportation be more closely involved with monitoring and regulating the financial state of the industry. They also suggested various changes to the Chapter 11 bankruptcy provisions, which had perhaps conferred unfair cost advantages on a number of airlines which had sought this protection from their creditors.

The Europeans reacted in a similar way, albeit a little later, to the early 1990s problems of the industry. The European Commission appointed a committee in 1993, which included five airline representatives (out of 12) as opposed to the US Commission's two (out of 15). In their early 1994 report, the European 'Committee of Wise Men' made the following financial recommendations:[10]

- The EU should work towards easing the ownership and control restrictions in bilateral agreements.
- The EU should try to maintain and improve the access of European airlines to credit insurance.
- The European Commission should try to expand the number of financing options available to airline management.

By the time that these two reports had been digested, the industry recovery was well under way, and little government action of this nature was required. Post 9/11 in 2001, the US airline industry was again in major crisis, and this time a direct transfusion of money was required (see Chapter 12).

Figure 1.5 gives an idea of the profitability of the various business models in the early 2000s. The best financial results were achieved by the regional airlines, especially those based in the US,[11] and LCCs, with the leisure (mainly those European airlines formerly called 'charters') next best. Majors are the network carriers with annual revenues of over US$2 billion, and these were adversely affected by some of the large US carrier losses. Flag carriers are the mainline, largely government-owned, network carriers that do not fit the other categories, while 'independents' are airlines like Virgin Atlantic that are owned by private interests.

---

9   The National Commission, To Ensure a Strong Competitive Airline Industry, (1993), *Change, Challenge and Competition*, A Report to the President and Congress, August, pp. 12–18.

10   Expanding Horizons, A Report by the Comité des Sages for Air Transport to the European Commission, (January 1994), pp. 29–31.

11   Many of these contract with US majors to operate their lower density routes on a cost plus basis that gives them a reasonable return at much lower risk.

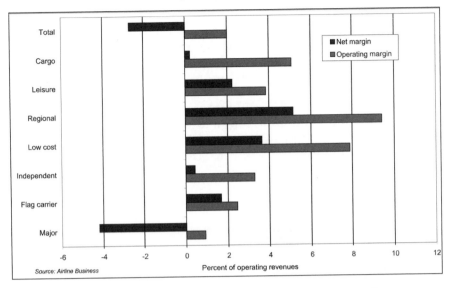

Figure 1.5 **Net/operating margins by type of carrier (average of 2003/2004/2005)**

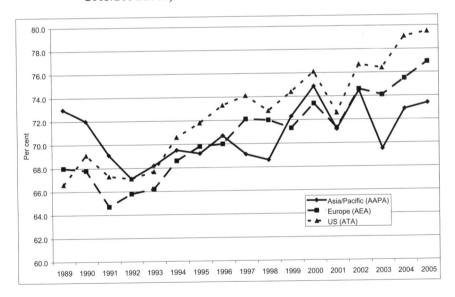

Figure 1.6 **Passenger load factor trends by major world region**

Source: Boeing, AEA, AAPA and Air Transport World Data

One of the key drivers in the subsequent airline recovery was load factors, although yield and cost trends were also clearly important. Figure 1.6 shows that the US carriers' passenger load factor was both the lowest and recovered the most. It is noticeable that load factors have converged for the airlines of the three major regions, reaching an effective ceiling given the nature of the service offered and the variation of demand by day, week and season.

Figure 1.7 shows airline return on capital over two five-year periods. It includes 30 airlines with strong coverage in each region, and together accounting for 64 per cent of the world market. Return on capital is defined as operating profit after taxes and adjusted for operating leases[12] expressed as a percentage of end-of year invested capital. The decline from the first period to the second was most marked for US airlines and to a lesser extent the European ones. However, none of the regional groups exceeded the weighted average cost of capital (WACC), which the IATA study assumed to be 7.5 per cent for the airline sector as a whole.

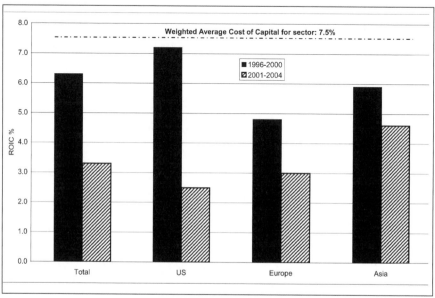

Figure 1.7   Airline Return on Invested Capital (ROIC)

Source: Value Chain Profitability, IATA Economics Briefing No. 04, June 2006

1.2   Factors Affecting Financial Results

Airline financial results are highly sensitive to small changes in either costs or revenues because of the historically high level of operational and gearing that has prevailed. Once the relatively high interest charges have been covered, increases in revenues or reductions in costs flow through to large improvements in net results, and *vice versa*. Financial gearing might be expected to decline somewhat in the future, as more assets are financed by operating leases, rather than with debt.

Airlines also display high operational gearing. This is caused by the fixed nature of operating expenses and relatively small margins on sales; this results in large swings in operating results, in the same way as described above for net results.

---

12 The interest component of operating leases is removed from aircraft rental expenses and added back into EBITA.

The degree to which operating costs are fixed depends on the time scale, and three periods can be identified:

a. *The medium term*: once the schedule has been determined, the costs associated with operating flights are relatively fixed, *i.e.*, aircraft related costs (capital), flying, technical and other skilled staff and general overheads.

b. *The short-term*: once the airline has committed to operate the flight, all the medium-term costs are fixed, as well as airport charges, fuel, ATC and certain flight related variable costs (*e.g.*, wear and tear on landing gear and tyres).

c. *The very short-term*: once the airline has committed to carry passengers on the flight, additional costs become fixed, *i.e.*, ticketing materials, in-flight food, agent commissions and fuel required to lift extra payload.

The additional costs in point b are often described as variable costs, while the additional costs in point c marginal or incremental costs. As long as the flight is not full, traffic and revenues can be increased at very little extra cost, but once additional flights need to be scheduled, costs start to escalate. Conversely, when there is an unexpected reduction in demand, induced by an economic recession or an event such as the Gulf War, airlines find it difficult to shed costs: aircraft cannot be sold, and staff contracts are difficult or expensive to break.

Many airlines have recently been trying to reduce this fixed cost burden by outsourcing and hiring part-time staff to meet traffic peaks. This allows them to return some aircraft to lessees, and adapt staff to levels of demand. There may be a trade-off in paying more for contracted out services during periods of traffic growth (and lower profits) against lower costs and reduced losses or higher profits in periods of recession.

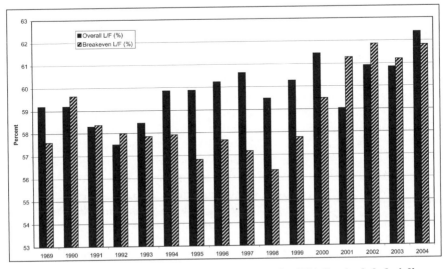

Figure 1.8   Actual and break even load factors for ICAO scheduled airlines

Source: ICAO

World airline financial results reflect the difference between the break-even and actual load factors. The former can be described as the ratio of unit costs to unit revenues (yields). This ratio remained surprisingly constant at around 58 per cent over the whole of the 1980s, dipping only in 1987 to just under 57 per cent as a result of reduced fuel costs. In the 1990s, both yields and costs declined, but the faster reduction in the latter at least until 1998 resulted in a gradual fall in break even load factor to just above 56 per cent in 1998. The continued decline in yields in the face of increased fuel costs pushed up the break even point above 60 per cent in the first half of the 2000s (Figure 1.8). The cause of declining yields was both increased competition and overcapacity that in less regulated industries might be removed by consolidation or market exit.

Overcapacity can be alleviated by grounding uneconomic aircraft. Some of these are subsequently brought back into service, but others are eventually broken up for spares or scrapped. The number of parked aircraft doubled to around 1,000 in the year following the Gulf War, as traffic declined and deliveries accelerated. This figure included a certain number that are parked even in good years on a short-term basis, either between operators or for major re-fits. It also included some brand new aircraft that went into storage direct from the factory. There were still 730 aircraft parked at the end of 1995, but, of those, 45 were Stage 1 and 230 Stage 2 aircraft, neither of which were likely to enter service because of the cost involved in hush-kiting them to meet current, more stringent, noise requirements.[13] A similar pattern emerged after 9/11 with 668 aircraft, or 6 per cent of the total IATA member airline fleet parked by 2005, down from 2002.[14] The average age of parked aircraft in 2005 was 23.6 years suggesting that many of these aircraft (such as B727s and early B737s) will never return to airline service.

1.3   Asset Utilisation

The airline industry appears to be a relatively labour intensive one in terms of the share of labour costs in total operating costs. These are between 25–35 per cent for the major scheduled airlines in North America and Europe, while capital costs, including depreciation, rentals and interest charges, amount to just over 15 per cent. This is not surprising, since it is a service industry that requires a substantial number of customer contact staff, particularly on the passenger side of the business.

However, the industry could also be described, at the same time, as capital intensive. A new Boeing 747-400 aircraft cost around US$200 million in 2005, and an increasing quantity of capital is required in the form of computers, component test equipment, ground handling automation and in other areas.

ICAO reported net fixed assets (after depreciation) of US$262 billion in 2004 for the world's scheduled airlines, compared to around $60 billion in 1985. One dollar of fixed assets produced 2.2 revenue tonne-kms (RTKs) in 1985, but this had fallen to 1.75 RTKs by 2002, increasing somewhat to 1.88 RTK by 2004.

---

13 Boeing (1996), *Current Market Outlook*, p. 4.
14 IATA World Air Transport Statistics, 2003 and 2006.

Based on an estimated 1.3 million staff employed by the world's airlines, the average net assets per employee was US$183,000 in 2002 (see Table 1.1). This had increased from about $50,000 per employee in 1986, or by over 8 per cent a year, compared to the US consumer price index increase of 3 per cent a year. Between 1999 and 2002, net assets per employee advanced by 4 per cent a year *versus* the general price index rise of 2.6 per cent a year. Inclusion of operating leased aircraft (at 7.5 times annual rental expenses) would increase the rate of growth between 1995 and 1999 and reduce it slightly between 1999 and 2002. On this basis it is clear that the industry is becoming more capital intensive although increasing less rapidly than in the early 2000s. This is caused by a combination of reduced staff numbers, increasingly expensive aircraft, and investment in new technology. It is also due to the outsourcing of the more labour intensive airline activities, for example ground handling and catering. Investment and outsourcing together led to strong growth in labour productivity of 4.8 per cent a year between 1985 and 2002, but only 2.7 per cent a year from 1999 to 2002. On the other hand, fuel efficiency gains accelerated over the latter period, as the late 1990s aircraft orders were introduced into the fleets.

Table 1.1   World airline productivity

	1985	1995	1999	2002	1985–2002 (per cent pa)
RTKs per employee (000)	144	258	295	320	4.8
RTKs per litre of fuel (index*)	187	213	213	234	1.3
Aircraft hours per year	2,179	2,751	3,031	3,001	1.9
Net assets per employee ($000)	50	153	162	183	7.9

* Index, 1965 = 100
Source: ICAO Cir 304 AT/127 and author using ICAO data

The average size of aircraft operated has been largely unchanged from 1985 to 2002, both for international services (36 tonnes) and domestic and international services combined (26 tonnes). However, the aircraft have been operated over longer sectors such that aircraft productivity in terms of ATKs per aircraft has increased in line with average sector length.

The average price of aircraft has increased at an average of 8 per cent a year between 1970 and 1995, based on the 1970 price of a B737-200 of US$4 million, and the 1995 price of the equivalent B737-500 of $28 million. This was faster than the rate of inflation of consumer prices in industrial countries, and has provided the stimulus for airlines to increase the utilisation of their aircraft. However, the price of a new B737-500 only increased marginally to $30 million by 2000, reflecting increased competition from Airbus and the slower increases in the consumer and producer price indices. Heavier discounting of new prices were evident in the period immediately after 9/11, with prices only starting to pick up again in 2003/2004.

Average aircraft utilisation for the world's airlines increased from just over 2,000 block hours per aircraft in 1985 to 3,000 hours in 2002, or by 1.9 per cent a year

(Table 1.1). However, a small dip occurred in the early 2000s, as a response to the unexpected downturn in traffic and a situation of overcapacity.

1.4   Key Financial Issues

As the industry approaches another downturn, it will be interesting to see if the same issues are as relevant as previously. Certainly, many more airlines are now privately owned (see Chapter 7) and thus might not be expected to receive the amount of state aid that they were given in the early to mid-1990s. Two national flag carriers went out of business in the early 1990s in Europe, and a number of major US airlines have been in intensive care. On the other hand, two previously privatised flag carriers in Federation of Malaysia and New Zealand were re-nationalised, and government support has continued to two or three more medium sized EU carriers.

Thus, *exit* does not seem quite as free yet as other industries, and the track record of existing airlines and other hurdles do not seem to deter new entrants unduly, at least for charter and LCC types of operation. Some rationalisation has taken place among network carriers through the bankruptcies mentioned above and the mergers of America West and US Airways, Air France and KLM and Lufthansa and Swiss. Bankruptcies and cross-border investments have also occurred in Central and South America. In other world regions, however, the national carrier is still the norm, more than likely to be still majority owned by its government.

Figure 1.9 shows how the major quoted airline stocks have performed against the world stock indices. The returns to shareholders should also include dividends paid, which are not reflected in these trends. Since airlines on the whole do not pay dividends and major industrials do, the comparison tends to overstate the airlines' performance, which has only beaten the Japanese index.

A survey of a cross-section of 25 large and small airlines based in North America, Europe and Australasia identified the most critical issues facing the industry.[15] Each airline finance director was asked to give the five most important financial issues, and those mentioned by more than six of the 25 airlines are stated hereafter.

Interestingly, debt/equity ratios were only mentioned as critical by four airlines and return on investment by three. The control of costs and the price of new aircraft are largely economic issues and not included in this book, although the financial planning aspects of fleet planning are (Chapter 8). Access to capital markets is considered in Chapters 5, 6, 7, 10 and 11, while foreign exchange exposure is covered in Chapter 9. Fuel price exposure is also discussed after exchange rates, since the two require similar approaches, and fuel prices can also have a major impact on airline profits.

---

15 IATA/KPMG (1992), *Accounting Policies, Disclosure and Financial Trends in the International Airline Industry*, August, p. 25.

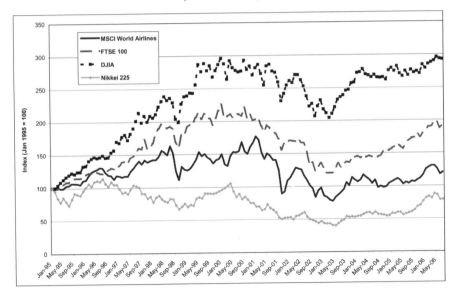

Figure 1.9   World airline stock index *vs* top share indices, 1995–2006

Issue	Number of airlines identifying as critical
Control of costs	15
Access to capital markets	13
Foreign currency exposure	9
Fleet replacement and price of new aircraft	8
Industry losses and inconsistent profitability	7
Cost of funds/low yield on surplus funds	7

More recently, airlines have devoted much management time to the formation of alliances, some tactical, but many of a more strategic nature which require the blessing of the regulatory authorities. This is arguably the easiest way for an airline to expand in scope and achieve the critical mass to compete against larger airlines and airline groups. Other ways, such as merger and acquisition can run into regulatory obstacles more quickly. Minority stakes or airline cross-investments were often used to re-affirm alliance commitments, but these have not always worked very well (e.g., KLM/Northwest and British Airways/US Air). However, the maximum stake permitted by foreign airlines has been creeping up from 25 per cent in many countries to 49 per cent in some. This may be expected to be further relaxed, and thus valuation techniques for airlines, as well as slots and route rights, should increase in importance (Chapter 4). For this, and many of the other topics discussed above, an understanding of airline financial statements and ratios is required, and these are addressed in the next two chapters.

Chapter 2

Airline Financial Statements

2.1 Introduction

The aim of this chapter is to provide an understanding of airline financial statements. The statements that are covered are the profit and loss or income statement, the balance sheet, and the cash flow statement. The value added statement and Cash Value Added (Economic Value Added) is also explained, although they are not widely used by airlines. While there are a number of introductory texts on financial statements (*e.g.*, ILO, 1995 and Reid and Myddleton, 2005), as well as more detailed texts (*e.g.*, Holmes and Sugden, 2004), they do not address specific airline industry aspects such as the treatment of frequent flyer programmes and aircraft leases. These will be discussed in this chapter, with the following chapter addressing the evaluation of airline performance by financial ratios.

There are considerable variations in the presentation and format of airline accounts world-wide, as well as the details provided in published reports. The statements of British Airways (BA) will be used throughout this and the next chapter as examples. This is because the published accounts of this airline:

- are in the English language.
- provide a reasonable amount of detail and supporting notes.
- reflect many of the more recent recommendations and standards from accounting bodies.
- were also shown in summary form according to US GAAP principles, illustrating how sensitive an airline's net profit is to accounting principles.

The financial statements of the AMR Corporation, which consists largely of the US major, American Airlines and its commuter airline subsidiaries, will also be presented and contrasted with BA. This will allow comparison between two major international airlines, incidentally both members of the same one-world strategic alliance, but based in different continents and applying different accounting standards.

The British Airways and AMR accounts will be compared, however, wherever possible with those of other airlines which use different accounting conventions and present the data in different formats.

The accounts describe the financial position of the airline at a particular moment or between two points in time. They are thus central to evaluating the performance of the management of the airline's finances. They enable the management and owners of an airline to answer two main questions:

- Is the airline operating at a profit?

- Will the airline be able to meet its financial commitments as they fall due, and so not have to close down because of lack of funds?

The system of accounts is not, however, ideally suited for management tasks such as pricing or product costing and planning, or for deriving economists' measures such as value added.

The record-making part of accounting is usually called *book-keeping*, performed by a *double-entry* system. The purpose of this chapter is not to explain how this is done, but rather how to make use of the *published* results of this system at a more general level. This analysis and interpretation of the published accounts of airlines could be the aim of the following interested parties:

- Shareholders;
- Banks, other debt holders and creditors;
- Financial analysts;
- Industry regulators;
- Employees.

Many airline managements are secretive about their financial data, and only release the minimum required by company law or stock exchange rules. Past data on yields and costs, even after some degree of aggregation, is considered to be useful to competitors. Government owned airlines are usually run as legally constituted corporations, and generally do publish annual accounts in some form, even though they may only be available a considerable time after the end of the financial year (for example through the ICAO statistical reporting programme). Airlines with stock market quotations are usually required to release financial information which is timely, in sufficient detail, and available to all at the same time. British Airways, for example, announce their results for the year ending 31 March in May of each year and publish their annual report and accounts in June. AMR report for a financial year ending 31 December, and their annual report is usually published in February.

Publicly quoted airlines generally control the release of information through an investor relations department, which in the case of British Airways also publishes a newsletter (Investor) circulated to all shareholders. This department also coordinates any special shareholder deals, such as the BA scheme whereby those owning a minimum of 200 ordinary shares receive 10 per cent off BA tickets (subject to various travel restrictions).

The directors of an airline will contract with a firm of auditors to examine the books and annual financial statements of the company on behalf of the shareholders. They will then issue a report which will conclude with their opinion as to whether the accounts give a true and fair view of the state of affairs of the company or group on a certain date, and whether they comply with company legislation. The way the auditors are hired (by management rather than directly by shareholders) has led to criticism of the objectivity of their opinions in certain cases. One answer to this has been for boards to appoint an audit committee composed largely of non-executive directors. However, it could be argued that these directors owe their position to the executives in the company in the same way as the auditors.

Individual accounts will be available from the airlines (with an increasing number now available from web sites), as well as through civil aviation authorities (*e.g.*, in the UK and Brazil), and from inspection of copies filed with governments as a result of company legislation (*e.g.*, UK Companies House). Sources giving the financial results and balance sheets of a number of different airlines in broadly comparable format are:

- International Civil Aviation Organization (ICAO), Financial Statistics, Series F.
- Stockbroker and finance house airline industry reports (distribution tends to be restricted to their clients).
- Datastream and other on-line data bases.

The last two cover only airlines with publicly quoted shares, which have sufficiently large daily trading turnover (and thus interest from institutional investors). The first is not consistent in coverage from year to year, and is only available more than a year after the end of the financial year (and from 2005 only in electronic form).

The financial year of an airline usually runs from January to December (almost all US and many other world airlines) or April to March (British Airways and many airlines based in British Commonwealth countries). Some airlines have recently changed their year-end to bring them into line at least with others in the region: Delta Air Lines changed from end June to end December. Air France moved away from a calendar year basis to a financial year ending at the end of March from 1994/1995.

2.2   Profit and Loss Account (Income Statement)

The Profit and Loss Account or Statement of Earnings summarises the revenues and expenses of the airline for the accounting period:

Revenue   Conversion of real assets into cash. Under the accrual basis of accounting, cash receipts are allocated to the period in which the related service took place.

Expenditure   Conversion of cash into real assets. Expenses are charged to Profit and Loss Account in the same accounting period as the one in which the related revenue is recognised. Certain large expenses will need to be charged over a number of years, since these assets will provide the potential to generate revenue over a period that extends well beyond the current accounting period:

- Aircraft and other fixed assets.
- Major aircraft and engine overhauls.
- Software development costs.
- Slots and new route start-up costs.
- Goodwill through the acquisition of other companies.

This process of allocation is called *depreciation* for tangible assets such as aircraft, and *amortisation* for intangible assets such as goodwill, software or the rights to routes or slots.

2.2.1   British Airways Group

British Airways (BA) only reports the Group profit and loss account, which includes the parent company and any subsidiary controlled by the parent (generally companies in which the parent owns over 50 per cent of the ordinary share capital). They do, however, report separate balance sheets for the Group (which totals all assets and liabilities from the parent and subsidiary companies) and the Company (only assets and liabilities of the airline operating company).

The Profit and Loss Account or Income Statement can be divided into:

- Trading or operating account.
- Profit and loss account or income statement.
- Appropriation account or statement of earned surplus.

The trading or operating account generally excludes interest paid or received, and any gains or losses from sales of assets, which appear in the profit and loss account.

From the presentation of BA's operating account in Table 2.1 it can be seen that some detail is provided of the breakdown of both revenues and expenses. The importance of cargo in scheduled service revenues can also be calculated (6.9 per cent in 2005/2006 compared to 8.1 per cent in 1994/1995). This report replaced the previous one that confined the breakdowns of both revenues and expenses to the notes to the accounts. The large increase in 'other revenues' occurred mainly as a result of the inclusion of fuel surcharges on air fares and cargo rates. Most airlines include these in passenger and cargo revenues but they could be identified separately or netted off against fuel expenses.

BA's 2005/2006 operating profit recovered with a 27 per cent increase from the previous year with both passenger and cargo yields up, as well as a 0.8 per cent point improvement in passenger load factor. It was also helped by keeping unit costs in check, in spite of the large increase in fuel costs.

Note 3 to the accounts gives a geographical analysis of both turnover and operating profit, which in percentage terms is shown in Table 2.3. Many airlines will show the regional distribution of turnover, but none now show the same for profits.

The network airline business accounted for 93 per cent of BA's 2005/2006 revenues, with the regional airline business 4 per cent and other non-airline activities with only 3 per cent. The latter comprised insurance, the London Eye and Air Miles Travel Promotions. Table 2.3 shows how important 'The Americas' are to BA's revenues, with the US probably accounting for a large part of this region. In previous annual reports BA gave a breakdown of operating profit for the same regions. This was discontinued since almost no other airline reported this, and it was thought to be commercially sensitive. For the last year that this was reported (2004/2005), £347 million of BA's operating profit came from the Americas, £224 million from Africa/ Mid East and India, offset by a loss of £5 million from the Far East and Australasia and £26 million from UK/Europe. The UK and Europe have historically broken even or made a small loss, but they provide valuable feed to the other regions, and the key focus is network profits. However, UK/Europe profitability has deteriorated in the early 2000s, possibly in part the result of a large increase in low cost carrier operations from the UK to Europe. The data are no longer provided, but BA reported that UK/Europe was showing a positive but small operating profit in 2005/2006.

The remainder of the profit and loss or income statement includes finance costs (*e.g.*, interest payable), finance income (*e.g.*, interest received) and any profits or losses from the sale of fixed assets. Table 2.1 above shows that in 2005/2006 BA's interest charges declined along with their debt reduction. Cash and equivalents recorded on the balance sheet rose from £1.882 million at the end of March 2005 to £2.44 billion at the end of March 2006, although finance income remained roughly the same. This cash was equivalent to 125 days of cash operating expenses (total operating expenses less depreciation) compared to only 95 days for the previous year end. Note 8 to BA's accounts shows that most of the profit from the sale of assets came from its sale of the London Eye in 2005/2006 (£26 million) and its disposal of its minority interest in Qantas (£86 million) the year before.

It also includes the share of profits from associates, which in BA's case amounted to £28 million in 2005/2006 from investments in Comair (a South African regional airline) and Iberia. An associate or associated undertaking is one where a company has a participating interest in a long-term investment. Participating means that it is able to influence the operational and financial decisions of its investment. This is usually considered to be in cases where between 20 per cent and 50 per cent of the voting shares are held. Where more than 50 per cent are held, the investment will be classed as a subsidiary and consolidated in the group accounts.

Under the old format, BA would have reported one-off restructuring costs (for example, staff redundancy schemes) under non-operating items. Now they are reported under the relevant item in operating costs (*i.e.*, redundancy under 'employee costs').

The importance of income from associates should not be underestimated: in August 2001, BA's share price fell by 10p to 315p following a report from Qantas that its profits would be £60 million lower as a result of ticket discounting in the domestic market in response to two low cost new entrants.[1]

BA's income statement includes a number of new items that now need to be reported under IAS and IFRS regulations. Part of the unrealised gains or losses from fuel hedging is shown (£19 million), and retranslation charges or credits on currency borrowings: these resulted in a net charge of £13 million, largely from US$ and Japanese Yen loans. The US$ strengthened by around 8 per cent over the financial year, increasing the sterling equivalent of the dollar loans and hence the charge to the income statement. Previously, this charge was taken from reserves (shareholders' funds on the balance sheet) and did not affect profits.

---

1   *The Times*, London, (17 August 2001).

Table 2.1   British Airways' Group consolidated income account

£ million for year ended 31 March	2005	2006
Traffic revenue	6,982	7,318
Passengers	6,500	6,820
Cargo	482	498
Other revenue (including fuel surcharges)	790	1,197
Total revenue	7,772	8,515
Employee costs	2,235	2,346
Depreciation, amortisation and impairment	739	717
Aircraft operating lease costs	106	112
Fuel and oil costs	1,128	1,632
Engineering and other aircraft costs	432	473
Landing fees and *en route* charges	556	559
Handling charges, catering and other operating costs	918	955
Selling costs	490	449
Currency differences	15	− 18
Accommodation, ground equipment and IT costs	597	585
Total expenditure on operations	7,216	7,810
Operating profit	556	705
Fuel derivative gains	—	19
Finance costs	− 265	− 221
Finance income	97	93
Financing income and expense relating to pensions	− 29	− 18
Retranslation (charges)/credits on currency borrowings	56	− 13
Profit/(loss) on sale of fixed assets and investments	71	27
Share of post-tax profits in associates	24	28
Income relating to fixed asset investments	3	—
Profit before taxation	513	620
Taxation	− 121	− 153
Profit for the year	392	467
Minority interests included in above	15	16
Earnings per share (pence)		
Basic	35.2	40.4
Diluted	34.1	39.8

Source: British Airways Plc Annual Report, 2005/2006

Table 2.2   British Airways' operating accounts

£ million, year to end March	2005	2006	% change
Passenger revenue	6,500	6,820	5
Cargo revenue	482	498	3
Other revenue	790	1,197	52
Total revenue	7,772	8,515	10
Operating expenditure	− 7,216	− 7,810	8
Operating profit	556	705	27

Table 2.3   British Airways' turnover/profit by area of sales

£ million, year to end March	2005	2006	% change
UK/Europe	5,079	5,406	6
The Americas	1,364	1,611	18
Africa, Middle East and India	747	826	11
Far East and Australasia	582	672	15
Total	7,772	8,515	10

The other new and significant item in the income statement relates to pensions: an additional amount has to be deducted from profits to make a contribution to the shortfall in pension scheme assets compared to actuarial assumptions on pension obligations that is not already reflected in 'employee costs'. It should be added that under IFRS BA now include the cost of share options granted to employees (since 2002) under 'employee costs', £1.8 million being introduced in 2005/2006 for the first time.

Finally, the statement of changes in equity shows the addition of the net income after any dividend payment, new shares issued and the various items that contributed to the net change in reserves. BA last distributed a dividend for the financial year 2000/2001 amounting to £193 million, giving retained losses of £79 million respectively. Paying out more than was earned in the year is highly unusual for an airline, and few US airlines pay dividends even in good years. BA, however, reckoned that a significant number of their shareholders (for example pension funds) would not invest in their shares without such continuity of dividend payments. However, since then BA has suspended dividend payments.

2.2.2   AMR Corporation

American Airlines (and other US carriers) show the past three years' operations whereas BA, other European and Asian airlines usually show only two years, although they generally include summary information for the past five to ten years in an appendix.

Of interest in Table 2.4 is American's success in reducing travel agent commission costs, in a year when their operating revenues increased by just over 10 per cent; these costs have declined by 22 per cent since 1994, the year before American took the initiative to cap the payments agents received for each transaction (which was followed by almost all other major US domestic carriers).

AMR's aircraft fuel costs can be seen to have risen by 41 per cent in 2005, significantly less than the increase in the spot price for jet kerosene on the US West Coast of just over 70 per cent. This difference can be explained by their hedging policy (a more general treatment of which is found in Chapter 9).

Table 2.4   American Airlines' consolidated statement of operation

US$ million, year to end December	2004	2005	% change
Passenger revenues	16,897	18,762	11
Cargo revenues	625	622	0
Other revenues	1,123	1,328	18
Total revenues	18,645	20,805	12
Wages, salaries and benefits	6,719	6,755	1
Aircraft fuel	3,969	5,615	41
Commissions to agents	1,107	1,113	1
Depreciation and amortisation	1,292	1,164	− 10
Other rentals and landing fees	1,187	1,262	6
Aircraft rentals	609	591	− 3
Food service	558	507	− 9
Maintenance: materials and repairs	971	989	2
Other operating expenses	2,377	2,809	18
Total operating expenses	18,789	20,805	11
Operating profit/(loss)	− 144	− 93	− 35

BA now include broadly similar items in their income statement as the US airlines in their statements of operations, although the expense breakdowns differ somewhat. Until 2005/2006, BA only gave the split of costs by item in a note to the then profit and loss statement. AMR already accounted for the value of stock options in their 2005 statements, but only if the price of the option was above the market value of the stock on the date of grant. From 2006, AMR will adopt new guidelines that require the application of the Black-Scholes option pricing model for calculation of their cost. Had they applied this in 2005, their loss would have increased by $42 million.

2.2.3   British Airways and AMR compared: Income statement

BA's depreciation charge for 2005/2006 amounted to 5.1 per cent of average gross fixed assets (fleet, property and equipment) employed during the year. This compared with 4.8 per cent for American Airlines (year to end December 2005), 6.6 per cent for Lufthansa (also for calendar year 2005), and 6.2 per cent for

Singapore Airlines (year to end March 2006). With the exception of Lufthansa, these values were broadly in line with the findings of a 1992 survey which showed the average per cent of cost for depreciating a B747 to be 6.8 per cent for Asian airlines, 5.1 per cent for European airlines and 4.2 per cent for North American airlines. For Boeing 737s the percentages were 8.2 per cent, 5.6 per cent and 4.2 per cent respectively (KPMG/IATA, 1992).

Singapore Airlines announced in 2001 that it would change its depreciation policy starting with the 2001/2002 accounts. Their policy for aircraft would change from straight-line depreciation over 10 years to 20 per cent residual value to 15 years to 10 per cent residual value. They had last revised their policy in 1990, and this change was to bring them more into line with other airlines. It would also be expected to boost 2001/2002 profits by S$265 million (around US$160 million).

2.2.4   Lufthansa Group and other airlines: income statement

The presentation of Lufthansa's group consolidated income statement is also prepared under IFRS, but has less detail in the main statement. However, footnotes show the breakdown in revenue, and other costs items. Traffic revenue for 2005 comprised €11,314 million from the carriage of passengers and 20 per cent or €2,590 million from freight and mail. Changes in stocks are included as a separate item, in addition to the cost of materials purchased from outside suppliers. This approach is adopted by many European airlines, but not by BA, US or Asian carriers.

Lufthansa gives a cost breakdown in footnotes to the main income statement. In 2005, the total cost of materials and services (€9.0 billion): €4,591 million for the cost of materials, of which €2,662 million was for fuel; and €4,416 million for services, €2,542 was for airport and *en-route* navigation charges, and €142 million from operating leases. The income statement also includes the financial (non-operating) result broken down into income from subsidiaries and associates, net interest and asset write-downs, minority interests and taxes.

Table 2.5   Lufthansa Group consolidated income statement

€ million, year to end December	2004	2005	% change
Traffic revenue	12,869	13,904	8
Other revenue	4,096	4,161	2
Total revenue	16,965	18,065	6
Changes in stocks and own work capitalised	85	127	49
Other operating income	1,753	1,545	− 12
Cost of materials/services	− 8,244	− 9,007	9
Staff costs	− 4,813	− 4,853	1
Depreciation, amortisation and impairment	− 1,112	− 1,398	26
Other operating expenses	− 3,680	− 3,760	2
Operating profit	954	719	− 25

With the growth of aircraft operating leases, an increasingly important inconsistency is the treatment of aircraft ownership costs. With owned aircraft, depreciation is treated as an operating cost and interest on any related finance is not. If the same aircraft is acquired under an operating lease, both depreciation and interest (combined as the rental cost) are included as operating costs. This distorts operating profit comparisons.

Other potential areas of distortion are depreciation policies, major maintenance of aircraft (which may be all included as an expense in one year, or capitalised and amortised over a number of years), and foreign exchange gains or losses. These may be further explained in the notes to the accounts. British Airways specify only a range of operational lives and residual values of their aircraft used for depreciation purposes in the notes to their accounts, but they do give the percentage rates of depreciation (which combine life and residual).

Lufthansa provide another example of the effect on operating profit of a change in depreciation policy: in 1992 the airline changed its policy from depreciating its aircraft over 10 years to a residual value of 5 per cent, to one of 12 years to 15 per cent (see Table 2.8 for example). This would have reduced the charge on a US$140 million B747 from $13.3 million to $9.9 million. The overall effect of the change was to increase Lufthansa's 1992 group profits by DM392 million (US$250 million).[2] Japan Airlines reduced their depreciation charge in April 1993 by Y17,842 million, thus reducing their operating loss for 1993/1994 to Y 29,627 million; this they did by increasing the useful lives of all aircraft except B747-400s from 10 years to 15 years (international) and 13 years (domestic).[3]

Agents' commission is generally recorded as an expense,[4] but some airlines deduct it from revenues. Frequent flyer points or credits can also be treated in a number of ways, the most common being to defer the incremental costs of providing the free travel awards. BA uses this approach for its Executive Club and Airmiles loyalty programmes, including incremental passenger service charges, security, fuel, catering and lost baggage insurance in accrued costs. Alternatively, a part of the revenue can be deferred and recognised when the free travel is provided (for a fuller explanation of how FFPs are accounted for, see Appendix 2.1 at the end of this chapter).

Goodwill arising from the acquisition of another company can be capitalised and amortised over a number of years (thus including its effect in the profit and loss account) or written off against retained earnings or reserves (and thus not appearing in the profit and loss account at all).

Finally, there are two ways of treating corporation tax: either full or partial provisioning. The first way assumes that profits will eventually be taxed, and that any generous tax allowances applicable in the year under question will only defer the tax liability to future years. A full provision for corporation tax at the applicable rate (the marginal rate in 2005 being 30 per cent in the UK, and ranges from only 12 per

---

2 Lufthansa Annual Report and Accounts (1995).
3 Japan Airlines Annual Report, 1995–1996.
4 This was the case with British Airways, which included commissions under selling costs.

cent in Ireland to almost 40 per cent in the US, Germany and Japan[5]) is made in the profit and loss account, even though this is not the tax actually charged for that year. This method in theory provides a better comparison of after tax profits over time.

However, it can be argued that the full applicable rate will never be paid, as long as the airline continues to invest in new aircraft and tax allowances of some sort continue to be available. This leads to the view that partial provisioning would give a better picture of net profits over time, based on the assumption that there will always be sizeable investment allowances against tax. The problem with this approach is the fact that investments often decline sharply, for example during recessions, and that tax allowances can also change significantly. For this reason, the UK standards board have recently come down in favour of full provisioning. Clearly, the choice of method makes a large difference to an airline's reported earnings per share, a key indicator for investment analysts.

Extraordinary items should also be given careful consideration for the following reasons:

- Treatment of ordinary or exceptional items as extraordinary (or *vice versa*) can make a very significant difference to earnings per share and other financial ratios.
- They may signal important changes in the nature of the business.
- They may give clues to the quality of management, and the future profitability of the airline.

There are two major traditions of accounting practice: one represented by the US, UK and the Netherlands whose emphasis is on providing information for investors and the capital markets, and the other, represented by Germany, France and Japan, which was driven by tax assessment requirements, and where banks rather than equity investors have tended to be more important in financing.[6] The first group produces one confidential set of accounts for the tax authorities, and publishes another for investors. The emphasis is thus on showing a good profit performance to investors. The other group are more concerned with minimising tax payments, and thus try to minimise declared profits. This group did not need to provide detailed information to investors, since they are likely to be large banks with seats on their board and access to detailed management accounts. Indeed, they see the provision of too much detail in published accounts as possibly conferring some advantages on competitors. The globalisation of capital markets and wider airline share ownership has led to a convergence of the two traditions.

There are also a number of significant differences between the UK and US accounting rules: BA made an after tax profit of £267 million in 2000/2001 under US GAAP rules, but an after tax profit of £473 million according to UK rules. The difference was largely due to the treatment of deferred taxation (£144 million) and foreign exchange losses (£72 million). Under the UK rules, certain aircraft operating

5   *The Economist*, (June 2006), p. 29.

6   McKenzie, W. (1994), *The Financial Times Guide to Using and Interpreting Company Accounts*, Pitman Books.

lease costs have been capitalised and shown as depreciation and interest; under US rules these would appear as an increase in operating expenditure (a reduction in net profits of £109 million), some of which would be offset by a reduction in depreciation (increase in net profit) of £23 million and a reduction in interest expense of £57 million.

2.3   Balance Sheet

The balance sheet (also called Statement of Financial Position) provides a classified summary at a particular date (end of the financial year or quarter) of where an airline has acquired its funds (liabilities) and how it has deployed those funds (assets). It also shows whether the funds have been borrowed on a long term basis (for periods of greater than one year), or short term basis (less than one year). The balance sheet shows the position at a particular date, while the Profit and Loss Account shows the results of transactions occurring between two dates.

The balance sheet can be presented in *Account* format or *Net Asset* format. Account format generally shows assets and liabilities on separate pages each with their own total, while the Net Asset format shows them on the same page with a total of assets less current liabilities.

The balance sheet shows what the airline *owes* as liabilities, and what the airline *owns* as assets. These must balance, or in other words total assets must always equal total liabilities (as shown by the items in *italics* below):

Net Asset Format balance sheet	
A.	Fixed (property and equipment) and other non-current assets
B.	Current assets
C.	Current liabilities
D.	Net current liabilities $(B - C)$
E.	Total assets less current liabilities $(A + D)$
F.	Long-term (fixed) debt and other long-term liabilities
G.	*Total assets less fixed and current liabilities $(E - F)$*
H.	*Capital and reserves or shareholders' funds $(= G)$*
Account format balance sheet	
Assets	*Liabilities and Shareholders' Equity*
Current assets	Current liabilities
Fixed assets	Long-term debt
(Property and equipment)	Other liabilities
Other non-current assets	Shareholders' equity (funds)
Total assets	Total liabilities

Airlines such as BA (up to financial year 2005/2006), Cathay Pacific, Singapore Airlines and AirAsia adopt the net asset format approach, albeit with some differences in the order of the main items, while the account format is used by all US and most European carriers. The first does not have a total assets line, whereas the second does. Qantas and Air New Zealand publish accounts in a format that combines elements of each. Assets and liabilities are described in more detail in the next two sections, with examples taken from British Airways Plc Annual Report, 2005/2006, followed by a comparison with the AMR Corporation. BA changed to an account format with their adoption of IFRS for their latest financial year.

2.3.1   Assets

Fixed assets   These are the physical and financial items that are intended to be used for the longer term operations and business of the airline. They should not therefore vary much from day to day. They can be converted into cash, but not always easily or at short notice. They can be divided into:

- Tangible assets: Physical property, plant and equipment (e.g., aircraft, engines and related parts)
- Intangible assets: Long-term financial investments, goodwill, patents, route rights, slots, etc.

Fixed assets will include aircraft and spares, including rotables (repairable items), but not expendable spare parts, which are shorter life items and generally included in current assets (stocks). They are generally valued at historical cost less depreciation accumulated up to the date of the balance sheet.

Advance and option payments in respect of future aircraft purchase commitments are recorded at cost and shown separately under the tangible assets heading. BA records these under 'progress payments'. On acquisition of the related aircraft, these costs are transferred to the cost of aircraft (fleet) and depreciated only from that date.

It should be noted that the values stated in the accounts at a particular date are not intended to reflect the market or realisable value of the assets at that date. They will also not reflect the replacement cost of those assets. Some airlines do re-value the balance sheet cost of their assets, as British Airways did to their Tristar fleet in 1992 (reduced their value to zero), and their properties periodically. Otherwise, tangible assets are valued at cost less accumulated depreciation.

Table 2.7 shows an overall decline in non-current or long-term assets (after deducting depreciation) of 5 per cent compared to the previous year. Intangible assets (goodwill) were set off against reserves up to 31 March 1998. After that date, where the cost of an acquisition exceeded the balance sheet values of such assets, under UK rules, the difference could be capitalised (as an intangible asset) and written off over a period not exceeding 20 years. This has now been modified to an annual decision on impairment based on the likely future cash flows that the asset will generate, rather than an automatic amortisation. Much of this amount came from BA's acquisition of CityFlyer Express, a Gatwick-based franchise. BA paid £76 million for the airline compared to its net assets of £16 million, giving rise to £60 million of goodwill. Other intangibles refer to software development.

Table 2.6   British Airways' Group balance sheet

£ million as at 31 March	2005	2006
Intangible assets	254	233
Fleet	6,944	6,606
Property	1,000	974
Equipment	385	302
Total fixed assets	*8,329*	*7,882*
Investments: in associates	126	131
Employee benefit assets	137	137
Other investments and financial assets	68	122
Total non-fixed assets	*331*	*390*
Total non-current assets	8,914	8,505
Current assets		
Expendable spares and other inventory	84	83
Trade receivables	685	685
Other current assets	301	458
Other current interest-bearing deposits	1,133	1,533
Cash and cash equivalents	549	907
Total current assets and receivables	*2,752*	*3,666*
Total assets	*11,671*	*12,174*
Shareholders' equity and liabilities		
Issued share capital	271	283
Share premium	788	888
Investment in own shares	− 26	—
Other reserves	152	690
Minority interests	212	213
Total shareholders' equity	*1,397*	*2,074*
Non-current liabilities		
Interest bearing long-term borrowings	4,045	3,602
Employee benefit obligations	1,820	1,803
Provisions for deferred tax	816	896
Other provisions	112	135
Other long-term liabilities	212	232
Total non-current liabilities	*7,005*	*6.668*
Current liabilities		
Current portion of long-term borrowings	447	479
Convertible borrowings	112	—
Trade and other payables	2,642	2,822
Current tax payable	36	75
Short-term provisions	32	56
Total current liabilities	*3,329*	*3,432*
Total equity and liabilities	11,671	12,174

Source: British Airways' Group Annual Report, 2005–2006

Table 2.7   British Airways' Group non-current assets

£ million at 31 March	2005	2006	% change
Intangible assets:			
Goodwill	72	72	—
Landing rights	122	115	− 6
Other	60	46	− 23
Total	254	233	− 8
Tangible assets			
Fleet	6,944	6,606	− 5
Property	1,000	974	− 3
Equipment	385	302	− 22
Total tangible assets	8,329	7,882	− 5
Investments in associates	126	131	− 4
Other investments	30	33	10
Employee benefits	137	137	—
Other financial assets	38	89	134
Total non-current assets	8,914	8,505	− 5

Landing rights or slots (all at London Heathrow Airport) have been 'purchased' from other airlines over the years, although this is technically not permitted. Thus, a deal is described as an exchange of an attractive slot for an off-peak one, with a payment made by the airline gaining the valuable one.

Depreciation is deducted from all tangible assets except land to account for the decline in the useful value of the asset due to wear and tear and economic obsolescence. The asset's historical cost is spread over its expected useful life, at the end of which it is often given a residual value of between 5 per cent and 40 per cent of its cost. The life or depreciation period and the residual value together define the rate of depreciation of the asset. The example in Table 2.8 selects an aircraft life and residual value that together are identical to BA's 2005/2006 policy of depreciating its B747-400s by 3.7 per cent a year.

The depreciation for the year will also be included as an operating expense in the trading (profit and loss) account. The cost of intangible assets was also spread over its expected future life (from anything between five and 40 years), and is called amortisation:

UAL Inc acquired Pan Am's Pacific route rights and other assets in 1986; total intangible assets acquired in this deal amounted to US$384 million, which were amortised over 40 years to zero residual value.[7]

Straight line is the most common method of depreciation. Alternatives are the progressive or regressive methods, and depreciation according to the number of

---

7   UAL Inc., (1986), Annual Report.

hours or cycles (take-offs and landings) of aircraft usage.[8] The regressive (or declining balance) approach is similar to that taken by some tax authorities in calculating capital allowances, whereby a given percentage is applied to the depreciated value. This would result in a net book value that corresponds more closely to actual aircraft values, particularly in the early years of its life. However, it produces higher charges, and lower profits, in the earlier years of aircraft operation, whereas management may prefer the reverse. Rather than charging a fixed amount every year, a (fixed) percentage of the remaining value of the asset is charged every year. For example, a £10,000 asset depreciated at 25 per cent a year will be depreciated by £2,500 in the first year, but by 25 per cent × (£10,000–£2,500) in the second year. Compared to the straight line method, depreciation is more heavily weighted towards early years.

Table 2.8   Airline depreciation example

B747-400: Cost: US$150 million (ex spares); depreciated over 23 years to 15 per cent residual value (or 3.7 per cent a year); straight-line method

Annual Charge: {$150 million − (15 per cent × $150 million)} ÷ 23 = $5.543 million

Period	Net book value (US$ million)**	Accumulated depreciation (US$ million)**
Year 0	150.0	0.0
Year 1	144.5	5.5
Year 2	138.9	11.1
Year 3	133.4	16.6
Year 4	127.8	22.2
… …	… …	… …
… …	… …	… …
Year 19	44.7	105.3
Year 20	39.1	110.9
Year 21	33.6	116.4
Year 22	28.0	122.0
Year 23	22.5*	127.5
Year 24	22.5*	127.5

* Residual value; ** Rounded to one decimal place

Although the reducing balance method may track more closely the actual the market value of an asset, the straight line method is generally preferable as it fits more closely with principle of matching. In the airline context, if the aircraft provides

---

8   Almost all airlines use straight-line depreciation for their aircraft now. However, between 1988 and 1993, SAS depreciated their fleet by applying an increasing annual rate to the cost of its aircraft: thus 2 per cent was taken in the first year, and increasing this by one-third of a per cent per cent in each subsequent year. The aircraft were fully depreciated to zero residual value after just over 19 years. Japan Air Lines still use the declining balance method for their older B747s and DC10s.

much the same benefit every year, the best matching is provided by charging the same depreciation every year. If not, linking annual depreciation to aircraft hours or cycles would be better.

It should be noted that for airlines in some countries such as Switzerland, extra or supplementary depreciation is charged in good years, but only normal depreciation in years when losses are reported. This is driven by tax considerations, and results in a distortion of profitability over time or comparisons with other airlines.

The table below supports the view that US airlines tend to depreciate their fleet slower than the European airlines. There was little difference between US network carrier, AMR, and low cost airline, Southwest. However, BA applied a much faster rate of depreciation to their short/medium-haul fleet than Ryanair, largely through their lower residual values (although these are not published).

Table 2.9   Depreciation rate comparison for 2005/2006: Short/medium-haul aircraft

	British Airways B737-400/A320	Ryanair B737-800	AMR Corp. B737-800	Southwest B737-700
Life (years)	*n/a*	23	30	25
Residual %	*n/a*	15	5/10	15
Rate: % pa	4.9	3.7	3.0/3.2	3.4

Source: Airline annual reports

The other category of long-term or non-current assets is minority investments in other companies (the majority owned ones will have been consolidated: their assets combined with those of the airline in question[9]): these are not depreciated, but included at cost, market value (where there is stock market trading and a listing) or a value estimated by the directors.

Current assets   Current assets generally include cash, marketable securities and those assets that can in the normal course of business be turned into cash in the near future, at least within one year of the balance sheet date. Cash includes petty cash and bank deposits of less than one year term. Marketable securities may be short-term government securities or other secure short-term investments for which there is a good secondary market to allow sale at short notice. These are both valued for balance sheet purposes at cost or current market value, whichever is the lower.

Trade receivables   The used to be described as 'debtors' and are amounts due from customers to whom goods were already shipped, or services provided. For an airline, these would consist largely of credit card companies, travel agents and tour operators, since passengers are usually asked to pay in full before travel. Travel

---

9   Those assets owned by minority shareholders are recognised under 'shareholders' equity' or 'capital and reserves'.

agents are generally allowed one month's grace after which they are expected to pay the airline, but this could be increased to twice monthly. From experience there will be some customers who will fail to settle their invoices (resulting from bankruptcy), and an allowance will be deducted from accounts receivable to allow for these bad debts. These will be assumed by credit card companies (themselves much less likely to fail), but airlines will be required to pay for this by providing a cash deposit or letter of credit to the credit card company (in addition to the fee for its collection services).

Expendable spares and other inventories   These will consist of raw materials, expendable or consumable spares, other supplies, work-in-progress (semi-finished products) and finished products. Since an airline's final output (seat-kilometres or available tonne-kms) cannot be stored, the last item is not relevant to the airline industry. Work-in-progress could, however, relate to aircraft or spare parts which are overhauled by the maintenance department. Raw materials and other supplies will consist of fuel stocks, maintenance, operations, office and other items of limited life. They will be valued at cost or market value, whichever is the lower. Some airlines deduct an allowance for expendable spares obsolescence, writing down parts that have not been used for two or three years by anything between 10–33.3 per cent.

The third and fourth items in this part of the BA balance sheet are sometimes called *Quick Assets*, since they are likely to be convertible into cash within a very short period, probably within one month. Inventories are not so easily sold, and debtors cannot be realised much faster than the credit terms allowed without damaging commercial relationships. Table 2.10 shows an improvement in BA's quick asset position.

BA had almost £2.5 billion in relatively liquid funds at end March 2006 compared to only £936 million at the end of March 2001. Trade receivables would normally be expected to be related to turnover, and for BA these declined from £853 million at end March 2001 to £685 million at end March 2006. A further amount of £458 million is reported as prepayments (or prepaid expenses) and accrued income, which would include such items as rents or rates paid in advance. Here the airline has the contracted right to goods or services which have yet to be delivered.

Table 2.10   British Airways' Group current assets

£ million at 31 March	2005	2006
Expendable spares and inventories	84	83
Trade receivables	685	685
Other current assets	301	458
Interest bearing deposits	1,133	1,533
Cash at bank and in hand	549	907
Total current assets	2,752	3,666

Deferred charges are similar to prepaid expenses, in that the payment is made in advance of receipt of related benefits, for example for office relocation costs. But here the benefits are usually considered to be of a longer term nature, and the deferred charge spread over a number of years. Deferred charges would thus normally be included under fixed or long-term assets.

2.3.2 Liabilities

Current liabilities   This item generally includes all debts that fall due in the 12 months after the balance sheet date. They are what the airline owes to other parties within this period, and are settled by drawing on the liquid resources that the airline owns or is likely to own in this period, namely the current assets. Thus, a comparison of current assets and current liabilities is an important step in balance sheet analysis. The difference between the two is described as 'working capital'.

Current portion of long-term borrowings   Those parts of the longer-term financial arrangements that fall due in the coming year.

Convertible borrowings   Represented the principal outstanding on convertible capital bonds issued by BA in June 1989 with due date in 2005. Thus, these were expected to be repaid in June 2005, but in the event all holders converted to ordinary shares priory to expiry, since the conversion price was lower than the market price of the equity.

Trade and other payables   The accounts payable by BA to its regular suppliers from which it has bought goods and services. The largest category of supplier is likely to be an oil company which has delivered aviation fuel, and grants the airline a given number of days' credit. Airports and air navigation authorities are also likely to be major creditors.

Table 2.11   British Airways' Group current liabilities

£ million at 31 March	2005	2006
Current portion of long-term borrowings	4,447	479
Convertible borrowings	112	—
Trade and other payables	2,642	2,822
Current tax payable	36	75
Short-term provisions	32	56
Total	3,269	3,432

Current tax payable   This is corporation and other taxes, duties and social security payments payable to the government within the next 12-month period.

Short-term provisions   Amounts owing to parties who have provided services, such as employees, but who have not yet been paid (they are likely to be paid by the end of the month). For outside services such as legal advice or consultancy, while the work has been completed, no invoice has been submitted, otherwise this would be recorded as trade creditors.

Sales in advance of carriage   These unearned transport revenues, shown in the BA accounts under 'Trade and other payables', are a significant source of short-term finance for many airlines (£1,045 million for BA at end March 2006), and are included under current liabilities. This is where a ticket has been issued and payment either received or expected, but the service is only deliverable at some time in the future (the ticket validity is unlikely to exceed a period of 12 months). BA increased this item by 19 per cent over 2005/2006, while revenues only climbed by 5 per cent. The main reason for this was the incidence of the Easter peak travel period in April in 2006 (just after the financial year end) and in March in 2005.

Overdrafts   (not used in either year by BA) are short-term loans from banks, which can usually be drawn upon, as and when necessary, up to a maximum figure (in BA's case up to £46 million and €20 million) and would generally not be secured against any of BA's assets.

Non-current (long-term) liabilities   Under current liabilities, an item was described as the current part of long-term loans, leases and hire purchase commitments. All the remaining sums owed by the airline under this heading will be placed under long-term or fixed liabilities. A breakdown is given in Table 2.12.

Table 2.12   British Airways' Group non-current liabilities

£ million at 31 March	2005	2006
Interest bearing long-term borrowings	4,045	3,602
Employee benefit obligations	1,820	1,803
Provisions for deferred tax	816	896
Other provisions	112	135
Other long-term liabilities	212	232
Total	7,005	6,668

Interest bearing long-term borrowings   This covers the principal of loans and capital/finance leases that is repayable one year or more into the future. Shorter term operating leases are treated as an annual operating expense, since the airline does not own the aircraft, nor does it have a long-term contractual commitment. Long-term financial leases, although similar in terms of ownership, are a long term commitment and are usually required to be included in the balance sheet, as in BA's case above (see Appendix 2.2 at the end of this chapter for a full treatment of leases). Of BA's total of £3.60 billion outstanding as at 31 March 2006, £1.03 billion was from bank and other loans, £1.42 billion from finance leases and £1.15 billion from Hire Purchase arrangements. Most of the reduction from the previous year came from repayment of the latter, and no new long-term loans were taken out during the last financial year.

Provisions These are defined as amounts which are retained to provide for any liability or loss which is either likely to be incurred, or certain to be incurred but uncertain as to the amount or the date on which it will arise. Major examples of this, usually falling into the latter category, are accelerated depreciation or write-downs on aircraft, pensions, retirement benefits, severance pay and legal damages.

BA had in the past provided for legal claims made by Virgin Atlantic Airways against them, but an outstanding claim was not considered by the directors to give rise to liabilities that would 'not give rise to a material effect' on the accounts.

BA's provisions are mostly for deferred tax, related largely to fixed assets and pensions. Other provisions relate mostly to aircraft leased to Eastern Airways and Swiss International, allowing for writing down the value of the aircraft and restoring the aircraft to return conditions. These have a current element, and will be gradually used up to 2011.

Other long-term liabilities For BA these consisted largely of accruals and deferred income. These accruals are expenses for which invoices have not yet been received, and will subsequently move to creditors in current liabilities. Deferred income is income received during the current financial year, but the services have not yet been provided. Sale of mileage credits to non-airline businesses is an example of this: these are reduced as and when the air miles are used accompanied by an addition to 'other revenues' in the income statement.

Shareholders' equity or funds The total equity interest that all the shareholders have in the airline is called the shareholders' equity or funds, and is equal to the airline's net worth (total assets less short and long-term liabilities). This is separated for legal and accounting reasons into three categories:

- Capital stock, called up or issued share capital.
- Capital surplus (share premium) or capital reserves.
- Accumulated retained earnings or deficits, revenue or other reserves, or profit and loss account.

Table 2.13   British Airways' Group capital and reserves

£ million at 31 March	2005	2006
Issued share capital	271	283
Share premium	788	888
Investment in own shares	− 26	—
Other reserves	152	690
Total	1,185	1,861
Minority interest	212	213
Total equity	1,397	2,074

Capital surplus consists of any adjustments which do not arise as a result of trading activities. These include the revaluation of fixed assets, currency gains or losses, premiums on the issue of shares and the capitalisation of goodwill. In some countries a part of retained earnings is required by law to be transferred into capital reserves, which cannot be distributed to shareholders in the form of dividends.

Capital stock, or issued (called up) share capital   This represents the nominal value of the share capital or issued share certificates, and is the proprietary interest in the company. There may be more than one class of shares issued (*e.g.*, Air New Zealand has class A shares for nationals, class B shares for foreign nationals, and one Kiwi share owned by the government with special rights). The share capital may be divided into ordinary and preferred, the latter having priority over the former in the distribution of dividends (and assets in the case of liquidation following bankruptcy), but only up to fixed maximum amount.

Share premium, capital surplus or capital reserves   This includes the amount paid by shareholders over the par or nominal value of the shares (share premium account), re-valuations of fixed assets, currency gains or losses and capitalised goodwill (revaluation reserves).

Investment in own shares   This practice was not permitted in some countries. In the UK it was allowed from 1999. BA originally accounted for these purchases in the open market as an investment (assets), but recently switched to recording a negative entry under reserves.

Accumulated retained earnings, revenue or other reserves   These are the net profits or losses, after payments of dividends to shareholders, accumulated from previous years' operations. From 2005/2006, BA describes these as 'other reserves'. Their change from the previous year total reflects the retained profit for the year adjusted for (reduced) hedging activity. In 2005, BA moved to the IFRS treatment of pension deficits which involved moving well over £1 billion from reserves to 'non-current' liabilities.

Minority interest   This reflects that part of total shareholders' equity that is attributed to the minority shareholders in the consolidated subsidiary companies that are not 100 per cent owned by BA. This would include the company established to jointly own the Iberia shares, with the AMR Corporation holding 10 per cent, and the minority shareholders in the London Eye (now sold).

2.4   Balance Sheet Comparison: BA *vs* AMR

The BA Group balance sheet is compared with that of the AMR Corporation in Table 2.14, first looking at their assets and then liabilities. AMR's total revenue in 2005 was 36 per cent higher than BA's. Their total assets were also significantly higher, especially in terms of equipment and property and other assets. BA's current assets were greater than AMR's thanks to over US$4 billion in cash and other liquid funds. BA also had a much larger portion of equipment and property (mostly aircraft) financed under capital leases.

Even larger differences between the two airlines are found on the liabilities side of the balance sheet. AMR has not produced a net profit since the 2000 financial year, and thus its stockholders' equity is now severely depleted and negative. It was last positive at the end of December 2003, but only by a small margin. The significance of negative balance sheet equity is that the airline is technically insolvent, even though it has not entered either Chapter 11 or Chapter 7 bankruptcy proceedings. This may be because in practice it could obtain sufficient cash from the sale of its assets to cover its outside liabilities; from the accounts this is not the case, but some of the aircraft may fetch more than their book balance sheet values. This is impossible to tell, but a similar exercise carried out at the end of June 2005 by Air New Zealand valued their fleet at NZ$1.224 billion on their books and only NZ$764 million on the open market.

Table 2.14   Balance sheet comparison: Assets, 2005/2006

US$ million	BA*	AMR**
Current Assets:		
Cash/short-term investments	4,246	3,814
Receivables	1,192	991
Inventories	144	515
Other	797	844
Total current assets	6,379	6,164
Equipment and property:		
Owned	6,725	17,249
Under capital/finance lease	6,793	1,019
Aircraft purchase deposits	197	278
Other assets:		
Route acquisition, slots and gates	200	1,194
Other	889	3,591
Total assets	21,182	29,495

* as at 31 March 2006 and applying US$1.74/£; ** as at 31 December 2005

The reason AMR continues trading normally with negative equity is that the creditors preferred this to forcing bankruptcy procedures. The airline generated just over US$1 billlion in cash in 2005, and the situation was improving. Aircraft lessors were being paid and their aircraft were flying.

BA on the other hand still had strongly positive equity, albeit reduced by the pension deficit provision it had to make for its latest financial years. BA, however, still had over $6 billion in debt and capital leases outstanding at end March 2006, whereas AMR had just under $1 billion.

AMR's outstanding long-term debt and capital leases were over double BA's, with capital leases and hire purchase arrangements contributing only 7 per cent *vs* 71 per cent for BA. The other difference between the two is the make-up of the liabilities, and the fact that BA's current assets less current liabilities (working capital) was positive, while for AMR it was negative. However, a much larger part of AMR's liabilities was air traffic liability, or sales in advance of carriage, and much of this is repayable in kind rather than cash, given the restrictions on many advance purchase tickets and FFP liabilities.

Table 2.15   Balance sheet comparison: Liabilities, 2005/2006

US$ million	BA*	AMR**
Current Liabilities:		
Accounts payable	2,173	1,078
Accrued liabilities	893	2,388
Air traffic liability	1,844	3,615
Other	1,061	1,239
Total current liabilities	5,971	8,320
Debt/capital leases	6,267	13,456
Other liabilities, provisions, credits	5,335	9,197
Stockholders' equity (deficit)	3,609	− 1,478
Total liabilities	21,182	29,495

* as at 31 March 2006 and applying US$1.74/£; ** as at 31 December 2005

2.5   Cash Flow Statement

The *cash flow statement* explains major changes in the balance sheet which occurred over the financial year in terms of cash flowing in and out of a company. Both the UK and US now both use the term cash flow statement to describe these changes, with the UK previously using the term *sources and applications of funds* or *funds flow statement*, and the US formerly presenting a *statement of changes in financial position*. It is usually shown in the annual report and accounts of US and UK airlines, and some European airlines (for example, KLM, Swissair, Air France and Lufthansa since 1998).

Neither the profit and loss accounts nor the balance sheet provide information directly on the cash position of the airline, and how the cash was generated for payments for aircraft and repayments of loans. This is shown in the cash flow statement. While an airline might be operating profitably over the year as a whole, it would still be possible for it to be forced to cease trading if it did not have sufficient cash to meet its invoices from suppliers and repayments on loans. This possibility is all the more likely in an industry such as air transport which is highly seasonal and is characterised by relatively high operational and financial gearing.

The cash flow statement will be explained here with reference to British Airways (BA), and therefore current UK practice. However, the statement is presented in a similar way in the US and by some European and Asian airlines. The statement shows cash movements under three main headings:

- Operations or operating activities:
  Dividends received from associates.
  Net return on investments and servicing of finance (interest charges).
  Tax.

- Investing activities:
  Purchase and sale of tangible fixed assets.
  Purchase of trade investments.

- Financing or financing activities:
  Changes in borrowings.
  Change in short-term bank deposits.
  Issue of shares or other securities.

Table 2.16   British Airways' Group cash flow statement

£ million	2004/2005	2005/2006
Net cash inflow from operations	1,247	1,607
Interest, dividends and tax paid	− 242	− 268
Net cash flow from operating activities (A)	*1,005*	*1,339*
Purchase of property, plant and equipment	− 356	− 275
Purchase of intangible assets	− 32	− 8
Sale of property, plant and equipment	57	9
Purchase of investments	− 12	− 7
Sale of investments	427	73
Interest and dividends received	101	100
Increase in interest bearing deposits	− 487	− 402
Net cash flow from investing activities (B)	*− 302*	*− 510*
Proceeds from long-term borrowing	116	—
Repayments of borrowing	− 168	− 64
Capital element of finance leases		
And HP agreements repaid	− 1,103	− 415
Exercise of share options	4	21
Other	− 9	− 14
Net cash flow from financing activities (C)	*− 1,160*	*− 472*
Net increase in cash/cash equivalents		
(A) + (B) + (C)	− 457	357

* less progress payments refunded

BA's cash flow statement has been summarised in Table 2.16. Cash flow statements can be confusing where net amounts are shown, for example 'Net cash from investing activities'. It is thus important to remember that a positive amount indicates an inflow of cash, and a negative amount an outflow. Thus, BA's negative net cash flow from investing activities reflects greater outflow than inflow, whether towards purchase of aircraft (under 'property, plant and equipment') or interest bearing deposits. BA's cash flow statement, however, avoids confusion by separating purchases and sales wherever possible.

BA generated £1.339 billion in cash from its operating activities in 2005/2006, after paying out £268 million for interest and tax (no dividend being paid). The main source of its cash from internal operations was its operating profit of £705 million and added back depreciation, amortisation and impairment (a non-cash item in operating expenses) of £717 million. An increase in trade and other payables also give them a boost of £150 million. This came from a longer delay in settling their invoices for goods and services provided by others.

BA invested only £275 million in fixed assets, mostly new aircraft, although this was offset by refunds of progress payments made since the contracts were signed. The need for new financing was further reduced by the net cash inflow of £78 million from the sale of BA's share in the London Eye.

After investments and disposals, the airline still had a positive cash inflow, as it had in the previous loss-making year. The positive inflow of cash was mainly used to pay off capital leases and other borrowings, still leaving a net addition to liquid funds of £357 million.

Cash flow statements are similar to funds flow or sources and application of funds statements in that they use balance sheet differences between two points in time (*e.g.*, between the beginning and end of the financial year). But they differ in adjusting these differences to eliminate all credit and accrued items.

A summary of the interpretation of BA's cash flow statement is as follows:

- The net cash inflow from operating activities increased in 2005/2006, principally from an increase in cash operating profits, helped by an increase in trade and other payables.
- The net cash required for investments increased from £302 million to £510 million, most of which was needed for interest bearing deposits (in both years).
- An increase in cash balances even after the repayment of almost £0.5 billion of debt and finance leases.

In theory, all items found in this statement can be derived from the profit and loss statement and the balance sheet, but in practice there is often not enough detail shown to be able to do this, as with the example above of changes in short-term bank deposits. In BA's case, one of the notes to the accounts provides a reconciliation of operating profit (from the P&L statement) to the net cash inflow from operating activities (from the cash flow statement).

BA's cash flow statement is in the UK recommended format of presenting the data. There are, however, a number of different ways of presenting these data, both with regard to netting off certain items and in terms of the ordering. Thus, interest paid and received may be shown separately, or as one net figure. Some statements show the financing activities before the investments made, and therefore give a figure of what was available for investment after changes in bank loans, rather than before.

Cash flow statements may be examined over a period of a number of years to see how an airline has financed its capital expenditure. One airline could also be compared with another, but this may be difficult resulting from different ways of presenting the information in different countries.

Summary cash flow statements are presented in a similar way for BA (2005/2006 turnover of US$15.2 billion) and the AMR Corporation (2005 turnover $20.7 billion). The three main activities are compared in Table 2.17.

Table 2.17   Summary cash flow statement comparison, 2005/2006

US$ million	BA*	AMR**
Cash flow from operating activities (A)	2,397	1,024
Capital expenditures	− 507	− 681
Other investing activities	− 406	− 858
Cash flow from investing activities (B)	− 913	− 1,539
Re-payments on long-term debt and capital lease	− 857	− 1,131
Proceeds from long-term borrowings and capital leases	—	1,252
Issues of stock/shares	—	223
Cash flow from financing activities (C)	− 845	533
Net increase/(decrease) in cash *(A) + (B) + (C)*	639	18

* year ended 31 March 2006 and converted at the average rate for the 12 month period:$1.79/£;
** year ended 31 December 2005

BA generated more than double AMR's cash provision from internal sources for the latest year, on lower total revenues. BA was thus able to be net repayers of loans (and repaid some of its more expensive debt early), whereas AMR needed to increase net borrowing. Both airlines kept capital expenditures well under control with most of AMRs other investing going towards interest-bearing short-term deposits. Both carriers re-paid a substantial amount of debt/capital leases, but AMR took out a very similar amount of new borrowing, as well as issuing new common stock. Without raising any new money, BA was still able to add US$639 million to cash.

The Lufthansa Group generated just under €2 billion in cash from operating activities, almost all of which was used to buy assets. It repaid €305 million of long-term borrowings and took out almost the same in new debt.

2.6   Value Added Statement

British Airways do not include a value added statement in their annual report and accounts, although they do give the essential ingredients to allow such a statement to be constructed (Table 2.18). The statement views the company from an economist's standpoint, and relates output to inputs of labour, capital and materials. In this way it is possible to see how much additional value has been created by the firm, after deducting all the goods and services bought in from other firms. This has special relevance in today's climate of the contracting out of an increasing part of the firm's activities.

Many interesting conclusions can be drawn from Table 2.18. First, the amount spent on purchasing goods and services from other firms increased by 12 per cent, compared to a 5 per cent rise in staff costs and 3 per cent fall in depreciation. This somewhat simplistic comparison does not necessarily suggest a shift to outsourcing. For the latest financial year, 56 per cent of turnover was bought in from other firms or government entities (69 per cent in 1985/1986), compared to the group results of 54 per cent for Singapore Airlines, 62 per cent for American Airlines, and 50 per cent for Lufthansa. The trend over time is not a good guide to the degree of outsourcing, since the large increase in fuel price would itself shift value added to outside suppliers. The cross-sectional comparison gives some indication but is similarly distorted by higher wage costs in some countries.

Table 2.18   Value added statement for British Airways Group[10]

£ million year ended 31 March	2005	2006
Turnover	7,772	8,515
Cost of goods and services	4,242	4,747
Value added by the group	3,530	3,768
Add investment income/profit from		
Sale of assets and other adjustments	222	136
Value added available	3,752	3,904
Applied to:		
Employees (salaries, *etc.*)	2,235	2,346
Government (taxes)	121	153
Suppliers of capital:		
Dividends	0	0
Interest paid	265	221
Minority interests	15	16
Retained in the business		
− Depreciation	739	717
− Retained profit	377	451
Value added applied	3,752	3,904

Estimated from information in the Income Statement

10   *The Times*, London, (17 August 2001).

BA distributed 60 per cent of their 2005/2006 value added available to employees compared to 63 per cent in 1995/1996, and 54 per cent for Lufthansa in 2005, 86 per cent for American Airlines in 2005, and only 45 per cent for Singapore Airlines in 2005/2006.

2.7   Cash Value Added

Cash Value Added (CVA) is designed to measure the shareholder value that the airline is adding, after providing for an economic return to long-term capital investors. It is similar to Economic Value Added (EVA), originally developed by the US firm Stern Stewart & Co, and is increasingly being used by firms, and more recently airlines such as BA and Lufthansa.

The starting point for CVA is cash flow, or EBITDAR, earnings before interest, tax, depreciation, amortisation and rentals. This is operating revenues less cash expenses, plus income from associates, dividends and interest received. However, the BA example below does not add in interest received. EVA takes as a starting point Net Operating Profit after Tax (NOPAT), which is similar to EBITDAR but after deducting tax.

From EBITDAR, tax is deducted, and an asset replacement charge designed to reflect the economic cost of replacing assets. For BA's 1999/2000 financial year, this resulted in a sustainable cash profit, before the capital charge deduction, of £466 million (see Table 2.19).

Table 2.19   Cash value added statement for British Airways Group

£ million	1999/2000
Operating revenues	8,940
Operating costs (less lease rentals and depreciation)	− 7,890
Other income	5
Asset replacement charge	− 379
Tax on the above	− 210
Sustainable cash profit	466
Gross assets at current cost	17,241
Capital charge	− 1,207
CVA	− 741

Source: British Airways Factbook, 2001

The asset replacement charge is where CVA departs from many of the ratios used in the past. This is the economic depreciation charge for assets that are owned, or on finance or operating leases. Its starting point is total depreciating assets: gross fixed assets from the balance sheet are adjusted for inflation and combined with the present value of leased assets. This is similar to replacement cost. For property and aircraft under operating leases, the annual rentals are multiplied by seven to give an estimate of present capital value.

The difficult part is inflating the historic costs of aircraft to current replacement values on a like-for-like basis. It appears that BA is currently taking equivalent new aircraft, since they are then depreciating the values over an average asset life of 22.5 years. This would imply, for example, that the historic balance sheet gross value of a B737-200 would be replaced by the *new cost* of a B737-200. Since these are no longer in production, in this case they would presumably take a B737-500, which is similar in most respects, but presumably has lower fuel costs. They did not apparently take the replacement cost of a B737-200, of *similar vintage and operating characteristics.* This latter approach would give roughly the right fuel and maintenance costs (which have already been assumed under cash operating costs), but the economic life would need to be 22.5 less the aircraft's vintage.

The annual asset replacement charge (£379 million in 1999/2000) is calculated by finding the annual amount, which, if discounted over the asset's economic life using the weighted average cost of capital (WACC which for BA was 7 per cent) as discount rate, would equal the total of depreciating assets.

From the BA figures published, it is difficult to determine the basis for the tax charge, but this appears to have been the full UK rate of tax (30 per cent in 1999/2000) applied to the cash profit.

The figure for gross assets at current cost is the total of depreciating assets plus debtors and stocks less provisions and non-interest bearing liabilities. This is equivalent to shareholders' funds and external liabilities, and this total (£17.241 billion in 1999/2000) was multiplied by WACC to arrive at the capital charge.

The total of the asset replacement charge and the capital charge amounted to £1.586 billion according to BA's figures. This compares with the conventional accounts figures for 1999/2000 of depreciation (£648 million), interest paid (£357 million), and rentals (£318 million), or a total of £1.323 million.

2.8   Progress Towards Greater Accounting Standardisation

The increasingly global nature of the airline business, together with a growth in airline privatisation, alliances and cross-shareholdings, is focusing attention on the wide variety of accounting principles used, and the differences in quality and quantity of financial data reported. This chapter has only described some of the more obvious differences, and the problems that they generate in inter-airline comparisons will be explored further in consideration of financial ratios in the next chapter.

The first authoritative survey of airline accounting policies was carried out by the accounting firm, KPMG, in association with IATA.[11] Questionnaires were sent out to 25 airline finance directors between May and July 1992. The sample covered six airlines in Australasia, 11 airlines in Europe, three airlines in North America and five in other world regions. The survey's findings fell into four main areas:

---

11 KPMG/IATA(1992), *Accounting Policies, Disclosure and Financial Trends in the International Airline Industry*, August.

- Accounting for fleet assets and related financing transactions.
- General accounting issues and disclosures.
- Treasury and foreign currency.
- Trends and developments.

The survey concluded with a recommendation that a single body be created to research and recommend policies for the international airline industry. This body would encourage airlines to adopt recommended accounting policies, and lobby international accounting standards bodies to take into account airline interests. Following this proposal, IATA established a sub-committee of its finance committee to produce accounting guidelines in a number of areas. So far, the following have been examined:

- Foreign currency accounting.
- Frequent flyer schemes.
- Depreciation.
- Recognition of revenues.
- Maintenance costs.
- Segmental reporting.
- Accounting for aircraft leases.

Discussions on the first topic focused on the translation of long-term foreign currency borrowings. An Exposure Draft was published which summarised the conclusions to the sub-committee's discussions.[12] This identified two markedly different accounting treatments of such borrowings, but did not recommend one in preference to the other. They did, however, say that whichever method were used, a comprehensive explanation should be included of the accounting policy used, and its effect on the profit and loss statement.

The second guideline[13] issued on frequent flyer programme recommended that the incremental cost approach was the most appropriate technique, if 'an airline can establish quantitatively that passengers flying as a result of awards under the FFP are incidental to the passenger revenue process' (see Appendix 2.1 for more detailed discussion of this).

The third guideline[14] described what should be taken into account when determining the cost of an airline's fleet, the useful life of aircraft and the residual value. It did not, however, recommend on aircraft lives or residual values, but did endorse the suitability of the straight-line method of depreciation 'in most circumstances'.

---

12 *Ibid.*, (1994), *Airline Accounting Guideline No. 1: Explanatory Foreword and Translation of Long-term Foreign Currency Borrowings*, Effective 1st August.

13 *Ibid.*, (1995), *Airline Accounting Guideline No. 2: Frequent Flyer Programme Accounting*, Effective 1st June.

14 *Ibid.*, (1996), *Airline Accounting Guideline No. 3: Components of Fleet Acquisition Cost and Associated Depreciation*, Effective 1st May.

The fourth guideline[15] examined the recognition of revenue and recommended that unearned revenue should be carried forward and included in current liabilities, agent commissions should be included as a cost of sales and recognised at the same time as the associated revenues, but that revenues should be recorded net of discounts. Unredeemed coupons should be recognised as revenue in the light of airline experience, with perhaps a write-back period of 18–24 months from the date of sale. The fifth guideline on accounting for maintenance costs[16] was originally published in 1996, but was revised in 1999. It suggested that routine maintenance costs are treated as expenses as and when they are incurred, but that heavy maintenance and overhauls are accounted for on an accruals basis, rather than deferred and amortised. For a large airline, they might be expensed as incurred if this resulted in a fairly even reporting over a number of years.

The guideline on accounting for leases endorsed the concept of economic ownership in accounting for leases, and suggested that the existence of options required careful consideration (see also Appendix 2.2 at the end of this chapter). It also argued that any lease structure under which the lessor is in substance merely a provider of finance and is not compensated for the risk of ownership should be treated by the airline as a finance lease.[17]

The guideline on segmental reporting considered that the segmentation of an airline's business should be viewed as a function of product or service rather than geography, which should be secondary. A more extensive allocation of costs and assets could, however, be made if the segmentation were by geographical region.[18]

It could be concluded, however, that these IATA initiatives did not bring any real benefits, regardless of whether they succeeded in persuading airlines to standardise their accounts. The real test is whether airlines can more easily access the world's capital markets, especially the huge US market. To do this, it could be argued that they need to comply with the US Generally Accepted Accounting Principles (US GAAP). Even the International Accounting Standards (IAS) does not yet meet US requirements, although they have moved much closer. An important step was taken in Europe, where companies that are listed on EU markets have to adopt most of the IAS for accounting periods on or after 1 January 2005. Thus, with the increasing convergence of IAS with US GAAP, larger EU companies are moving closer to US requirements. From the beginning of 2007, all companies whose shares are traded on mainland Chinese stock exchanges will need to apply the Chinese Accounting Standards System, largely in line with IAS.[19]

---

15 *Ibid.*, (1996), *Airline Accounting Guideline No. 4: Recognition of Revenue*, Effective 1st May.

16 *Ibid.*, (1999), *Airline Accounting Guideline No. 5: Accounting for Maintenance Costs.*

17 *Ibid.*, (1997), *Airline Accounting Guideline No. 6: Accounting for Leases of Aircraft Fleet Assets.*

18 *Ibid.*, (2000), *Airline Accounting Guideline No. 7: Segmental Reporting.*

19 *The Wall Street Journal,* Europe, (12 July 2006) XXIV, No. 113.

Appendix 2.1   Frequent Flyer Programme Award Accounting

Frequent Flyer or Loyalty Programmes (FFPs) allow passengers to accumulate points each time they travel with a certain airline, or FFP partner airlines. These are earned under most schemes each time a passenger buys a first or business class ticket, and for some airlines economy class tickets. Once a threshold is reached, the points or miles can be exchanged for:

- A free ticket.
- A free companion ticket.
- An upgrade to a business or first class ticket.
- Other non air travel awards.

These would be valid on the flights of the sponsoring or any participating airline. It is likely that many of the points earned will be redeemed at some time in the future. There will therefore be a future liability to the airline that must be accounted for; otherwise profitability in the period the points are earned will be artificially inflated, and profits for some future period understated.

FFPs were adopted by airlines to differentiate their brand from other airlines, and thus to increase market share. This effect is reduced once all their competitor airlines have similar programmes, although the total market will probably have been stimulated by their introduction. Airlines will also compete through their FFP through special offers, more generous upgrades, or longer validity periods. Traffic on new or problem routes, or flights in off-peak periods, can also be stimulated by offering double or triple FFP points for those services.

The effect of FFPs on profitability depend on the adoption of blackout dates over Christmas or peak holiday periods during which no awards will be granted. This is to ensure that seats are not occupied by FFP award passengers that would otherwise have been sold to revenue generating passengers. It is generally assumed that any such displacement is minimal. Airlines sometimes demonstrate the negligible likelihood of the displacement of fare paying passengers by giving figures of seat factors, or the percentage of FFP award passenger-kms in total passenger-kms. For US airlines this latter figure has increased from around 3 per cent in 1991 to between 6 per cent and 10 per cent in 2005. United reported 1.9 million miles redeemed in 2005, 70 per cent of which for travel within the US and Canada. This amounted to 6.6 per cent of United's total passenger-miles, down from 9.0 per cent in 2003. For Northwest, the miles redeemed on Northwest's flights were 7.3 per cent of total passenger-miles, or 8.9 per cent including those redeemed on partner airlines. British Airways recorded only 1.4 per cent of total traffic travelling on awards in 1993/1994, increasing to 2.1 per cent in 2000/2001 and 3.2 per cent in 2004/2005, dropping back to 2.8 in 2005/2006.

There are three possible approaches to FFP accounting. The first treats the redemption of the points as a contingent liability, on the basis that it is impossible to quantify accurately the timing and amount of awards. This was rejected by IATA's Accounting Policy Task Force because FFPs are specially designed to stimulate traffic, and there is a high probability of a future liability being incurred.

The second method is called the *incremental cost* technique. This recognises the future liability in providing for the future costs of carrying those passengers that have passed the points threshold (for example 25,000 miles for American Airlines) and are likely to be granted an award. This is done through the profit and loss statement by increasing passenger services (or other) expenses by the incremental costs of carrying the award passengers at a future date. The same amount is recorded in the balance sheet as an accrued liability. When the passenger is eventually carried under the award, the incremental cost of carrying that passenger is deducted from expenses (since there is no matching revenue for this period), and the liability in the balance sheet extinguished. This means that the operating profit in each year is not distorted by the FFP award.

Incremental costs used to include only the cost of in-flight catering, fuel, reservations, passenger taxes, fees and insurance, and ticket and baggage tag delivery, and would be calculated for each class of service. No contribution to overheads or profit is included in these costs. However, many airlines (such as BA) now impose a separate charge for airport charges, insurance and security and fuel surcharges. Any government taxes would also be extra. In-flight catering is now much reduced and in some cases charged to the passenger. These would be paid by any passenger using free mileage allowance, and thus incremental costs are probably now lower than they were. It also means that the value of FFP miles to passengers has been reduced. Few airlines provide data on what they include in incremental costs. At end December 2005, Delta Air Lines recorded a liability of US$291 million for 7 million expected FFP redemptions, giving an average cost of US$42 (Delta Form 10K Report, 2005). This compared with US$35 at the end of 2004 and US$23 for end 2003.

The third method is called the *deferred revenue* technique. This defers a certain proportion of the revenue earned from the sale of the tickets which conferred FFP points until the award is granted and used. The proportion of revenue is normally based on the yield derived from a discount fare ticket with similar restrictions to the award ticket. This amount is also recorded in current liabilities, and added to revenues when the passenger uses the award. Some airlines account for their own FFPs in this way, and American Airlines uses this method for mileage credits or points sold to other airlines and companies participating in its FFP (although it uses the incremental cost method for credits earned by its own members).

Most airlines use the incremental cost method because:

- They consider the displacement of revenue generating passengers by award passengers to be insignificant.
- The share of free ticket award passengers is not material in the context of total passengers.

For both the last two methods, it is necessary to estimate the number of future awards likely to be granted under the FFP. This will depend on the thresholds established, the future cut-off when points must be redeemed or lost (*e.g.*, Swissair had a two-year limit, and US carriers such as United and Delta introduced a three-year expiry date[20]), and the redemption experience of the airline. Airlines either consider only those members who have reached the threshold for awards, or they account for a liability as the qualifying miles are flown. From the 1992 IATA/KPMG survey, in fact two-thirds (6) of the airlines used the latter approach, even though it must be difficult to estimate how many with fewer points will eventually reach the threshold. Only one-third (3) of airlines used the first approach.

TWA assumed in 1991 that 80 per cent of the potential awards outstanding would be translated into free tickets, a similar level to that adopted by United and Delta. By 1996, however, Delta had reduced their estimate to 66 per cent, partly because of the acquisition of Pan Am's frequent flyer members, many of which were considered to be dormant. Delta's marketing department may wish to activate these 'dormant' accounts by promoting loyalty to their own services, but the downside of this would be the incremental costs of providing free tickets that otherwise might not have been requested.

By 2000, Delta had increased their estimate of the share of award holders who will actually use their awards for travel to 75 per cent, somewhat lower than United's 82 per cent for the same year. European airlines do not give such estimates, nor do they divulge marginal costs.

Canadian Airlines International provoked a rush to cash in frequent flyer points in December 1996 by issuing a warning that they may have to stop service if their unions and creditors failed to agree a restructuring. Award requests were running at over 50 per cent normal levels, but they could easily be accommodated since this was the low season for the carrier and many seats were available. This provided a solution for the FFP liabilities, which had risen to rather a high level, but caused alarm amongst creditors which had not been desired.

Some airlines have been encouraging FFP members to use their awards for merchandise rather than flights. This avoids any dissatisfaction that might arise in failure to obtain a flight at the right time and to the preferred destination. Airlines need to continue to apply tight restrictions, but still value the FFP programmes as a competitive tool. Table 2.20 shows that product redemptions are still a small part of overall redemptions.

The discussion so far has focused on airline frequent flyer schemes. Airlines also sell air miles to non-airline businesses, and frequent buyers on non-airline goods and services probably now account for more miles than frequent flyers. These are sold by airlines for between one and two US cents a mile, with 25,000 miles needed to earn a US domestic trip. As mentioned above, the airline would incur the marginal cost of up to US$100 for a ticket sold for US$250–500.[21]

---

20 Membership can be reactivated by means of a payment or the purchase of a qualifying flight.

21 *The Economist*, (24 December 2005).

Table 2.20   AAdvantage award distribution in 2005

	Miles (000)	%
American Airlines flights	2,378	52.2
Upgrade awards	864	19.0
Product redemptions	359	7.9
Flights on other airline and other awards	956	21.0
Total	4,556	100.0

Source: AAdvantage website (American Airlines)

These air miles schemes are generally accounted for by the deferred revenue approach, while the same airline would probably use the deferred cost method for their own scheme. American Airlines takes part of the revenue from air miles' sales to the revenue in the income statement of the year in which they are sold to cover the cost of administration; the remainder is deferred and recognised over the following 28 months (the period of time AA expect the miles to be used).

Appendix 2.2   Accounting for Finance and Operating Leases

Operating or short-term leases are almost always accounted for by including the actual rental payments as an operating expense as it is incurred, or equalised over the term of the lease (see Chapter 10 for a detailed description of both operating and finance leases).

There are a number of ways of accounting for finance leases, with the majority of airlines using the following method:

- Calculate the present value of future lease or rental payments, using as the discount rate the implicit interest rate applied to the fair value of the asset to arrive at the rental amounts; if this is not known then the lessee's cost of borrowing may be used.
- Add this present value, or aggregate of the capital elements payable during the lease term, to the fixed tangible assets on the balance sheet, and depreciate the leased aircraft in exactly the same way as for a similar owned aircraft, i.e., over the same period and to the same residual value.
- Record the present value of future lease payments as a liability on the balance sheet (long-term obligation together with a current portion under current liabilities), reducing this each year by the appropriate part of the lease or rental payments made.
- Separate the lease payments into interest expenses and depreciation, or a reduction in the lease liability, for inclusion in the profit and loss statement (instead of rental expenses).

An alternative way of capitalising the value both of the asset and the liability is to take the fair market value (adopted by six out of 18 airlines in the KPMG/IATA survey), or to take the lower of the present value and the fair market value (four out of 18 airlines).

One or two airlines use a different value for the finance lease asset and the long-term lease liability, the difference being added to, or subtracted from, the interest expense over a given period. In the second step shown above, some airlines depreciate the leased asset over a different period to that which owned aircraft are depreciated. Almost all the airlines in the survey calculated the interest portion of the payment on an actuarial or effective yield basis over the lease term.

As will be demonstrated in Chapter 10, it is becoming more and more difficult to distinguish between operating and finance/capital leases. The following criteria are used by most airlines, and conform to their national accounting guidelines:

- Substantially all the risks and benefits of ownership are transferred from or to lessee.
- The term of the lease is equal to or greater than a certain portion of the asset's estimated useful life.
- The present value of minimum lease payments exceeds a certain proportion of the asset's fair value.
- Ownership of the asset will be transferred to the lessee at the end of the lease term, possibly for a very small consideration or residual value payment.

The UK rules for accounting for leases define a financial or capital lease which requires to be placed on balance sheet as:

> a lease that transfers substantially all the risks and rewards of ownership of an asset to the lessee. It should be presumed that such a transfer of risks and rewards occurs if at the inception of a lease the present value of the minimum lease payments amounts to substantially all (normally 90 per cent or more) of the fair value of the leased asset.

The US rules classify a lease as a capital lease if either ownership is transferred to the lessee, or there is a bargain purchase option, or the lease term covers 75 per cent or more of the remaining economic life of the aircraft, or the present value of the minimum lease payments is more than 90 per cent of the aircraft's fair value.

The international accounting standard bases its recommendation for inclusion of a finance lease on balance sheet on economic rather than legal ownership. In many European countries and Japan, finance leases were often excluded from the balance sheet because the airline did not have legal title or ownership. In the UK and US, however, these leases are capitalised and placed on the balance sheet.

A more difficult problem occurs with extendible operating leases, which usually have a lease term that covers the economic life of the aircraft, but give the lessee airline the opportunity to break the lease at no penalty (walk away from the deal) at various intervals over the term. British Airways have a number of aircraft leased in this way, and originally left them off balance sheet. However, from March 1995 onwards, they decided to place these on balance sheet, in line with latest UK financial reporting guidelines. The effect was to add £870 million to tangible fixed assets and £905 million to borrowings (at 31 March 1995). This also boosted operating profit for 1994/1995 by £53 million, since the interest payable part of the rental payment (£54 million) would have been transferred to non-operating items. It would also have reduced net profit in the earlier years of the lease term, but increased net profit in later years. This is because an equalised rental charge would have been replaced by depreciation and a declining interest charge over the lease term.

The IATA/KPMG guidelines have already been discussed in Section 2.8 above, and these are summarised in the diagram shown in Figure 2.1, which is quite widely used in decisions on whether a particular lease structure should be considered as a finance or operating lease.

Classification of a Lease

Figure 2.1 represents examples of situations in which it could be inferred that substantially all of the risks and rewards of the ownership have been transferred. See also Glossary of Terms for definitions.

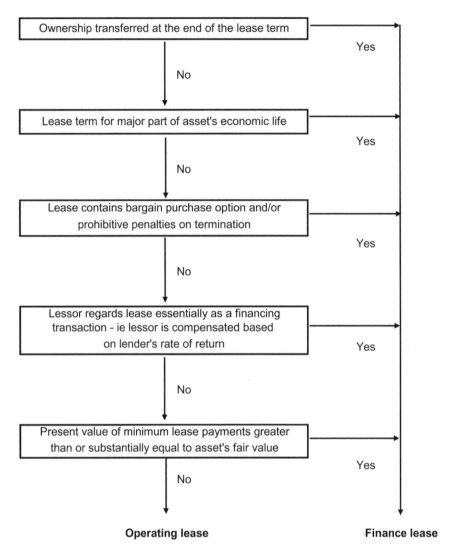

Figure 2.1   Aircraft lease classification guidelines

Source: Airline Accounting Guideline No. 6 (IATA/KPMG)

Chapter 3

Airline Financial Ratios

The previous chapter explained in some detail the individual items in an airline's profit and loss account, balance sheet and cash flow statement. Some idea can be gained of the airline's size, capital structure, profitability and the financing of its investments from an examination of these figures and the notes attached to them. However, performance ratios will need to be calculated to be able to assess past trends of a particular airline or to compare different airlines. These could be helpful in evaluating a shareholder's investment in an airline, or in an assessment by banks or lessors before entering into a loan or lease agreement. The ratios can be categorised under the following headings:

- Performance/earnings.
- Risk or solvency.
- Liquidity.
- Market valuation or investment.

The first group of ratios are designed to evaluate how the airline is trading, whether in relation to turnover, assets or equity, while the second deal with the risk of the firm being unable to meet its financial commitments overall, and continue trading. The third provides a measure of the airline's ability to meet its short-term financial commitments. The last group are concerned with value, and are based on the market price of the airline's shares or bonds and can thus only be calculated for companies that are traded on a stock market.

Some ratios use only profit and loss account data, some use only balance sheet data, and some combine data from each of these statements. The latter need to take into account the fact that balance sheet items are measured on a particular date, whereas profit and loss account items are summed over a particular period (usually one year). The balance sheet items may need therefore to be averaged over the same period.

The next part of this chapter explains how the more important and widely used ratios are calculated with reference to British Airways' last two financial years. In some cases it was impossible to compute comparable ratios for the previous year, as a result of the change in accounting rules in 2005. This affected equity in particular. The ratios for 2005/2006 were also compared with those for AMR using 2005 data. Ratios for a selection of major international airlines are then compared, before concluding with some of the principal problems with interpretation and comparison.

3.1 Performance/Earnings Ratios

Operating Ratio

The operating ratio is defined as operating revenue expressed as a percentage of operating expenditure; operating margin is an alternative expression that is similar to margin on sales.

Table 3.1   British Airways Group – Operating ratio/margin

	2004/2005	2005/2006
Operating revenues (£ million) – A	7,772	8,515
Operating expenses (£ million) – B	7,216	7,810
Operating profit/(los) (£ million) – C	556	705
Operating ratio (per cent) = A^* 100/B	107.7	109.0
Operating margin (per cent) = C^* 100/A	7.2	8.3

The operating ratio or margin gives an indication of management efficiency in controlling costs and increasing revenues. However, it can be distorted by changes in depreciation policy, or a switch from ownership of aircraft (involving both depreciation and interest charges, only the first of which is shown under operating costs) to operating leases (all of which annual cost is shown under operating costs). Ignoring these distortions, BA achieved a higher operating ratio in 2005/2006 than the 2004 ICAO preliminary world average of 103.5 per cent, and was also ahead of the 2005 IATA international scheduled average operating margin of 2.3 per cent.

For comparison, the AMR Corporation made a margin of -0.4 per cent in 2005, only a small improvement from the -0.8 per cent in 2004.

An alternative formulation of this ratio that avoids the operating lease/owned aircraft distortion is operating profit (after interest charges) expressed as a percentage of operating revenues. BA's interest expense (before capitalised interest) was £223 million in 2005/2006: adding this to operating expenses would have resulted in a decline in operating ratio from 109.0 per cent to 106.0 per cent, or a fall in margin from 8.3 per cent to 5.7 per cent (both for 2005/2006).

The possible distortion from a comparison of operating margins is clearly shown with AMR and Continental Airlines. Only 24 per cent of the former's fleet was on operating lease in 2005, whereas for Continental it was 77 per cent. Continental reported an operating margin of -0.3 per cent in 2005, which became -0.4 per cent if interest expense were deducted from operating profit (added to operating loss). In AMR's case, the margin increased from −0.4 per cent to −5.1 per cent, after accounting for almost US$1 billion in interest expense (US$410 million for Continental).

It is difficult to define a satisfactory target for this ratio (pre-interest), since it will depend on the airline's tax rate, financial gearing and other non-operating factors. A recent IATA study[1] suggested a minimum operating margin of between 9 per cent

---

1   Value Chain Profitability, IATA Economics Briefing No. 04, June 2006, p. 21.

and 10 per cent to meet their cost of capital. Delta Air Lines has in recent years used a target of 12.5 per cent, BA have a target operating margin (or EBIT margin) of 10 per cent for financial year (FY)2007/2008 (also a longer term corporate target across the business cycle), while Finnair apply a lower target of the same ratio of 6 per cent, without specifying year. Lufthansa aim to achieve a total EBIT of €1 billion by FY2008 (without specifying a ratio).

An alternative measure of operating profit increasingly used is EBIT, EBITDA or EBITDAR (also called EBITDRA). EBIT is earnings or net profit before deducting interest and tax (and before other items are added or subtracted such as profits from associates or gains from the sale of assets). This is effectively another word for 'operating profit'. Iberia uses the EBITDAR margin for their target of 16 per cent by FY2008. EBITDA is EBIT with depreciation and amortisation charges for the year added back to give a proxy figure for cash flow.

The last, EBITDAR is EBITDA with rental expenses added back. EBITDA and EBITDAR can be substituted for operating profit (or EBIT) in the above to calculate, for example, the EBITDA margin, instead of the operating margin. They have the advantage of being free of distortions from depreciation policy or method of aircraft financing. But they present a new distortion in that they total disregard capital costs and their relationship to other operating costs.

Net Profit Margin

The net profit margin is after tax profit expressed as a percentage of operating revenue or turnover.

Table 3.2   British Airways Group – Net profit margin

	2004/2005	2005/2006
Operating revenues (£ million)	7,772	8,515
Profit after tax (£ million)	392	467
Net profit margin (per cent)	5.0	5.5

This ratio was calculated for the world airline industry as a whole in Chapter 1 (Figure 1.3). BA's 2000/2001 ratio was the same as the margin for the industry, while for 2005/2006 the industry achieved a -0.8 per cent margin. This ratio has the advantage over the operating ratio or margin in that it is free of the operating lease distortion. However, the margin for a particular year may be increased or reduced by large asset sales, restructuring costs or asset write-downs.

Return on Invested Capital (Capital Employed)

Return on invested capital (ROIC) is the pre-tax profit before interest paid as a percentage of average total long-term capital employed. For some airline accounts, the figure for interest paid or payable is not given. Here the ratio could be calculated before *net interest*. Some airlines define this ratio as operating profit as a percentage of capital, but it is more logical to include any income from asset sales and investments to show the profit available to provide a return for the two classes of long-term capital providers, debt holders and shareholders.

Some investment banks use what is known as NOPAT for the numerator and adjust the denominator to include short-term debt and add back accumulated amortisation to goodwill. NOPAT is defined as EBIT plus interest received (income) together with the goodwill amortisation that has been added to the denominator. EBIT can also be reduced by the full tax rate.

The ratio can be calculated with or without minority interests, but if they are included (as in the example above), they should be included in both numerator and denominator of the ratio. Capitalised interest has been subtracted from interest payable, to reflect interest on lending for current, rather than future operations.

Table 3.3   Return on Invested Capital (ROIC)

	BA: 2005/2006[1]	AMR: 2005
Profit before tax and interest payable (US$ million)[2]	1,505	96
Average shareholders' equity (US$ million)	3,107	− 1,030
Average long-term debt (US$ million)	6,844	13,490
Av. long-term capital employed (£ million)	9,951	12,460
Return on capital (%)	15.1	n/a

1. Converted into US dollars at average rate over 2005/2006 of US$1.79/£
2. Profit/loss before tax plus interest expense (*i.e.*, adding back interest expense)

This percentage gives an indication of how successful the airline or group is in its investment of all the long-term capital under its management. It can move up and down significantly from year to year, so that more valid comparisons between airlines or industries might be better made using averages over a number of years. Comparisons are also distorted by greater use of aircraft and other assets on short-term operating leases.

While BA does not publish a figure for return on capital, Austrian Airlines modify the above formulation using earnings before interest (and not tax) and dividing by long-term and short-term debt less cash and cash equivalents (the denominator thus identical to the numerator of the net debt to equity ratio – *see below*). SAS use CFROI which is adjusted EBITDAR divided by a non-book measure of asset value (*see below*) for their 20 per cent target. Air France-KLM have a target ROCE of 7 per cent that it aims to achieve by FY2010.

A less common way of calculating return on investment is employed by Lufthansa. Profit is defined in the same way as Table 3.3, but investment is taken to be the balance sheet total assets or total liabilities (including current liabilities and provisions). Taking total liabilities may be too broad a definition, since it includes such items as accounts payable, which do not demand a return in any strictly financial sense. Lufthansa also use total assets at the year end, rather than using an average over the year. Averaging gives a better ratio (ideally a weighted average should be used), but the year end position is easier to calculate, and provides a similar ratio unless there have been major changes in assets over the year.

Return on Equity

Return on equity is the net profit after interest and tax expressed as a percentage of shareholder's funds. The numerator is before deducting minority interests and the denominator includes the capital belonging to these interests. This percentage gives an idea of how successful the airline's management is in using the capital entrusted to it by the owners of the company, or equity shareholders. It is sensitive to method of financing. Similar comments apply as for the return on capital employed, in terms of marked year to year fluctuations.

Table 3.4   Return on Equity (RoE)

	BA: 2005/2006[1]	AMR: 2005
Profit after tax and interest (US$ million)	836	− 861
Average shareholders' equity (US$ million)	3,107	− 1,030
Return on equity (%)	26.9	*n/a*

1. Converted into US dollars at average rate over 2005/2006 of US$1.79/£

AMR's ratio could not be calculated for 2005, since both profit and equity were negative. This makes the ratio meaningless. The ratio is usually calculated after tax, but some airlines (Austrian Airlines and Lufthansa in 2005) take profit before tax.

Target rates of return on equity are generally around 15 per cent and this is currently used by a major German bank, while the insurance company Hannover Re uses 12 per cent. A French utility uses a range of 10–15 per cent, and the bank ABN AMRO set a target of an average of 20 per cent for their future performance over 2005–2008. In 2005, the UK based low cost carrier, easyJet, adopted a RoE target of 15 per cent to be achieved within three years. Meeting the target would give senior staff an award of shares equivalent to their total annual salary. The agreement also allowed for smaller awards for smaller gains in RoE from its 2004/2005 level of 7.4 per cent.

As with ROIC, this ratio can be calculated both with and without minority interests. They have been included in the table above.

3.2   Risk or Solvency Ratios

Interest Cover

Interest cover is the profit before *net* interest payable and tax divided by *net* interest expenses.

Table 3.5   British Airways Group – Interest cover

	2004/2005	2005/2006
Profit before tax and net interest (£ million) (A)	681	748
Net interest payable (£ million) (B)	168	128
Interest cover (A) ÷ (B)	4.1	5.8

This is the formulation used by BA, defining it as the number of times that the profit/ (loss) before tax and excluding net interest payable covers net interest payable. This ratio is one of the more important ones, showing the ability of the airline to meet the interest payments on its debt. Without a clear margin of cover (well over 1.00), there will be little profit remaining for distribution to shareholders or ploughing back into the company. Banks and investors generally look for interest cover of at least 2.5:1, while an IATA industry capital needs study suggested that it should be not less than 1.5. The UK airports group, BAA, sets in internal target of 3.5 for its long-term plans, and BA more than achieved a substantial margin above this target in both years.

Some investment banks use the above formula using only interest payable. However, it is not always possible to calculate this, since many airlines show only net interest, without any breakdown between income and expense.

An alternative used by SAS is operating profit plus interest income divided by interest payable. For BA's FY2005/2006, this would mean a slightly lower cover of 3.6. AMR had negative profit before tax and net interest in 2005, and thus had no cover for its net interest payable of $808 million.

Interpretation of such trends as well as comparisons with other airlines needs to take into account key variables such as depreciation and leasing policies.

BA believes that the formulation shown in the table above is useful to investors when analysing their 'ability to meet its interest commitments from current earnings' (BA's Form 20K submission to the SEC for 2005/2006).

Finally, another way of approaching interest cover is to take the cash flow from operating activities before interest paid from the cash flow statement and relate that to interest paid. That would give a 7.3 times cover for BA in 2005/2006. For AMR it would have been 2.1 times covered for FY2005.

Debt/Equity Ratio

The debt/equity ratio, or gearing, is the long-term debt or borrowings divided by shareholders' funds.

Table 3.6   British Airways Group – Debt/equity ratio

At 31 March	2005	2006
Long-term debt (£ million)	4,045	3,602
Stockholders' equity (£ million)	1,397	2,074
Debt/equity ratio	2.90	1.74

BA's gearing has fallen below the 2:1 level, in spite of a large movement of £1.8 billion from equity to pension provisions. Under the UK GAAP accounting rules, its debt/equity would have been close to 1:1 at the end of FY2005/2006. As with the ratios discussed above, operating leases will also affect this one. Leaving this aside, BA's debt/equity ratio of 2.01 at the end of March 2000 was higher than the ICAO world airline figure of 1.32 at the end of December 1999, and by 2004 (the latest year for which complete ICAO data were available) BA was well below the industry average of 1.76 (before inclusion of pension liabilities). Comparisons over a longer period of time would show the marked cyclical effect on this ratio, with latest cyclical downswing causing a marked deterioration for the ICAO world airlines from 1.42 in 2000 to the 2003 position of 2.46.

It is also common to find gearing expressed by the long-term debt as a percentage of total capital employed: thus, BA's end March 2006 gearing would be £3.602 billion expressed as a percentage of £(3,602 + 2,074) billion, or 63.5 per cent.

A better measure of debt to equity, however, should include all outside liabilities, rather than only long-term ones, and debts should be net of any cash and deposits shown as current assets. In this form it can also be called the solvency ratio. BA define this ratio as net debt to total capital, with net debt being the sum of all loans, finance leases, hire purchase arrangements and capital bonds, net of short-term deposits and cash less bank overdrafts. Total capital is capital and reserves plus net debt. This approach produces an end March 2006 net debt to capital ratio of 44.2 per cent compared to the above 63.5 per cent, or a net debt to equity ratio of 0.79 *vs* 1.74 in 2005/2006. Another definition of net debt (used by SAS) is interest bearing debts minus interest bearing assets; this would be difficult to calculate using published data, but would in any case be very close to the BA definition.

The lower the debt/equity or solvency ratio the greater the firm's capacity for borrowing more outside finance, due to the lower risk to potential lenders. Banks sometimes include a covenant or condition on loans requiring the debt/equity ratio to be kept below a certain ratio (say, 2:1) otherwise the borrower would be in default.

The impact of debt/equity ratios or gearing is illustrated by the hypothetical example in Table 3.7. An airline which is more highly geared will display a larger variation in return on equity (the measure used by existing and potential shareholders). Thus, in good years the rate of return will be higher than that of the lower geared airline, other things such as profit and total capital employed being equal. In bad years, however, the return will be worse than the lower geared airline. Conversely, the lower geared airline will produce smaller variations in return on equity.

Southwest Airlines has one of the best financial records of any US airlines, and has consistently kept its long-term debt between 20 per cent and 30 per cent of total capital throughout the second half of the 1990s, or a debt/equity ratio averaging 0.35:1.[2] Even at the lowest point in the last recession (1991), Southwest's debt/equity was still only 0.97:1. At the end of 2005, Southwest's equity was 47 per cent of total liabilities and its debt/equity back down to only 0.21:1.

---

2   Southwest Annual Report, 1999.

Table 3.7   Effect of gearing on ratios

	Airline A	Airline B
Capital and reserves (£)	200,000	400,000
Long-term debt (£)	300,000	100,000
Total capital (£)	500,000	500,000
Debt/equity ratio	1.5	0.25
Pre-interest profit: year 1 (£)	30,000	30,000
Average capital and reserves (£ million)	− 30,000	− 10,000
Net profit after interest (£)1	0	20,000
Return on capital employed (%)	0	4
Return on equity (per cent)	0	5
Pre-interest profit: year 1 (£)	60,000	60,000
Average capital and reserves (£ million)	− 30,000	− 10,000
Net profit after interest (£)1	30,000	50,000
Return on capital employed (%)	6	10
Return on equity (%)	15	12½

1. Interest assumed to be 10 per cent of long-term debt

Swissair, or its parent company that was then called SAir Group, suffered a sharp deterioration in financial fortunes in 2000: worsening profits and large provisions in 2000 resulted in the debt/equity ratio deteriorating from 1.01:1 at end December 1999 to 4.68:1 at the end of 2000.[3]

Austrian Airlines uses shareholders' equity as a percentage of total assets (and liabilities) for their target. It has a medium-term target of keeping this above 25 per cent. It was only 17.7 per cent at the end of December 2005, with BA just below this figure at end March 2006. Lufthansa has a medium-term target to raise its percentage from 23.5 per cent in 2005 to above 30 per cent. Lufthansa also has a target band for its net debt to equity ratio (gearing) of between 40 per cent and 60 per cent (0.4–0.8), but from 2004 it included pension provisions in the calculation.

3.3   Liquidity Ratios

Current Ratio

The current ratio is the ratio of current assets to current liabilities.

A ratio of 1.00 is normally considered for industry in general to be broadly sound. Any ratio falling substantially below this level indicates that the business may not be generating adequate cash to meet short-term obligations as they become

---

3   The SAir Group Annual Report, 2000.

due. Airlines' current liabilities often include significant amounts relating to sales in advance of carriage (in BA's case £1,045 million at the end of March 2006). These might be excluded when calculating the current ratio, since they are mostly non-refundable claims on the airline. Such an adjustment was not necessary for BA's ratio at end March 2006, but it was more appropriate to AMR. This US airline's current assets totalled $6,164 million at the end of December 2005 compared with current liabilities of $8,320 million. This gave them a current ratio of 0.74, well below industry norms. However, they had $3,615 million of air traffic liability in current assets: these included some refundable tickets, but many that were not in addition to a sizeable FFP liability that is not reimbursable. Excluding this from current liabilities leads to an adjust figure of $4,705 million and an adjusted current ratio of 1.31.

Table 3.8   British Airways Group – Current ratio

At 31 March	2005	2006
Current assets (£ million)	2,752	3,666
Current liabilities (£ million)	3,269	3,432
Current ratio	0.84	1.07

If the current ratio is too high (well above 1.00), it suggests that the business is generating more cash than can be profitably re-invested for longer term expansion. The airline may, however, be building up a *war chest* for acquisition of other companies, or be expecting a period ahead of bunching of aircraft deliveries.

Liquidity covenants may be applied to bank debt, especially in cases where the airline does not have a high credit rating. For example, American Airlines has borrowed on the basis of being required to keep it liquidity equal to or above US$1.25 billion, or risk default. A covenant that requires a current ratio of 1.5 or above could also be applied in some cases.

A small number of airlines include rotatable items, or those spare parts that can be repaired and reused, as current rather than fixed assets. Other airlines would do the same with repairable items, which can only be repaired and reused a limited number of times (*e.g.*, tyres). These airlines would thus have inflated stock levels, and current ratios which would not be strictly comparable with the majority of airlines.

Acid Test/Quick Ratio

The ratio of liquid assets to current liabilities. The purpose of this ratio is to identify current assets that can be easily and readily converted into cash. There are no rules or targets on the desirable level of this ratio, but BA has a comfortable margin of liquidity.

BA's quick ratio improved to a healthier level at the end of FY2006, although the same adjustment for sales in advance of carriage applies here. Removing this non-cash liability would give BA a quick ratio of around unity.

Table 3.9   British Airways Group – Quick ratio

At 31 March	2005	2006
Liquid or quick assets (£ million)	1,682	2,440
Current liabilities (£ million)	3,269	3,432
Quick ratio	0.51	0.71

AMR's end 2005 cash and short-term investments amounted to $3,814 million compared to $4,705 million of current liabilities excluding its air traffic liability. This results in an adjusted quick ratio of 0.81, lower than might be expected, but no cause for alarm.

Another test that investors make is the number of days of cash operating expenses that the cash and short-term investments would cover (see 8.2.3 for this calculation).

3.4   Stock Market Ratios

Performance

Dividend cover   Net profit attributable to shareholders divided by dividend payable.

Table 3.10   British Airways Group – Dividend cover

	2000/2001	2005/2006
Profit for the year (£ million)	67	467
Dividend payable (£ million)	193	0
Dividend cover	0.35	*n/a*

There are no rules as to how high the level of dividend cover should be. Some investors, such as pension fund managers, require an adequate and continuing income stream, but others perhaps driven by rates of taxation look for capital gains. In a capital intensive industry, or one that requires the frequent application of new technology, it is prudent to keep the dividend cover high. In general, cover should exceed 1.00 by an adequate margin, and an earlier IATA study adopted a target of 2.00.

BA chose to maintain its dividend per share (17.9p) in 1999/2000 in the face of a net loss for the year, following profitable trading throughout the 1990s, including in the aftermath of the Gulf War recession. A dividend was also paid in the following year, despite very low cover.

Dividend yield   Dividend per share expressed as a percentage of the cost or market value of one share.

This is a useful ratio for investors to evaluate their investment in BA ordinary shares compared to other investment opportunities. But it only takes account of dividends returns, and not of expected future capital gains. BA's yield on 26 July 2001 was 4.4 per cent compared to the yield on the companies in the *Financial Times* all-share index of 2.6 per cent. No calculation has been possible between 2001 and 2006.

Yields on firms in the services sector (3 per cent) tended to be lower than those in the general industrial sector (4.4 per cent). Higher yields tend to compensate for slow or variable growth in earnings per share, as was the case for BA.

Market capitalisation   Market share price per share multiplied by the number of shares outstanding.

Market capitalisation will change in line with changes in share price, and the number of shares issued. Normally, the share price would be depressed by any large new issue of shares. Market capitalisation is shown for other airlines in Table 6.2.

Table 3.11   British Airways Group – Market capitalisation

At 31 March	2005	2006
Shares issued at end of year (million)	1,060.20	1,130.90
Share price (£) at year end	2.64	3.53
Market capitalisation (£ million)	2,799	3,992

Earnings per share   Profit after tax attributed to the parent company shareholders (*i.e.*, after allowing for minority interests) divided by the number of ordinary shares issued.

The absolute value and growth in this ratio has traditionally been a key target for the management of quoted companies, and one of the most important benchmarks for investment analysts. While it is still in widespread use, increased emphasis is now being placed on cash based ratios (see Equity value/EBDRIT above), as well as measures of economic value added. This is because, like many other ratios, it is susceptible to distortion by one-off items.

Table 3.12   British Airways Group – Earnings per share (EPS)

	2004/2005	2005/2006
Weighted average no.shares (million)	1,071.10	1,116.20
Net profit for the year (£ million)	377	451
Basic earnings per share (UK pence)	35.2	40.4

The ratio has the advantage over measures such as net profit by itself. This is because a company could increase net profit merely by acquiring another profitable company by issuing new shares. Earnings per share, however, would not automatically increase.

Earnings per share can also be calculated on a *fully diluted* basis. This allows for the future issue of further shares for employee share options, and from the convertible capital bonds. This would have increased the number of shares issued by BA over 2005/2006 to 1,138.5 million. Profit would also be increased by £2 million to allow for the elimination of convertible bond interest (for only part of the year). The net result of these changes would be to reduce BA's earnings per share to 39.8 pence in 2005/2006 on a diluted basis.

BA used this metric in their share option plan between 1999 and 2006: options were granted if EPS increased by more than 4 per cent above the retail price index (averaged over three consecutive years).

Price/earnings ratio   Market price per share divided by earnings per share.

The price/earnings (*P/E*) ratio shows how many years of current earnings are necessary to cover the share price. However, the stock market is always looking ahead, and if earnings are expected to increase strongly over the next few years this will push up the share price and result in higher *P/E* ratios as measured against current or latest historical figures. That is why growth or high technology shares often have high *P/E* ratios. To take some of this effect into account, the *P/E* ratio is sometimes calculated on a *prospective* basis, using a *forecast* of earnings per share for the year ahead.

It can be seen from Table 3.13 that BA's share price increased faster than earnings in 2005/2006, but its *P/E* is still well below the 20 plus levels achieved by the fast expanding low cost carriers.

Table 3.13   British Airways Group – Price/earnings ratio

As at 31 March	2005	2006
Market price per share (£)	2.64	3.53
Basic earnings per share (p)*	35.2	40.4
Price/earnings ratio	7.5	8.7

* for latest 12 month period

Value

Net asset value per share   Total assets less outside liabilities divided by total number of shares outstanding. This is the book (not market) value per share.

The book value of net assets per share gives only a very broad indication of the break-up value of the airline, depending on whether the assets were re-valued recently and the rate of inflation. BA re-value their properties from time to time, and have written down certain aircraft types. The market value has moved much in line with book value over the past year or so, reflecting limited opportunities for high earnings growth, or any substantial gains from sales of aircraft at higher than book values.

Table 3.14   British Airways Group − Net asset value per share

At 31 March	2005	2006
Book value of assets (£ million)	11,671	12,174
Total creditors (£ million)	10,274	10,100
Net book value of assets (£ million)	1,397	2,074
Shares issued at end of year (million)	1,082.90	1,130.90
Net asset value per share (£)	1.29	1.84
Market price per share (£)	2.64	3.53
Ratio of market to book value	2.05	1.92

Operating Cash Flow Multiples

An operating cash flow multiple is the ratio of the market value of debt and equity to EBDRIT (earnings before depreciation, rentals, interest and tax); an alternative formulation is based on the market value of equity alone. These multiples are used by investment banks to try to avoid the accounting biases that can distort the conventional ratios described above. They also use the market, rather than book value of shareholders' equity, which is an improvement (but only applicable to airlines with a market quotation for their equity). The main disadvantage of these ratios is that by avoiding accounting bias they are also removing the effect of efficiency in the use of capital. Airlines that operate very new high cost aircraft have these aircraft related costs removed from cash flow, which gives them an unfair advantage over those that have traded low capital costs for high fuel and maintenance costs. One bank does try to adjust for maintenance cost variations, but this involved some fairly heroic assumptions in the absence of detailed data.

Table 3.15   British Airways Group − Equity value/EBITDAR

	BA: 2005/2006[1]	AMR: 2005
Profit before tax and interest payable ($ million)	1,505	96
Depreciation, amortisation and rentals ($ million)	1,733	1,755
EBDRIT ($ million)	3,238	1,851
Average market value of equity ($ million)	6,115	3,487
Equity Value/EBDRIT	1.89	1.88

1. Converted into US dollars at average rate over 2005/2006 of US$1.79/£

The market value of equity in Table 3.15 has been calculated by taking the average of the share price times the number of shares issued at the beginning and end of the year. This information is given in the annual report. The EBITDAR can also be used in any of the other ratios described in this chapter, which involve measures of operating or per-tax profit. Market value to EBITDAR is an alternative to the more traditionally used price-earnings ratio (see Table 3.13).

The numerator in the above ratio can also include debt and other liabilities, or 'Enterprise value'. This is what it would cost to buy the airline free of debt and other liabilities (such as pension fund deficits). This is in contrast to the equity value which values the airline with these liabilities. Ideally the market value of debt should be included, but in practice most debt is not traded and thus book debt is used (see 4.3.2).

Other Ratios

Other measures which may be used, such as the average collection period, will be discussed in the chapter on working capital. Stocks/spare parts can also be expressed as a percentage of investments in aircraft and equipment.

The self-financing ratio is defined as internal sources of funds expressed as a percentage of the increase in fixed assets. Basing the ratio on the cash flow statement described in Section 2.5 would mean cash flow from operating activities expressed as a percentage of cash required for investing activities. This would have been a healthy 177 per cent for BA in 2000/2001 and 96 per cent for the AMR Corporation in 2000. Clearly, a ratio that is substantially below 100 per cent over a number of years would imply a deteriorating financial position.

Turnover to capital employed ratio   Turnover or operating revenue expressed as a ratio of average net assets employed (long-term debt plus shareholders' funds). In general, the higher the ratio (BA 0.90 in 1999/2000 and 1.53 in 2005/2006) the better the utilisation of assets. There are however dangers in comparing airlines with other industries, and between airlines where there are large differences in off-balance sheet financing of assets (*e.g.*, operating leases) or in degree of outsourcing. BA's 2000/2001 ratio of 0.91 looked somewhat low compared with American Airlines' 2000 ratio of 1.56, taking into account the percentage of their respectively fleets financed off-balance sheet of 33 per cent for BA and 25 per cent for American. American's ratio in 2005 was 1.66, not as far above BA's ratio as previously.

β Value   This gives an indication of the degree of risk in investing in airline shares. It is based on the capital-asset pricing model (CAPM), and can only be calculated for airlines with stock market quotations for their shares. The approach usually taken is to examine the relationship between airline stock market returns and the returns to the market relative to a risk-free rate. Major stock market indices such as S&P500 are taken as a proxy for the market, and long-term government bonds for the risk-free rate. Dividend income should be included in the data on total returns, and most analysis covers the previous five-year period. The β *Value* is the coefficient determined from the regression of airline *versus* market returns. In the early 1990s, values were generally between 1.2 and 1.6, with reasonably good correlation coefficients.

An earlier study examined the airline industry as a whole and found that airlines had a β value of 1.80, compared to retailing with 1.45, construction with 1.30, drugs and cosmetics with 1.15, banks and oil companies with 0.85 and energy utilities with 0.60.[4]

More recent studies have shown some deterioration in the degree of correlation (*e.g.*, BA), with β Values often close to or below one.[5] For example, Qantas had a value of 1.51, Singapore Airlines 1.33 and Lufthansa 1.21. The corresponding values from Datastream were 0.86, 0.92 and 1.14.

This implies that some airline stocks are less volatile than the 'market,' and thus less risky, it also suggests some analysts are making a significant number of adjustments to the figures. However, this may be because the market has become more volatile, following the inclusion of a greater weight of IT and telecoms companies.

β Values are used in determining the cost of equity capital in Weighted Average Cost of Capital (WACC), which is discussed in more detail in 8.3.3. This is in turn used as the discount rate in Cash Value Added (CVA) calculations (see 2.7 above), as well as in the appraisal of new investments. Lower betas imply lower discount rates and the acceptance of more capital investment proposals.

3.5   Inter-airline Comparison of Financial Ratios

So far in this chapter, examples of ratios have been given for only 2 years of data for British Airways to assist in an understanding of how they can be calculated in practice. Some comparative figures have also been shown for one or two other major international airlines, in particular AMR. In this section, the comparison will be broadened to include some of the major airlines from North America, Europe and Asia.

The comparisons are shown in Table 3.16 for the 2004 calendar year for the majority of airlines, April 2004 to March 2005 for some airlines, and years ending in September (Thai) and June 1999 (Qantas) for two airlines. Given the variations in the ratios over the economic cycle, a stricter comparison would have adjusted the figures to the calendar year. Most of the major airlines were profitable, having recovered from 9/11 (for the US, and to a lesser extent, European airlines) and SARS (for some of the Asian airlines). Ratios were not calculated for some airlines because of negative results or negative equity, either of which produces meaningless figures. There are numerous problems associated with comparisons such as these, which have been discussed earlier. They are also summarised below. In spite of these problems, it is considered worthwhile presenting a view of the financial position of the major world airlines after some recovery had occurred.

---

4   Rosenberg, B. and Guy, J. (1988).

5   Morrell, P.S. and Turner, S.A. (2002).

Table 3.16   Key financial ratios for major airlines, 2004/2005

Airline (Financial year end)	Operating Ratio (%)	Return on Equity* (%)	Debt/ Equity	Interest Cover
Asia/Pacific Airlines				
Cathay Pacific (December 2004)	110.7	14.6	0.5	6.4
JAL Group (March 2005)	102.7	15.5	6.1	2.3
Korean Air (December 2004)	105.6	17.4	1.0	n/a
Malaysia Airlines (March 2005)	102.6	9.5	0.0	n/a
Qantas Group (05 June)	109.7	11.9	0.8	5.3
SIA Group (March 2005)	108.5	13.6	0.1	12.1
Thai Airways (September 2005)	115.3	26.1	1.4	4.8
North American Airlines				
AMR (December 2004)	97.8	n/a	n/a	n/a
Continental (December 2004)	97.1	n/a	19.2	n/a
Delta Air Lines (December 2004)	90.4	n/a	n/a	n/a
Northwest (December 2004)	96.3	n/a	3.1	n/a
Southwest (December 2004)	109.3	8.9	0.3	11.3
UAL (December 2004)	93.1	n/a	n/a	n/a
US Air (December 2004)	95.3	n/a	n/a	n/a
Air Canada (December 2004)	99.2	n/a	11.6	n/a
European Airlines				
Air France (March 2005)	100.5	4.1	2.0	n/a
Alitalia (December 2004)	91.5	n/a	3.7	n/a
Austrian Group (December 2004)	103.4	8.5	2.4	2.2
British Airways (March 2005)	109.0	14.4	1.7	2.8
Iberia (December 2004)	104.3	28.9	0.5	n/a
KLM (March 2005)	103.6	6.8	1.9	1.8
Lufthansa (December 2004)	101.2	13.5	0.9	0.4
SAS (December 2004)	97.0	n/a	1.7	n/a
Virgin Atlantic (December 2004)	100.9	4.1	1.0	2.1

* Year-end shareholders' equity

Operating Ratio

Asian airlines such as Cathay Pacific, Singapore Airlines and Thai Airways International have traditionally achieved operating ratios of between 110 per cent and 120 per cent. However, only Cathay and Thai achieved this for 2004/2005, and only by a small margin. Singapore Airlines' ratio was well below past levels but reasonable good by airline standards. Malyasian Airlines had been privatised in 1994, but sold back to the government in 2001 in a poor financial state. Its operating result was positive but very low, faced with uneconomic fares on domestic routes, poor productivity and growing LCC competition.

In other world regions, only Southwest in the US reached a reasonable level, with the remaining majors still in deep financial trouble. Apart from BA, the main European airlines were scarcely above break even, in a year when fuel price rises were combined with adverse currency trends and weak yields, with Alitalia and SAS making a loss. Continental and Iberia have a much higher percentage of their fleet off-balance sheet, and thus high rentals, which tends to depress operating ratio relative to net profit margin.

3.5.1   Return on Equity

Return on equity, rather than investment or assets, has been chosen to reduce the distortion arising from off-balance sheet assets. More highly geared Asian airlines, such as Thai and JAL thus generated a relatively high return on equity, commensurate with the risk taken by shareholders. On the other hand, three relatively highly geared airlines in Europe, Austrian Airlines, KLM and Air France, recorded low returns on equity. Only Iberia, Lufthansa and BA generated the levels of return that investors might expect. In the US, Southwest's RoE was somewhat low, but it also has very low gearing. None of the other US carriers made a net profit upon which to base a meaningful return.

Debt to Equity Ratio

This ratio is still considered one of the most important ones for an assessment of risk and solvency, although some analysts now rely more on the less problematical interest cover. Ideally net debt to equity should be calculated, but some sources (such as ICAO) only allow the more traditional debt/equity to be determined.

From Table 3.16, only Iberia, Lufthansa and Virgin Atlantic had satisfactory ratios, with Alitalia and Austrian too high. It is notable that the latter were still partly owned by their respective governments. Four of the US airlines had negative equity, and thus the ratio could not be calculated. Of the others, the very low level for Southwest has already been mentioned. Northwest and Continental had levels that would indicate near-insolvency, and Northwest subsequently filed for Chapter 11.

Most of the Asian airlines had satisfactory debt/equity ratios. The exception was the privately owned JAL, which has made poor returns over the past few years. JAL did not have very large cash balances to use to offset against their debt.

Interest Cover

This ratio was calculated as operating profit divided by interest expense (which for many airlines was effectively net interest). Interest cover varied widely amongst the sample airlines shown in Table 3.16. None of the European airlines had comfortably high levels, but Austrian, BA and Virgin were adequately covered. In North America, Southwest had no problem with this ratio, given its low debt and interest costs. The other airlines all made an operating loss for the year, and were unable to cover their interest. If depreciation were added back to operating profit to give cash operating profit, only AMR would have covered interest expense. Some of the remainder were even recording negative cash operating profits. All the Asian airlines except Malaysian and JAL showed excellent cover, while Korean indicated that it received more interest than it paid.

3.6   Interpretation Problems

Distortion of Comparative Data

Inflation affects comparative profitability, primarily through depreciation, which is usually based on the historic cost of assets. Seasonal factors will also distort ratio analysis, and many balance sheet amounts will be sensitive to the choice of financial year end in relation to the point in the seasonal cycle. For example, BA's financial year ends at the end of their low season, which means that many ratios will be lower than would be the case for their second quarter results. SAS changed in 1987 from reporting annual financial results to the end of September, to a calendar year basis. Air France has also changed from a calendar year to a financial year ending 31 March.

Differences in Accounting Treatment

Different depreciation periods will affect the comparability of ratios, as well as whether aircraft leases are on or off balance sheet. Writing off route rights or slot acquisitions against reserves will increase the debt/equity ratio. Other distortions are the capitalisation of interest payments (or turning an expense into an asset), and different treatment of foreign exchange gains and losses. Earnings per share can be distorted by the definition of extraordinary items, and the way taxation is accounted for will affect in particular the debt/equity ratio. Many of these have already been discussed, but the three areas of major concern can be summarised as follows:

- Asset lives and cost (capitalisation of interest on advance payments, manufacturers' credits, historical cost *vs.* market value), and residual values used for depreciation.
- Treatment of leased aircraft, or more generally whether aircraft financing is on or off-balance sheet.
- Accounting for foreign exchange gains and losses, and the treatment of foreign exchange hedging and foreign operations.

These and other possible distortions will affect most of the ratios to a greater or lesser degree, although some, such as interest cover, will be less affected than others, such as debt/equity ratio. An attempt to address most of these areas, together with many airline examples, was made in a special report published by Airline Business in 2004.[6]

Ratio Analysis Used to Assist Judgement

It is impossible to generalise as to whether one particular ratio by itself is good or bad. For example, a high quick ratio shows a strong liquidity position, but the firm may not be earning a high enough return on its total assets. The airline analyst should therefore use a number of ratios together. In a study of the performance of US firms over a 20 year period, Peters and Waterman used six indicators to identify 43 excellent companies. They were asset growth, equity growth, market to book value, return on capital, return on equity and return on sales.[7]

Window Dressing

Balance sheets are only a snapshot on a particular date and firms can employ techniques to make their position look better on that day. Sometimes profit and loss accounts can be made to look worse.

---

6   Milne, I.R. (2005), Bridging the GAAP, *Airline Business*, July.
7   Peters, T.J. and Waterman, R.H., Jr (1982), *Search of Excellence*.

Chapter 4

Airline Valuation

Airline accounts are not expected to show how much the airline is worth or even the value of its fixed assets. Fixed assets are generally included at their original historical cost, less an allowance for depreciation. It is unlikely that this book value of tangible assets at a given date would coincide with the market or re-sale value of the same assets. The last part of the previous chapter highlighted these differences in terms of the stock market value of an airline and its relationship to the book value of its assets.

This chapter will expand on this, and introduce the further issue of the absence of sizeable intangible assets such as route rights and slots in most airline accounts. It will first examine how these might be valued for international airlines, and then go on to review various approaches to valuing all or part of such airlines. This problem is faced by advisers to governments on the privatisation of their national airlines, which is the subject of Chapter 7.

4.1   The Valuation of Intangible Assets

4.1.1   Route or Traffic Rights

An airline's intangible assets would include mainly its route/traffic rights, and the rights to take-off and landing slots at congested airports. They might also include items such as brand value, and management and staff experience and training.

Scheduled airlines operate international air services using traffic rights granted to them by governments. Most of these rights are still negotiated bilaterally between two countries, with each country designating one or more carriers to take advantage of the traffic rights that the designating states have negotiated.

The negotiation of these rights was originally pursued according to a *quid pro quo* approach, with countries exchanging routes of comparable value. This was later to become the doctrine of an *equal exchange of economic benefits*, which dominates most bilateral negotiations today. For one country to negotiate effectively with another, it needs to evaluate a complex web of options, which would encompass fifth and even sixth freedom rights in addition to third and fourth freedoms.[1] It would also need to consider the so-called *soft rights*, including such areas as transfers of foreign exchange, and the opening of sales offices, as well as increasingly code-sharing and ground handling.

---

1   Doganis, R. (2002), *Flying off Course: the Economics of International Airlines*, London: Routledge. Third edition.

Most governments view these traffic rights as government property, and if an airline ceases to operate or goes into liquidation they revert to the state. For example, the UK's Civil Aviation Authority considered the possible sale or franchising of route rights before the privatisation of British Airways, but took the following view:

> Route licenses are not property. British Airways did not purchase its licenses .... Insofar as the state, through the licensing of air services, gives airlines an opportunity to operate profitably, these opportunities remain at the disposal of the state.[2]

On the other hand, when one scheduled airline acquires another as a going concern, it has usually acquired its traffic rights in addition to its tangible assets, existing staff and other contractual obligations and arrangements.

Any premium paid for the airline might be thought of as goodwill, but this would probably include the value of traffic rights. This was the case when British Airways acquired British Caledonian, and it was also the case more recently when British Airways acquired CityFlyer Express. In both cases British Airways inherited a substantial number of scheduled routes out of Gatwick Airport, which were not returned to the state for re-allocation, although the competition authorities made various stipulations relating to market entry by other airlines. In the case of the CityFlyer take-over, British Airways were capped on the share of slots that they could hold at London Gatwick Airport.[3]

A stricter definition of goodwill would be the amount by which the value of a business as a whole exceeds the value of its individual assets less its liabilities. Assets, here, should include all intangible assets such as traffic rights, airport slots, concessions, patents or trademarks. But it is difficult in practice to separate the goodwill and other intangible asset elements in any premium paid for an airline, since intangible assets are not valued and placed on the balance sheet.

In the USA, there was a considerable debate in 1982 when Braniff's Latin American routes were purchased by Eastern Airlines. But the Department of Transportation (DoT) finally approved the deal, with Judith Connor, then Assistant Secretary at DoT, proposing that 'this freedom to deal in what had once been valuable gifts from government should be made a permanent right'.[4]

United Airlines acquired the Pacific Division of Pan American World Airways in 1985, including aircraft, route rights and valuable slots at Tokyo's Narita Airport. The transfer was opposed by the US Department of Justice, but was approved by the Transportation Secretary after an evidentiary hearing. Out of the total price of US$750 million, it was estimated that only $365.8 million was accounted for by aircraft and other tangible assets.[5]

---

2   CAA (1984), *Airline Competition Policy*, *CAP*500, Civil Aviation Authority, London.

3   Jasper, C. (1999), BA CityFlyer take-over approved, *Flight International*, 28 July-2 August.

4   Howard, B. (1982), The Iron Lady at DOT, *Forbes*, 7 June.

5   Fisher, F.M. (1987), Pan-American to United: The Pacific Division Transfer Case, *Rand Journal of Economics*, 18, No. 4, winter.

Billions of dollars were spent by US airlines in purchasing traffic rights from other US carriers during the 1980s, and the US Government no longer questions these route rights aspects of any deal, but is rather concerned with its competitive consequences. In the 1990s, however, very liberal open skies agreements, and the promise of further liberalisation, reduced the importance of such acquisitions (see 4.1.2).

In other parts of the world, there have been few complete take-overs of scheduled airlines up to the late 1990s (see 6.6 for events since then), apart from the British Airways deals mentioned above and Air France's acquisition of UTA and Air Inter, both of which were within national boundaries.[6] In all these cases, the traffic rights have been transferred with the sale, although some routes have had to be handed back at a later stage following government (or European Commission) investigations of the anti-competitive implications of such deals. However, the practice of buying and selling route or traffic rights by themselves has so far only been observed in the US, although Air Canada did attempt (unsuccessfully) to buy all the international traffic rights held by Canadian Airlines International in 1993. However, in January 2000 Air Canada purchased the entire company, including all slots and route rights.

The value of traffic rights can only be realised once they are exercised by an airline. Some airlines can make more use of such rights than others, perhaps due to their greater marketing presence, or the fact that they complement their existing route structure and provide greater opportunities to feed traffic to other routes.[7]

Thus, the value of these rights can only be realised in conjunction with the production process, which is the carriage of passengers and cargo. In this respect they are similar to brands, which, although they can also be sold separately, only have value when applied to a particular product or service. The establishment of brand value involves considerable expenditure in improving product quality and consistency across the network, as well as communication to the marketplace. The successful brand should result in an airline achieving and sustaining both above average yields and load factors.

Virgin Atlantic Airways franchised their brand to the Greek scheduled airline, SEEA, and the Irish carrier, Cityjet. These two independent airlines used the Virgin brand in conjunction with services they operated between London and Athens and Dublin respectively. In the first case, there was limited opportunity to feed traffic to Virgin Atlantic services, and, in the second case, none at all. SEEA services were taken over by Virgin upon the airline's demise, and the Cityjet arrangement has been terminated. Virgin Blue holds a license from Virgin Enterprises for its operations

---

6   The acquisition of a controlling interest in an airline outside the country of the purchasing airline was considered highly unlikely under the present international regulatory system, since it would put at risk all the traffic rights granted to that airline under its existing bilateral agreements. That is now changing at least within the EU.

7   For example, Continental Airlines were given approval to operate the Seattle–Tokyo route in 1988, hoping to generate US$126 million in annual revenues. They actually only managed to generate US$28 million in revenues in 1989, and in late 1990 sold the route to American Airlines for US$150 million. American clearly expected significantly higher revenues than Continental could generate.

in Australia which expires at the end of 2015. In return it has contracted to pay an annual fee of A$100,000 or 0.5 per cent of gross sales, whichever is the greater.

In accounting terms they would both be considered as intangible assets, since no physical equipment or facilities are involved. In the US, where airlines have acquired route rights they are general included in their balance sheets and amortised over 40 years.[8] This latter figure is presumably based on their likely future useful or economic life. In other parts of the world, the premium arising on the take-over of another airline (including traffic rights) would either be written off against reserves, or amortised in a similar way.

4.1.2   Factors Determining the Value of Traffic Rights

A large number of factors may contribute to the value of traffic rights on a route, but they might be grouped in three main categories:[9]

- Route characteristics.
- Management characteristics.
- Transaction characteristics.

The first refers to the existing and expected level of traffic on the route, the degree to which it fits an airline's existing network, as well as the mix of traffic and variation in demand by season, month, day or hour. The existing degree of economic regulation of the route will be important, and will dictate the degree to which frequency can be increased, and market-based air fares introduced. It will also indicate the number of competitors on the route, reflected in the air services agreement between the countries at each end of the route. Competition and the ability to add frequency might also be constrained by the availability of slots at airports (*e.g.*, Tokyo Narita and London Heathrow).

Under perfect competition, with open skies and little economic regulation, the value of route rights would be expected to fall to close to zero. The more regulated the routes, the greater the potential for earning monopoly profits, the discounted present value of which would be the value of the rights. Under the present system of licensing air carriers, these monopoly profits do not have to be paid to the state in the form of public franchise fees. Liberalisation of air services agreements is seen in many countries as the preferred way to introduce competition and reduce monopoly profits. However, even in more liberal countries such as the US the bilateral system still gives route rights considerable value, which accrues to the carrier rather than the government. At present, there seems little likelihood of a world-wide introduction of open skies, so that these traffic right values will continue, albeit reduced by increased competition, or the prospect of greater competition.

---

8   KPMG/IATA (1992), *Accounting Policies, Disclosure and Financial Trends in the International Airline Industry*, KPMG in Association with IATA, Geneva.

9   Hai, N. (1994), *An Evaluation of Scheduled Airline Traffic Rights*, MSc thesis: Cranfield University, England.

The second of the above categories refers to management skills in combining routes into an effective and profitable network. Strategic issues are also relevant, as well as the efficiency of the airline in controlling costs and enhancing revenues. For example, some of Pan-American's loss making international routes were turned into profit by the management of airlines that acquired them (helped by far better domestic feed).[10] These factors are clearly difficult to quantify, but can be captured indirectly through their effect on the first group of factors mentioned above.

The third category relates to the characteristics of the transaction. These would depend on the type and timing of the transaction: whether it was incremental to an airline's network or the acquisition of a division or airline; whether it was combined with other assets such as slots or aircraft; its timing in the economic cycle; and whether it was a distress sale. Some of the US route rights acquisitions, especially those bought from Pan Am, concerned a large number of routes comprising the regional operations of the vendor. These would include both aircraft and slots. Others related to only a few international routes, but usually connecting with one of the hubs operated by the purchaser, and therefore having strategic importance. Often there were no serious competing bids, which together with a distress sale resulted in a bargain price being accepted. The AMR Corporation acquired TWA from Chapter 11 bankruptcy in April 2001 for $625 million in cash, and agreed to honour over $3 billion in debt. There was no other bidder for the airline, although both Continental and Frontier bid for TWA's Washington National slots, and Galileo bid for the airline's shares in Worldspan.

Sometimes one serious competing bidder pushed up the price significantly, as in the case of SAS bidding against British Airways for British Caledonian. A large premium was also thought to have been paid by American Airlines to acquire TWA's London Heathrow routes and slots in December 1990, following United's purchase of Pan Am's Heathrow rights in October of the same year.

4.1.3 Rights to Airport Slots

A growing number of capital city airports are suffering from runway congestion at peak periods. At such times, demand for take-off or landing times (slots) far exceeds the available supply. Examples of this are the slot controlled or 'high density' airports in the US (New York Kennedy and La Guardia, Washington National and Chicago O'Hare), London Heathrow and Frankfurt in Europe, and Tokyo Narita in Asia. Some additional capacity can often be obtained by improved air traffic control techniques or technology, but badly needed extra runways are usually ruled out because of environmental restrictions or lack of green fields for expansion. New airports are sometimes possible (*e.g.*, Hong Kong Chep Lap Kok or Munich), but these take considerable time and money to build.

Slots are allocated by a system of historical precedence or 'grandfather rights'. An airline that has used a slot in the previous season can use it again in the next corresponding season. Since airlines need both take-off slots at the origin airport

---

10 AAE (1990), Pan Am: What Will it Sell Next?, *The Avmark Aviation Economist*, April.

and landing slots at the destination airport to be able to offer a viable service, this procedure needs to be coordinated internationally. This has historically been done through the airline trade association, IATA.

To try to allow greater competition than would be available through this system of self-regulation, the European and US authorities have both introduced legislation to provide a pool of available slots for new entrants, as well as stricter 'use it or lose it' rules. However, many observers do not think these regulations go far enough, and do not allocate sufficient and timely slots to new entrants to allow them to operate at competitive frequencies on short to medium haul routes.

It is generally thought that it is the airports or government, rather than airlines, that own slots. US legislation denies the existence of any right of ownership of slots, but the Federal Aviation Administration (FAA) does allow airlines to exchange, sell or lease the slots that it has allocated to them.[11] In the US the sale or lease of slots to another airline needs to be accompanied by access to gates and passenger handling facilities which are usually owned or controlled by the vendor or lessor.

The European Commission's proposal for a Regulation amending their previous rules on the allocation of slots at Community airports defines slots as 'entitlements to depart or arrive at an airport on a specific date and time', and avoids assigning their legal rights to either airlines or airports. It adds in paragraph 12 that 'slots are allocated as public goods, based on certain rules, to the most deserving air carrier'.[12]

In Europe and other parts of the world, slots can be exchanged but not bought or sold. Unofficially, however, trading does take place, although not on a large scale. Legalised slot trading was suggested by British Airways as a solution to the demands for increased access to Heathrow Airport by US carriers, in return for their approval of their June 1996 proposal for an alliance with American Airlines.

4.1.4   Valuation Methods

The value of an airline's intangible assets and goodwill could be inferred from a comparison of its total market capitalisation and the market value of its net tangible assets. The value of the traffic rights would then need to be separated from the other items of goodwill or intangible assets. For this method of valuation, the airline would also have to be quoted on a stock market, and a market price would have to found for all tangible assets. However, the market capitalisation of an airline that did not have a share price quotation could be estimated by applying the price-earnings ratio of a comparable airline which was quoted.

A discounted cash flow approach could also be used, given that the purchase of traffic rights could be seen as an investment which produced a stream of net benefits

---

11   Haanappel, P.P.C. (1994), Airport Slots and Market Access: Some Basic Notions and Solutions, *Air and Space Law*, XIX, No. 4/5, pp. 198–199.

12   Commission of the European Communities (2001), *Proposal for a Regulation of the European Parliament and of the Council amending. Council Regulation (EEC) No.95/93 of 18 January 1993 on common rules for the allocation of slots at Community airports,* COM(2001)335, Brussels 20 June.

over its useful life. The present value of the net benefit stream, discounted at an appropriate rate, would then be the value of the traffic rights.[13] This approach is difficult to apply in practice, principally because:

- The useful life would be difficult to estimate, but judging by the accounting treatment of such rights would probably be over a long period.
- Future revenues and costs would be impossible to forecast with any precision over a relatively long period principally due to uncertainties relating to the future economic regulation of the industry and the economic environment.
- Re-investment requirements would need to be considered, and possibly the terminal value of the assets.

A final method of valuing traffic rights is to analyse them as a function of one or more causal variables, and calibrating the resulting model against actual prices paid by airlines for route rights. These variables were discussed above, and can be grouped as:

- Revenue or income related variables.
- Traffic or traffic related variables.

The transactions used for the model would almost entirely be limited to various US deals, and thus the model's relevance to other parts of the world might be questionable. At its simplest level, this approach implies that if American Airlines pays US$195 million for TWA's Chicago–London route which carries 190,000 passengers a year, then Pan Am's North Atlantic services which carry around 3.7 million passengers would be worth around US$3.9 billion, or 20 times as much.[14]

Rather than trying to forecast variables such as revenues or income over the useful life of the investment, current year or one year ahead projections can be used. This type of approach is often used by financial institutions in the form of a price/ earnings (*P/E*) ratio. This was described in Section 3.4 in its application to valuing a company, but it could also be applied to a single or group of investments.

Thus, the value of the traffic rights would be the product of the current (or projected) year net profit or earnings from the route and *a P/E* ratio. The ratio used should be based on the market ratio for an airline operating similar services. For example, Pan Am sold its Internal German Services to Lufthansa in 1988 for US$300 million. Given that Pan Am made an estimated US$43 million operating profit on the route in 1987, this purchase price implied *a P/E* ratio of around seven, which was thought to be an undervaluation according to some observers.[15]

Relating actual or potential earnings from a route to its value in this way requires the choice of *a P/E* ratio, which can only be inferred from data produced by deals of

---

13 Key, S.L., ed. (1989), *The Ernst and Young Guide to Mergers and Acquisitions*, New York: John Wiley & Sons.

14 AAE, supra.

15 AAE, supra.

a similar nature. However, it is often impossible to obtain estimates even for latest year's earnings at the level of individual or even groups of routes.

The valuation of slots has received attention as a result of proposals in Europe for the introduction of slot trading (see 4.1.3 above). The implications of such a change for BA's balance sheet and return on capital were explored by equity research analysts using two methods of slot valuation.[16] They suggested one approach based on previous slot trades by US carriers and another based on the treatment of landing and *en route* charges as operating leases, and calculating their discounted present value (over an unspecified number of future years at a 9 per cent discount rate). Under the first method, they valued BA's Heathrow and Gatwick slots at around £1 billion, and under the second method at £710 million. The first method was based on an average price per slot of £4,200 (£5,000 at Heathrow and £2,500 at Gatwick), compared to their estimated slot prices of £10,200 and £17,200 paid by United and American respectively. The US airline prices probably included at least 50 per cent of the total of 11,000 annual slots in the peak period, but was also based on some fairly crude assumptions on the part of the total consideration paid that was attributable to the slots at the US end of the routes. No value appeared to have been assigned to the route authority as a separate asset from the slots. The early 1990s going rate for US slots was thought to be around $1.5 million a year, or $4,100 for each slot.[17] A later estimate of £2 million a year ($3.2 million), or £5,500 ($8,800) a slot, was made by Continental Airlines in connection with the proposal for BA to relinquish some of their Heathrow slots.[18] KLM recorded a gain of US$25 million in their 1997/1998 accounts relating to the 'sale' by KLM UK of the Heathrow slots used for their four daily flights to Jersey.[19] This was equivalent to $8,560 (around £5,800) per slot. Swiss International Airlines 'sold' eight daily slots at Heathrow to BA for SFR43 million in the first Quarter of their 2005 financial year.[20] These slots were originally used to secure a loan from BA to Swiss in the second half of 2003. In US dollar terms this amounted to just under $5m per take-off/landing slot over a full year. In early 2004, Qantas paid what was probably the highest price for Heathrow slots to flyBe: A$47.3 million for two slot pairs, or an average of US$16 million per annual take-off/landing slot.[21] BA was reported to have been outbid by their alliance partner in this case.[22] The high price reflects competitive bidding, as well as the likelihood of all the slots being in the peak period. The deal exceeded the previous high price paid in 2003 of US$21 million or $10.5 million per pair by BA to United for two slot pairs at the airport.[23] United also leased slots at Heathrow to the Indian carrier, Jet Airways, for three years.

---

16 HSBC James Capel (1996), *British Airways: Selling Slot(s)*, November, pp. 31–33.

17 Doganis, R. (1992), *The Airport Business*, Routledge, p. 109.

18 *Travel Weekly*, 5 (15 January 1997).

19 *Flight International*, 8–14 July 1998.

20 Swiss International Financial report for the first half of 2005.

21 Qantas Annual Report (2005).

22 BA Outbid for Heathrow Slots Package, *Financial Times*, 21 January 2004.

23 Virgin, United Airlines in Heathrow Deal, *Financial Times*, 7 November 2005.

Most of the deals for slots at the US slot constrained airports have been on a lease basis, although buying and selling there is legal. Average slots prices between 1990 and 1997 were around US$1 million, with a US Airways deal in 2000 valued at just under $1 million per air carrier slot, and much lower for commuter slot. The same source also highlighted the large variation in value between peak and off-peak period, the difference at New York, La Guardia Airport being four times.[24]

4.2 The Valuation of Tangible Assets

Tangible assets cover both the fixed or physical assets of an airline and the long-term investments in other companies or airlines. The first consists largely of aircraft and related spares, but also buildings, land, vehicles and equipment. The second could be in shares of quoted companies, in which case valuation can be based on the market price. In the case of unquoted companies, the approach described in 4.3 below could be taken. This section will focus on tangible fixed assets, the balance sheet valuation of which was described in the previous chapter as historical cost less accumulated depreciation. Depreciation rates, however, can vary markedly for the same aircraft type, according to the policies adopted by the airline.

For airlines with stock market quotations, the market capitalisation will show investors' valuation of the airline as a whole on a day-to-day basis, but this will include intangible assets, management strength and business prospects, or what has been described as the airline 'franchise'.

A way to separate the value of the fleet and other tangible assets would be to examine the market value for these assets according to used aircraft transactions. There are three problems with this: first, there are very few transactions involving airline ground facilities; second, aircraft are far from commodities and it would be difficult to find a comparable market transaction in terms of aircraft age, number of hours flown and cycles completed, time to major overhaul and modifications incorporated; and third, the used aircraft market is cyclical which makes modelling aircraft price behaviour problematic.

One way of avoiding these problems is to estimate the replacement value for each aircraft in an airline's fleet. If aircraft are no longer in production, such as the DC10-30, then the nearest equivalent, the MD-11, is taken. A standardised depreciation rate is then applied to the replacement values to allow for the fleet's age. One finance house has used a straight line depreciation method over 20 years' useful life to a residual value of 10 per cent. They then deducted depreciation according to the average fleet age in years, weighted by replacement costs, to arrive at the current market value of the airline's fleet.[25] A major problem with this approach is that the new replacement is likely to incorporate lower fuel, maintenance and possibly crew costs, such that a higher profit stream would be generated.

---

24 Flight and Slot Valuations under Alternative Market Arrangements, *William Spitz, GRA, Paper to German*, Hamburg: Air Transport Association Workshop (16 February 2005).

25 Warburg, S.B.C. (1996), *Airline Valuation Guide*, September.

4.3   The Valuation of the Airline as a Whole

A market price per share would be available for an airline which is quoted on a stock market. Given the total number of shares issued, this would give a market valuation for the airline as a whole, or market capitalisation (see Section 3.4). Such valuation would change by the minute, by the hour or day, depending on supply and demand for the shares. This in turn would be determined by changes in investors' desire to hold shares in general (*versus* cash), and their wish to hold shares in the sector and the company.

The share price quotation will consist of a bid and offer price. For a share like British Airways which has a daily turnover of an average of some 2 million shares per day, the spread between the two will be around ½-1 per cent. For other airlines which are quoted on a stock market, but whose shares are rarely traded, the spread will be very much larger. The shares of these airlines might not be traded very often, either because very few shares have been issued to the public (*e.g.*, Cyprus Airways or China Airlines), or because private owners wish to hold on to their shares (as was the case with Malaysia Airlines before re-nationalisation). Where turnover is low, the stock market will not be a very efficient method of valuation.

However, investment bank analysts assume that the stock market is not efficient and their clients can make money by trading the shares. They estimate their own values for companies which are then divided by the number of shares issued and compared to the market price. This results in a recommendation to investors in the form of 'buy', 'hold', 'add' or 'sell'. The stockbrokers tend not charge their clients for their detailed analyses of companies, but make their profits on the subsequent commissions earned on any share trading. This is a controversial area with some proposing that share analysis should be performed by completely independent companies that might charge for their advice. Investment bank valuation is usually based on a combination of ratio analysis and the Discounted cash flow (DCF) method. These will be described starting with DCF.

4.3.1   Discounted Cash Flow (DCF) Method

The first method of valuing an airline's value is often described as a 'three-phase DCF'. The first phase is the initial period over which detailed forecasts for the airline are prepared. This would be at least three years into the future, and probably not more than five. The second phase is characterised by investment opportunities and the potential for expansion over the next, say, five to 10 years, while the third phase the return on capital is expected to gradually fall towards the company's cost of capital. The maximum for all three phases would be 40 years. Cash flows are forecast over each of the three periods and discounted to present values using the airline's WACC. Total Enterprise Value is then the addition of the opening invested capital, the DCF value and the present value of any terminal value at the end of the period. This may be adjusted by the addition of any non-airline assets and minorities to give an equity value, which, divided by the number of shares issued, gives a value per share of the equity.

4.3.2   Ratio Method

The alternative method that is commonly used by financial advisers is the application of price-earnings and related ratios. The steps taken to price shares using price-earnings ratios would be as follows:

- Estimate the airline's earnings or net profits for the current year and at least one future year.
- Estimate the historical or projected *P/E* ratio for the airline, based on a comparison of *P/E* ratios of similar airlines, and perhaps with reference to the relationship of the *P/E* of airlines quoted in the market to the *P/E* ratio of the market as a whole.
- Calculate the airline's market capitalisation (earnings multiplied by the *P/E* ratio).

The main problem with the above procedure is the estimation of the *P/E* ratio. There are a number of distortions that could be introduced to the valuation, such as variations in depreciation policies, off-balance sheet financing and operating leases. Tax policies might also differ, and local markets introduce added bias to the comparisons.

Sometimes, attempts are made to remove some of these by computing, for example, the cash *P/E* ratio. This is broadly the *P/E* ratio with depreciation (and any other non-cash items in the profit and loss statement) added back. But this favours those airlines operating new fleets which are owned rather than leased. Alternatively, depreciation could be adjusted so the same policy is applied to all airlines, but the other distortions still remain.

An alternative technique that is now used by a number of financial advisers in support of valuations is 'Enterprise Value,' also known as 'Firm Value'. This takes as a starting point the company's market capitalisation and adds the book value of its net debt (long-term and current portion of debt less cash and marketable securities). This is supposed to value both the equity and debt sources of finance, and is thus free of any gearing distortion. The market rather than book value of debt finance cannot normally be used, since the majority of airline long-term debt is not issued against a tradable security.

Enterprise Value (EV) improves the denominator of the traditional *P/E* ratio; for the numerator, earnings are adjusted to take into account the other distortions described above. Thus, earnings are considered before deduction of interest, tax, depreciation and amortisation (EBITDA). An alternative formulation subtracts also lease rental payments (EBITDAR or EBDRIT). The ratio of EV to EBITDA or EV to EBDRIT is then used for valuation purposes, and compared with other airlines. Some analysts also use EV/Sales, usually expressed as a percentage.

Figure 4.1 compares the major international airlines in North America, Europe and Asia in terms of ratios that relate income statement measures to stock market prices. The LCCs included have much higher ratios than the network carriers. This is expected from the high growth prospects that they have and thus a higher market rating. Some airlines, such as Thai perform worse on the *P/E* ratio compared to their ranking on the EBITDART his suggests high capital charges that have been removed from EBITDAR, thus inflating this ratio. Alternatively, it might have high net debt.

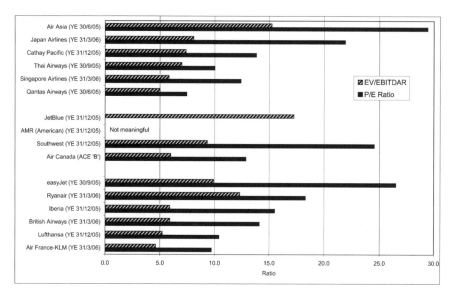

Figure 4.1   Income statement valuation ratios for selected airlines by region (June 2006 stock prices and FY2005/2006)

The opposite is true for easyJet, which has low net debt and capital charges. AMR's ratios could not be calculated because it reported a net loss in the comparable financial year (negative *P/E* ratio), and even EBITDAR was negative by a small margin.

Figure 4.2 gives two more ratios that are used by investment banks to assist in valuing traded airlines. These combine stock market price based metrics (MV and EV) with ones that draw from balance sheet values (Invested capital and book value). The LCCs also enjoy a high rating using these ratios with the exception of jetBlue. The overall ranking is identical for the European airlines and similar for the Asian ones. Those airlines with older fleets or that depreciate aircraft in their books at a faster rate would tend to have high MV/BV ratios, as would those with a large number of off-balance sheet aircraft. The first two did not apply to Air Canada (ACE) that depreciated its fleet over 20–25 years and had an average age of fleet that was somewhat lower than the IATA average. However, Air Canada had just under half of their fleet on operating lease, and thus off-balance sheet.

In January 1996, NatWest Securities valued BA's shares at between 540p to 570p, compared to the share price at that time of 465p. This was based on an analysis of BA and the airline industry, as well as forecasts of BA's earnings to the year 2001. Table 4.2 shows the key valuation ratios that they used, calculated on forecasts of 1997/98 earnings and sales.[26] The *P/E* ratio over the range of values for the share price was broadly in line with the range of values over the same phase of the previous

26 NatWest Securities (1996), *Strategic Assessment of British Airways*, January.

business cycle (1988–1990), although the other ratios appeared to have been based on more recent (1993–1995) performance.

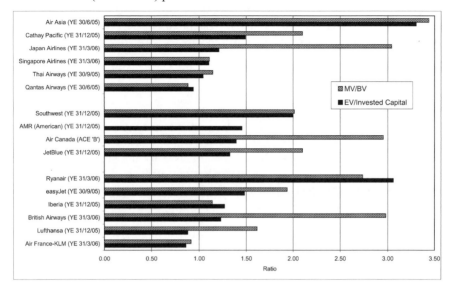

Figure 4.2   Balance sheet valuation ratios for selected airlines by region
(June 2006 stock prices and FY2005/2006.)

Table 4.1   British Airways' valuation criteria

	At Target Price (540p–570p)	Range 1988–1990
P/E Ratio	9.0–9.5	9.1–10.9
P/E Ratio relative to UK market	80–85	52–74
Price/cash flow Ratio	4.9–5.2	3.3–4.6
EV/Sales (%)	92–95	49–61
EV/EBITDA	5.4–5.5	3.5–5.1

Source: NatWest Securities, Strategic Assessment of British Airways, January 1996

Market capitalisation is the current measure of how much the airline's equity is worth to investors. Based on the June 2006 data used in Figure 4.2, Lufthansa had the highest valuation of the European airlines with €6.5 billion (US$8.2 billion) followed by BA with €6.0 billion and Ryanair with €5.5 billion. It may appear surprising that the much smaller low cost airline, Ryanair, has a market capitalisation approaching BA's. This is due to the very high rating that the market gives it (and easyJet) based on expectations of continued very high growth in traffic and earnings.

Amongst the North American carriers, Southwest is by far the largest with US$13 billion, with AMR at only $4 billion. Singapore Airlines was the largest Asian carrier with US$9.6 billion, followed by Cathay Pacific with US$5.9 billion, and LCC Air Asia a much smaller $0.9 billion.

Interestingly, BA's market capitalisation was over six times that of KLM. In August 2000, the two airlines were seriously discussing a merger, which was reported to give KLM 25 per cent of the merged entity, implying valuing BA at only three times KLM (KLM was believed to be negotiating for 33 per cent).[27] The talks broke down, as had a previous attempt in early 1992.

4.4   Ratings Agencies

The two main agencies that publish ratings for quoted debt securities, including those issued by airlines, are Standard & Poor's and Moody. A third is called Fitch. They rate all the obligations of all industries, but will have a key role in commercial bank regulation from 2007. They have been criticised for not predicting collapses such as Enron and Parmalat, but their defenders argue that in these cases they are supplied with fraudulent data. It is also argued that competition is restricted by entry requirements, but this is being addressed in the US by Congress and the Securities Exchange Commission (SEC).

These firms earn their revenues from companies, including airlines, which wish to issue securities (bonds, commercial paper or preferred stock), as well as from selling reports to investors. For example, both Standard & Poor and Moody received US$30,000 for rating a $100 million unsecured placement of Southwest Airlines' securities.[28]

Table 4.2   Selected airline debt ratings, June 2001 and December 2004

	Standard & Poor's		Moody	
	2001	2004	2001	2004
Southwest	**A**	A	**A3**	**Baa1**
British Airways	**BBB+**	BB+	A3	Ba2
Qantas Airways	**BBB+**	**BBB+**	**Baa1**	**Baa2**
American Airlines	**BBB-**	B-	**Baa3**	Caa2C.A.A.2
Delta Air Lines	**BBB-**	CC	**Baa3**	Caa2C.A.A.2
UAL Corp.	BB+	D	**Baa3**	Withdrawn
Northwest Airlines	BB	B	Ba2	Caa1C.A.A.1
Continental	BB	B	Ba2	Caa2C.A.A.2
Japan Airlines	BB	BB-	**Baa3**	*n/a*
Air Canada	BB-	B	B1	Withdrawn
America West	B+	B+	B2	Caa2C.A.A.2
US Airways	B	D	B2	Ba2

Note: Ranked in descending order of creditworthiness (S&P) in June 2001; investment grade highlighted in bold letters.
Source: Standard & Poor's and Moody

---

27   *Airline Business* (August 2000), p. 21.
28   *Airline Business* (April 1995), pp. 54–7.

The agencies' analysis aims to evaluate the likelihood of the timely repayment of principal and interest relating to debt securities, or dividends for preferred stock. The analysis covers both the airline industry in general, and the particular circumstances and prospects for the airline concerned. The latter will examine operational and management quality, success in controlling costs, revenue and yield management, cash flow and capitalisation and other financial issues. The two major agencies together have over 100 analysts making detailed analyses of company financial statements, making any necessary adjustments for variations in accounting practice.

Investment grade:

Standard & Poor's: AAA, AA, A and BBB

(+ and − indicate relative standing within each grade)
All have capacity to pay interest and repay principal, with increased susceptibility to adverse economic conditions as grades fall.
Moody: AaaAAA, Aa, A and Baa

Speculative grade:

Standard & Poor's: BB, B, CCC

(+ and −indicate relative standing within each grade)

All have speculative characteristics regarding the payment of interest and repayment of principal, with increased vulnerability to default as grades fall. C is highly vulnerable to non-payment, while an obligation rated D is in default.

Moody: Ba, B, Caa, Ca and C

Standard & Poor's (S&P) rated BA and Japan Airlines much more highly back in October 1996 than shown in Table 4.2: BA was graded A, and Japan Airlines BBB+. While BA was still investment grade before 9/11, it was subsequently downgraded. Japan Airlines has also moved from investment grade to speculative (more colloquially referred to as 'junk'). Swissair were also downgraded by Moodys from Baa3 (just investment grade) to Ba3 (speculative) following their 2001 difficulties. As the above table shows, only two of the major rated airlines were rated investment grade by either agency.

Moody use different abbreviations, and also ranked the above airlines somewhat differently. They gave Southwest and BA the same rating (A3) in 2001 whereas S&P rated BA just below Southwest. Moody gave United Airlines investment grade by a very small margin in 2001, while S&P rated them speculative. TWA was rated CCC by S&P in October 1996, the only C amongst the airlines in Table 4.4, and in 2001 went into Chapter 11 and was acquired by the AMR Corporation. In December 2004, Moody rated Southwest somewhat lower than it did in 2001, although still investment grade; this contrasts with S&P maintaining their 'A' rating in both years.

In addition to the above passenger airlines, one air cargo integrator and transport company (UPS) was rated AAA by S&P in 2005, while another, FedEx was BBB. Low cost airline, JetBlue was just below investment grade at BB-.

Chapter 5

Sources of Finance

Airline finance has in the past generally been readily available to the majority of airlines, in spite of a worse record of profitability than many other industries, and the cyclical nature of airline earnings. This was because of government involvement, either directly through ownership of the national airline or through loan guarantees. However, even privately owned airlines have found little difficulty in financing aircraft (historically 80–90 per cent of total capital expenditure), due to the possibility of re-possession and re-sale of the asset.

The origin of finance for the airlines, as for any other industry, has been individual and corporate savings. Money from individuals would be channelled through banks as well as pension funds, insurance companies, mutual funds, investment and unit trusts. These institutions would in turn lend to banks, which would act as intermediaries in lending on to airlines, buy airline shares or bonds, or participate in leasing arrangements. Corporations would place surplus funds with banks or participate directly in aircraft leases. Leases might also attract wealthy individuals paying high marginal rates of tax.

In the 1980s, Japanese financial institutions supplied around half of the US$20 billion per annum in loans to the air transport industry.[1] This share has declined significantly in the 1990s, principally because of the gradual application to Japanese banks of the 8 per cent capital adequacy level agreed through the Bank for International Settlements (BIS). Those financial institutions which are most heavily involved in lending to the airline industry will be examined in more detail later in this chapter.

Airline capital expenditure can be financed internally from cash or retained earnings or externally from lenders or lessors using a variety of financial instruments. It is difficult to obtain comprehensive data on the sources of finance for aircraft deliveries. Acknowledging the dangers of taking only one year's data, jet aircraft deliveries totalled 911 in 2004, of which 457 were narrow-bodies, 135 wide-bodies and 319 regional jets. Taking average aircraft prices in 2004 US$ for each category of aircraft gives a total delivered value of US$58 billion. ICAO reported that airline operating profits before depreciation and after interest/tax payments (approximate cash flow) was $16 billion in the same year. They would thus have financed only 28 per cent of deliveries from cash flow leaving a further $42 billion to be financed by banks and leasing companies. Export credit supported bank lending totalled around

---

1   Jet Finance S.A. (1995), *Analysis of the Comparative Ability of the European Airline Industry to Finance Investments*, Economic Research Prepared for the Commission of the European Communities.

$15 billion (including some operating lessors), operating lessors $10 billion leaving more than $17 billion for unsupported lending, new equity and finance leasing.

It is possible to get a rough idea from the financial statements of the world's scheduled airlines (published by ICAO) of how the stock of airlines assets are financed. In the table below operating lease rentals have been multiplied by seven to give an approximate capital value:

Table 5.1   Scheduled world airlines balance sheet long-term financing

Financial year	2004 (US$ billion)	% total
Operating leases capitalised	194.5	42.3
Finance leases	36.0	7.8
Long-term debt	159.6	34.7
Capital stock and surplus	69.6	15.2
Total	459.7	100.0

Source: ICAO

The figures above show the high share of operating leases, although perhaps the amount reported to ICAO includes some finance leases. Finance leases may also be underestimated by being included by some airlines under long-term debt.

5.1   Sources of Internal Finance

Internally, generated funds come from the cash retained in the business, or net profits (after paying interest, tax, and dividends) but before providing for depreciation. Deferred taxes and the profits from the sale of assets will also be internal sources of finance. For many airlines, depreciation is the largest single internal source; some airlines, such as Singapore Airlines, have also in the past generated substantial cash from aircraft sales. The identification of the cash available for investment from an airline's financial statements was described in Chapter 2. The amount of retained earnings available for capital investment will depend on:

- The airline's dividend policy.
- The government's taxation policy.

The proportion of capital expenditure financed from internal sources is often called the *self-financing ratio*. This was examined in Chapter 3. The ratio is subject to very wide swings from a low at the low point in the airline economic cycle, when aircraft deliveries and investment is high and cash flow low, to a high when cash flow is improved and investment lower.

Taxation for the world's scheduled airlines averaged at just under US$3.5 billion over the six profitable years to 2000, or 35 per cent of pre-tax profits. Few major airlines pay dividends, given the need to find finance for capital expenditure. No major US airline pays a dividend apart from the more profitable all-cargo carriers such as FedEx. British Airways has traditionally paid a dividend, but did not pay one from 2001/2002 to 2005/2006.

5.2   Sources of External Finance

5.2.1   Short-term

Bank overdraft   Most airlines will have a facility with one or more commercial banks to run a deficit on their current account up to an agreed limit, which will be based on the overall financial health of the company. This may be secured against certain assets. The rate of interest charged will vary with market rates.

Short-term loans   These will differ from overdrafts by being for fixed amounts to be re-paid at a fixed future date. A fixed or variable interest rate will be charged, and security or other conditions may be stipulated (such as a maximum debt/equity ratio).

Trade creditors   Goods and services purchased by airlines do not generally have to be paid for upon delivery in cash, such that some short-term finance will be available. This will either be free credit, or there will be an implicit cost in terms of cash discount foregone. This should be offset against trade debtors, where the airline is providing short-term finance to others (see Section 8.2).

5.2.2   Long-term

Shareholders' equity capital   Finance from owners of the airline. These owners or shareholders have the right to vote at meetings of the company, the right to a dividend (if one is paid), and the right to a capital distribution on liquidation (if sufficient cash is available after settling all other claims). Outside the USA and many European countries, many of the world's scheduled airlines are still more than 50 per cent owned by their governments (see Chapter 7). Other categories of shareholder might be:

- Other airlines.
- Financial institutions.
- Employees.
- Other individuals.

Lufthansa's shareholding in 2005 was 30 per cent held by private and 70 per cent institutional investors. Employees or other individuals do not generally hold shares unless they can be traded either on a stock market, or through a special company arrangement. United Airlines in the US used to be 55 per cent owned by three labour unions that held shares on behalf of their members.

A large shareholder may wish to sell their holding by offering it to another company or the public (*e.g.*, the UK Government privatisation of British Airways). Care must be taken to comply with company law, which grants all owners of the same class of shares certain rights, relating both to profit distribution and share acquisition. Certain protection may also be given to minority shareholders.

Financing assets by raising additional equity has the advantage of improving the relationship between equity and both output and existing debt, and permits further borrowing. It may, however, dilute the control of existing owners and facilitate a take-over by another company. Thus, share issues are not often used by private companies to fund equipment purchases.

It should be added that in some countries it is possible for a company with a large cash holding to buy back its own shares from shareholders. This would have the effect of improving its earnings per share, a ratio that is given some weight by airline share analysts (see Section 3.4), and possibly of strengthening its share price.

Such a buy-back was carried out by KLM and the Dutch Government in December 1996. The government holding in KLM was reduced from 38.2 per cent to 25 per cent, by the sale of 17.3 million ordinary shares to KLM for Fl 1.1 billion (US$569 million).[2] The price paid per share was decided on the basis of a formula, whereby KLM would pay the weighted average of the market price over a four-day period, less a discount of 2.5 per cent. The discount would seek to quell any demands from other shareholders that the offer be made to them.

As a result of the deal, KLM's earnings per share rose by about 20 per cent, although its debt/equity ratio deteriorated from 0.95 to 1.3. KLM had Fl 2.8 billion (US$1.7 billion) in cash and marketable securities at the end of March 1996, and this amount would have been almost halved as a result of the buy-back. The Dutch Government had further reduced its stake to 14.1 per cent by the end of March 2001, but retained the option to acquire sufficient 'B' preference shares to give it control; this could be exercised in the event of restrictions being placed on KLM as a result of bilateral nationality clauses. It was later sold to Air France.

It is difficult to estimate the cost of equity capital, whether from new issues or from retained profits. While the cost of dividends is identifiable, the key consideration is the long-term ability of the airline to attract capital and the price that must be paid to do this successfully. If the airline's shares are traded, the price-earnings ratio indicates the approximate price level of new equity capital.

A high price/earnings ratio (or the inverse of a low earnings yield) means a low cost of new capital; thus Japanese airlines have in the past had access to cheap equity finance as a result of their high *P/E* ratios. A fuller discussion of equity capital is to be found in the next chapter.

Preference share capital   This is similar to equity capital but there is a maximum return or fixed dividend payable (as long as the airline makes a profit). It ranks before equity shares for the payment of dividend and distribution in the event of bankruptcy, and is therefore less risky. Preference shares can either be redeemable, whereby the company can buy them back from shareholders at a future date, or perpetual (in the same way as ordinary shares). Other features can be:

- Cumulative, where any unpaid dividends are carried forward to the next financial year, or non-cumulative.
- Participating, where a basic dividend is paid, plus an additional variable mount depending on how much is left for distribution after paying a dividend to ordinary shareholders.

---

2   *Financial Times*, 6 December 1996.

British Airways acquired convertible preference shares in US Air as part of their alliance link up in 1993 (see box below). The advantage of preference shares is that losses (or the share of losses) do not have to be shown in the investor's profit and loss account, where the company invested in is an associated company (*i.e.*, the investment is between 20 per cent and 50 per cent). Only the dividends are shown.

Bonds/debentures/unsecured loan stock   These are financial securities or long-term promissory notes which pay a fixed or variable rate of interest and a have a fixed term. They are negotiable which means that the general public can hold, buy or sell them in the same way as shares. Bonds can sometimes be traded on the Eurobond or US bond markets. They are re-paid or redeemed at par on the due date. In the case of debentures they can be secured by a *fixed* or *floating charge* on the airline's assets. A mortgage debenture is secured on specific land or buildings. A fixed charge is on specific assets, a floating charge is a general charge on all assets owned.

Convertible Preference Shares: British Airways' Investment in US Air

Federal Aviation Act prohibits foreign owners from controlling more than 25 per cent of voting stock of a US airline.

July 1992:
BA announced intention to invest US$750 million in US Air (44 per cent of equity). BA would buy $230 million in convertible preferred shares with full voting rights. BA would also buy $520 million in form of non-voting convertible preferred shares.

January 1993:
BA acquired US$300 million (£198 million) of new convertible preferred stock in US Air; this stock earns cumulative cash dividends of 7 per cent *per annum* (paid quarterly), and gives BA the right to convert it into US Air common stock at any time on or after 21 January 1997. This gives BA an estimated 21 per cent of the voting rights in US Air (other foreign owners hold around 4 per cent). Flight code sharing agreement was also signed.

BA also has the option to buy another $450 million of US Airpreferred stock in two tranches over the next five years, at similar terms to the first investment, which if fully converted would bring BA's share of equity to a maximum of 40.7 per cent on an undiluted basis or 31.2 per cent, allowing for the exercise of all stock options and all other conversion rights (*i.e.*, on a fully diluted basis). If this option is not exercised before 21 January 1996, US Air has the right to redeem any of the initial investment in preferred stock (or in any event on 21 January 2008 if this had not already been converted into common stock).

After conversion, BA will hold 24.6 per cent of voting rights on an undiluted basis, or around 17 per cent on a fully diluted basis. BA receives three out of 16 US Air board positions, and would thus hold veto over certain board decisions. BA to lease and operate the aircraft and crews on US Air's routes to London from Charlotte, Philadelphia and Baltimore. US Air (and BA) remain interested in TWA's transatlantic rights and assets.

May 1993:

US Air issues a further $231 million in common stock and US Air employees exercise rights under certain stock option agreements, and BA exercises its pre-emptive rights to subscribe to a further $100.7 million of new convertible preferred stock in US Air in order to maintain its share at just under 25 per cent. This new stock is entitled to cash dividends of 0.5 per cent over LIBOR.

March 1994:

Code sharing agreement extended for a further year; US Air reports a first quarter pre-tax loss of $200 million and predicts a worse full year result in 1994 than the $350 million in 1993.

BA indicates that it will not increase its investment in US Air unless labour concessions and restructuring are forthcoming

March 1995:

US Air reports a net loss of $685 million. Continued uncertainty about agreement with the unions, but British Airways considered that US Air's cash position would continue to be adequate until such time that an agreement could be concluded. BA consider further investment of $450 million extremely unlikely.

US Air suspend dividend on preferred stock, and BA write-down their investment in US Air by 50 per cent, primarily because of a change in US accounting rules.

March 1996:

US Air posts a net profit of $119 million in 1995, and achieves $500 saving in annual non-labour costs. Labour cost reductions have yet to be realised. BA retains its 50 per cent provision against its US Air investment.

December 1996: BA offers their stock for sale on the open market, after deterioration of relationship with US Air following plans for link up with American Airlines. US Air decided not to exercise their option to buy back this stock.

May 1997:

BA realises total proceeds of US$625 million from the sale of its holding.

Source: British Airways' Annual Report and Accounts, and BA News

They can be issued in various classes to finance assets, each of the classes having different rates of interest and claims on the underlying assets. Debentures and bonds are practically the same, with small legal differences.

Convertible bonds   These are bonds that give the holder the option to convert to ordinary shares within a certain time 'window'. They allow finance to be raised, often at a time when the share price is weak, on a fixed interest basis, but with rights attached to convert to ordinary shares at a future date, and at a given conversion rate. They can also usually be traded on a stock market. The coupon or interest rate is lower than would be the case for loan stock without the conversion rights.

British Airways issued convertible capital bonds in June 1989 entitling the holders to interest payments of 9¾ per cent a year up to the maturity date of June 2005. They also had the right to convert the bonds into ordinary shares at any time between June 1993 and June 2005 on the basis of one ordinary share in British Airways to each £2.34 of bonds held. Many holders ran the bonds for the full term and benefited from the attractive interest rate, in spite of the BA share price reaching over £7 for a time.

Lufthansa issued convertible bonds totalling €750 million in January 2002, with the relatively low interest rate of 1.25 per cent *per annum*, maturing in 2012. The conversion price was €19.86 per ordinary share. These were quoted on the Luxembourg stock exchange. In January 2006, the Lufthansa ordinary share price was well below the conversion price; the interest paid was also by then unattractive, such that around €700 million worth of bondholders exercised an option they were granted to redeem the bonds.

Equipment Trust Certificates (ETCs)   These are similar to a secured bond, but arranged in the form of a lease. The airline sells the certificates to investors to pay for aircraft, which is then owned by a Trust on behalf of the investors. This can be done for single aircraft or multiple aircraft, and certificates issued to finance new aircraft can be secured against aircraft already in the fleet. Lease payments are made to the investors through the trustee. On maturity, title to the aircraft passes to the airline. This form of finance was largely restricted to the US market in the 1990s because of the protection it affords investors when the airline lessee enters 'Chapter 11' (a form of bankruptcy administration unique to the USA – see Chapter 12). However, it has recently become more popular in Europe, with an issue from Iberia in 1999 followed by deals for both Air France and Lufthansa, reported to be each totalling around $1 billion.[3] The certificates are also a type of securitisation which is discussed more fully in Chapter 11.

Term loans   These are generally negotiated from banks or insurance companies, and are easier and cheaper to arrange than bonds. They could be arranged on a bilateral basis for smaller amounts, or on a syndicated basis for larger loans. For the latter, a lead bank will organise a number of banks to participate in the loan, with fees distributed according to the bank's share of total funds and depending whether or not it is the lead bank. For this type of borrowing there will be a closer relationship between the lead financial institution and airline borrower. This will allow closer monitoring of the airline's performance than for bonds or other sources of finance.

Loans are usually to finance aircraft and will often be secured against these assets. They may be used to fund advance payments to aircraft manufacturers, which typically begin two years years before delivery and amount to some 30 per cent of the total cost. Banks will only lend for up to about five years years on an unsecured basis, except to large airlines (*e.g.*, KLM at 19 basis points over LIBOR), and have the usual debt advantage of the tax deductibility of interest payments. If an aircraft is to be exported to a foreign country, the loan could be offered or guaranteed by

---

3   *Airfinance Journal*, (2001), More euro EETCs on the way, July/August.

a government backed Export Credit Agency (ECA). The agencies involved are described later in this chapter.

France and Germany will support 95 per cent and the UK 100 per cent of the aircraft cost (less a down-payment made by the airline, or with a commercial bank loan, of 15 per cent). The maximum term is 10–12 years at fixed interest rates of 120–175 basis points above the 10-year government bond yields. The terms and rates are laid down in the Large Aircraft Sector Understanding (LASU), an agreement between aircraft exporting countries to prevent unfair competition. The 12-year maximum term is considered much too short, especially for large high cost jets such as Boeing 747s, but discussions between the US and European ECAs aimed at extending this limit have not in the past been successful. There is also an agreement between the European ECAs and Ex-Im not to support aircraft sold to airlines in each other's territory (although operating lessors could benefit since the aircraft would not necessarily be operated there).

Export credit bank loans can be relatively expensive for larger creditworthy airlines, and, in addition to interest rates at levels considerably higher than could be obtained by many good name airlines. The following fees are likely to be charged by banks for an Ex-Im Bank type credit to a small airline:

- Commitment fees (payable on undrawn portions of the loan), say ¼ per cent to ½ per cent.
- Management/arrangement fees on the total loan, say ¾ per cent.
- Agency fees (usually a flat fee per participating bank) to cover the administration costs of the agent or lead bank.

There would also be a guarantee fee payable to Ex-Im Bank for the part of the loan for which they provided a 100 per cent guarantee. This was increased from 2 per cent to 4 per cent in 1994, but was subsequently reduced to 3 per cent. In 2004, this fee was reduced by one-third for airlines and lessors based in countries that had adopted, ratified and implemented the Cape Town Treaty.

An example of this type of financing was Asiana's purchase of one B747-400 and one B737-400 in 1996. Of the total cost of the two aircraft of US$195 million, $166.5 million was financed by a 12-year Ex-Im Bank backed loan at eight basis points over six-month LIBOR, the remaining $28.5 million with a commercial 12-year loan at 100 basis points over LIBOR.

However, under LASU, agencies can offer a fixed rate alternative, whereby airlines have the option of locking into a low fixed interest rate at least three months in advance. When interest rates are rising, this is extremely attractive and amounts to a one-way option (if interest rates fall, the option does not have to be exercised, at no cost to the borrower). The airline also benefits in that the loan has no impact on its borrowing capacity from the bank making the loan, since the bank will book the loan against the government of the Export Credit Agency country.

Because there is an element of subsidy in export credits, rumours circulate continuously that they will be discontinued, or made less attractive. So far, there are no signs of this happening.

Aircraft Purchase Alternative: Term Loan

> The three key variables associated with a term loan are the loan amount, the loan term and the rate of interest. The currency of the loan is also important. The term and interest rate will depend on the airline's creditworthiness, intended use of the loan (*e.g.*, type of aircraft), and the repayment prospects.
>
> The financial institution has a legal recourse to the recapture of its loan, but loan defaults are an expensive inconvenience. Thus, the lender will take a close interest in the intended use of the loan, and will require detailed information on this (cash flow projections and loan repayment schedules), as well as the financial health of the airline. They will need to be satisfied that the equity base is adequate, the borrower has a long-term commitment to the business, and financial contingencies are in place for possible business downturns. Covenants are frequently applied in the form of ratios that must be satisfied: if airlines to not meet these ratios (see Chapter 3 for examples) default may follow.
>
> One advantage of term loans was the ability to match the financing to the expected life of aircraft. However, the economic lives of aircraft have been increasing to the extent that this rarely now happens. The loan period could be between 10 to 15 years, depending on airline creditworthiness.
>
> The nominal interest rate depends on general economic conditions, as well as the airline's creditworthiness. The London Inter-Bank Offered Rate (LIBOR) or the US Prime Rate may be used as benchmarks for the loan. A floating or fixed rate may be adopted. Fixed interest rates are usually slightly higher, and tend to increase in magnitude with the lengthening of the loan term.

Leases   These are contracts between airlines and banks or leasing companies where the airline obtains use of the aircraft without ownership. Financing is therefore arranged by these other parties, although the aircraft specification may be determined by the airline, and the aircraft may be delivered directly to the airline and be operated by one airline throughout its life. Leasing is covered more fully in Chapter 10.

Manufacturer's support   This is usually provided in the form of deficiency payments or buy-back guarantees on the aircraft. It could also be in the form of a loan to the airline or equity investment in the airline. For example, in May 1987 Boeing made a loan of US$700 million to United Airlines in the form of 7.52 per cent notes which could have been converted into a maximum of 15 per cent of the airline's equity. These notes were repaid in full in January 1988, including a pre-payment premium of $50 million.[4] At the end of 1995, Continental Airlines had $634 million in secured borrowings from engine manufacturer, General Electric and associated companies.[5] British Aerospace has in the past provided minority equity stakes in a US regional

---

4   Allegis Corporation (1988), *Addressing Airline Issues, 1987 Annual Report.*
5   *Continental Airlines Annual Report* (1995), p. 25.

airline and a Caribbean start-up airline, as a means of supporting sales of its BAe 146 aircraft. Neither airline survived for very long.

An example of a deficiency guarantee related to a secured loan to an airline, on a 'first loss' basis would be:

Table 5.2   Hypothetical example of manufacturer's support for aircraft finance

US$ million	A	B	C
Outstanding debt	100	100	100
Net proceeds from aircraft sale	90	75	60
Loss on sale	10	25	40
Paid by manufacturer	10	25	25
Paid by lender	0	0	15

The above table shows three scenarios for the forced sale of an aircraft in the open market, because of a loan default or bankruptcy. Under scenarios A and B, the manufacturer makes good the loss and the lender is not out of pocket. Under scenario C, the lender is required to cover part of the loss. The part paid by the manufacturer could be a pre-agreed amount of the unamortised loan principal, or a pre-agreed share of the sale loss. The aircraft could also be bought back by the manufacturer for storage and later sale or lease to another airline. The manufacturer might also be required to give technical advice on re-marketing the aircraft and/or arrange for maintenance or refurbishment.

A survey of 20 firms involved in aircraft manufacturing estimated that their exposure to customer financing increased by 54 per cent between the end of 1991 and the end of 1995, to US$27.8 billion. This was offset by receivable sales to banks of $4.1 billion to reduce the end 1995 exposure to $23.7 billion, down from $25 billion in 1994.[6] This latter figure was 15 per cent of total ICAO world airline debt and equity estimated at end 1994, or 22 per cent of total airline long-term debt.[7] More recent figures have not been published.

5.3   Institutions Involved in Aircraft Finance

5.3.1   Banks

Banks act as intermediaries between savers and users of funds. Bank loans to the airline industry might be from money deposited with them or their own capital. They would appear on their balance sheet and be subject to lending limits and liquidity ratios. Banks will have limits up to which they can lend to a particular company, a particular country, or a particular industry. They might also underwrite debt or equity

---

6   Philippakkos, T. (1996), Support System, *Airfinance Journal*, September, 42.
7   *ICAO Journal (1996)*, July/August, 8.

issues, but this would be off-balance sheet. Some observers see banks focusing more on off-balance sheet activities in the future, such as underwriting and fee earning services. This has traditionally been the preserve of the smaller merchant banks, which did not have a large balance sheet.

Many of the larger international banks have traditionally been involved in aerospace and aircraft financing, and have often had specialist departments dealing with this industry. Up to 1990, the big US banks, such as Citibank and Chase Manhattan Bank headed the table of top loan providers for aircraft transactions. By 1990, however, these two names had disappeared from the top 20, and were largely replaced by Japanese banks, such as Fuji Bank, Sumitomo Bank and the Mitsubishi Trust and Banking Corporation. More recently, the position has been reversed, with the Japanese Banks being replaced by the large US and European banks, and some new entrants from the UK, such as the Halifax and Abbey National (both formerly building societies).

An indication of the banks most involved in aircraft financing can be obtained from those doing export credit deals. In 2004, BNP Paribas and Barclays were offering low cost export credit backed finance to airlines such as Ryanair at rates close to LIBOR, and happy to bid for a large number of deals. Then came banks like Calyon (The Crédit Agricole Group that incorporated Crédit Lyonnais), Citigroup, Natexis Banque Populaire and Rabobank that would be more selective, preferring deals for relationship airlines. Other banks were that had previously had a significant presence in aircraft finance, such as Deutsche Bank, Bank of Scotland and WestLB, were less active in the market.[8]

Airlines invite banks to compete for the mandate which would give the winner the authorisation to be the lead bank in any subsequent financing. For larger airlines, there may be 15–20 banks competing for the lead mandate, with a further 100 or so banks happy to accept the smaller level of risk implicit in a secondary role in syndicate financing.

5.3.2 Export Credit Agencies

Most of the major exporting countries will have export credit agencies (ECAs) which are either a part of government or a government supported organisation. Their purpose is to encourage exports of goods from their countries, generally by guarantees or insurance rather than direct loans. Thus, they are there to provide support or complement bank lending, especially in cases where banks would be reluctant to assume 100 per cent of the risk. This could be where the country is high risk or low credit standing, or the purchaser of the goods is high risk, or a combination of the two.

The export credit volume varies significantly from year to year, with just under US$10 billion of deals reported in 2004,[9] compared to $16.5 billion in 1999. For 2000, 35 per cent of backing went to airlines in Asia, followed by 27 per cent in Latin

---

8   *AirFinance Journal*, December 2004/January 2005, pp. 20–21.

9   *AirFinance Journal*, December 2004/January 2005. Reported US$15 billion of business done between November 2003 and November 2004, but this referred to the total

America, 17 per cent Europe, 15 per cent Middle East and Africa, and 6 per cent in North America.[10] The following are the Export Credit Agencies in the countries which have some aircraft or aircraft component manufacturing capability, and could therefore be involved in aircraft financing:

- Ex-Im Bank (USA).
- Export Credit Guarantee Department (UK).
- COFACE (France).
- Euler Hermes (Germany).
- NEXI (Japan).
- Export Development Corporation - EDC (Canada).
- ESACE (Italy).
-

The above institutions generally provide only guarantees, although the Exim Bank and ECGD have also lent money directly, with the actual finance being provided by banks under *syndicated loans*. This is a way of spreading the risk between a number of commercial banks, with a lead bank inviting others to participate jointly in the financing.

Under a *gentleman's agreement*, the US Eximbank does not support exports of US aircraft to airlines based in UK, France, Germany and Spain, and the European ECAs does not assist Airbus aircraft exports to US airlines.

Where an export of an aircraft from one country incorporates a substantial share of airframe or components from another country, then two or more ECAs would be involved. This would be essential for Airbus aircraft, with financing support generally proportionate to each ECA's national manufacturer's share in the production of the aircraft (*e.g.*, for an A320 with IAE engines: UK 32 per cent France 32 per cent and Germany 36 per cent ; or an A321 with CFM engines 17 per cent, 52 per cent and 31 per cent respectively). Another example would be the involvement of both Eximbank and the ECGD in the financing of a Boeing 757 with Rolls-Royce engines.

Eximbank　　(USA) Ex-Im Bank provides official support for aircraft finance through long-term guarantees for up to 85 per cent of the US cost of aircraft exported. It also offers loans and subsidies, but this is a small part of its overall business. It complies with the LASU guidelines. Ex-Im Bank provided little support for aircraft exports in the 1980s, since finance was relatively easy to obtain from US and Japanese banks. When many Japanese sources dried up in the early 1990s, however, the bank expanded its aircraft lending and support. For example, the agency only provided two aircraft loan guarantees in 1988 compared to 67 during 1992/1993.[11]

The agency has recently been restructured and a dedicated aviation department established, as opposed to supporting all sectors through geographic regional

---

value of the aircraft, not that portion guaranteed by the ECAs; there may also have been some double counting.

10　*AirFinance Journal, Export Credit Survey*, March (2001).

11　Verchère, I. (1994), *The Air Transport Industry in Crisis*, EIU Publishing, Chapter 8.

divisions. This was necessary because of the increasingly complex asset-based financing, which now comprise around two-thirds of total bank transactions.

For the financial year ended September 1993, Ex-Im Bank provided cover worth US$15.5 billion, of which $3.4 billion related to commercial jet aircraft. For 1993/1994, this increased to $20 billion and $3.0 billion respectively, but for the two subsequent fiscal years aircraft activity fell to $1 billion a year. In 2000, its support had increased again to $3.5 billion of cover for 63 aircraft, reaching $4.3 billion in 2005 on 78 aircraft. Its largest single aircraft deal in 2005 was guarantees worth $530 million for Emirates, followed by $402 million for WestJet. Two separate deals for Ryanair totalled $687 million.

European ECAs The three major European ECAs involved in Airbus financing are the Export Credit Guarantee Department in the UK, COFACE in France, and Hermes in Germany. They are estimated to support around 30 per cent of total Airbus sales.

The ECGD insures UK exports, with aerospace now ahead of defence as the second largest sector of the agency's business. In 1993/1994, guarantees for commercial aircraft sales were issued for a total value of £1.14 billion, falling to £786 million in 1995/1996, of which around three-quarters was for Airbus aircraft, and the rest for regional aircraft and Rolls-Royce engines. ECGD covers 100 per cent of the principal and interest of the loan, up to a maximum of 85 per cent of the aircraft cost. Bank commitment or management fees are not covered. Both COFACE and Hermes cover only 95 per cent of the principal and interest on 85 per cent of the aircraft cost, but they do cover 95 per cent of a bank's fees. Neither cover the interest payable from the due date of the loan to the date of payment of a claim.

Hermes differs from the other two European agencies in being a wholly owned subsidiary of the Allianz Group (in turn 76 per cent owned by German banks), acting on behalf of the German Government. It structures its support in the form of an insurance policy.

Spare parts are normally allowed to be added to the cost of the aircraft by European ECAs, but only up to a maximum of 15 per cent of the aircraft cost for the first five aircraft, and up to 10 per cent of aircraft cost for subsequent aircraft.

In 2000, the European export credit agencies provided $1.6 billion of support for 21 Airbus aircraft, significantly less than the US Ex-Im cover.[12] However, it was thought that by 2005, the European agencies were supporting a similar value of aircraft to the US Ex-Im Bank (*i.e.*, almost $5 billion). The largest guarantee provided by ECGD in FY2005–2006 was £178.4 million (over $300 million) on Airbus aircraft for Thai Airways, covering only the value of the aircraft manufactured in the UK.

NEXI (Japan) The role of this agency differs somewhat from those described above, in that Japan does not have its own civil aircraft manufacturing programme. It is, however, an increasingly large supplier of components and is involved with Boeing on the B767 (15 per cent of the airframe value) B777 and B787 projects. The agency normally finances 60–70 per cent of the aircraft cost, with the remainder coming from commercial sources, not necessarily Japanese.

---

12 *Airline Business*, (February 2001) p. 57.

Most of the agency's business comes from import credits. It provided finance for the acquisition of foreign aircraft by domestic airlines, for example 50 per cent of the value of JAL's purchase of three B747-400s which were delivered in 1993.[13]

5.3.3 Operating Lessors

The operating lease business has until recently been dominated by two firms: International Lease Finance Corporation (ILFC) and General Electric Capital Asset Services (GECAS), which effectively took over the failing GPA in the mid-1990s. At the end of 1994, these two firms owned 62 per cent of the 1,820 commercial jet aircraft leased by 40 companies. By 2005, this had fallen to 42 per cent of the jet fleet numbers owned by the top 50 lessors. The two companies accounted for a larger share of total jet fleet value, 52 per cent in 2005.

ILFC started in 1973 (at the height of the early 1970s energy crisis) with the lease of a DC8 to AeroMexico. It subsequently expanded to reach turnover of US$30 million and pre-tax income of $5.5 million in 1980. By 1985, turnover was $58 million and profits $20 million, but the fastest period of growth was the second half of the 1980s, with 1990 revenues approaching $500 million and profits $124 million. The number of aircraft owned by ILFC grew to 106 in 1990, and at the end of 2005 was 911 (see Table 5.3). ILFC's turnover in 1994 was $1.11 billion, and $2.5 billion in 2000 (93 per cent of which came from the rental of flight equipment). Airlines in Europe provided the largest part of ILFC's business with 45.8 per cent of the total rentals, followed by Asia/Pacific with 20.1 per cent and the US and Canada with 19.1 per cent. It is the only lessor of the B747-400, and the only operating lessor to order the A380 (up to mid-2001).

ILFC was originally owned by the founders, and operated until 1990 with a staff of only 28. This gave it one of the highest ratios of turnover to employee of any US company. In 1990, they were acquired by the large US insurance company, AIG, for $1.3 billion with the increasing need for access to cheap debt finance that its new parent could provide.

GPA was founded in 1976, principally as an aircraft management services company. Initially, GPA was involved with wet leasing aircraft and some operating leases of used aircraft. It was not until 1984 that they made their first order for new aircraft. They then switched emphasis from aircraft trading and acquiring aircraft for known customers to ordering aircraft purely on the basis of expected industry growth. This culminated in a 1989 order at for 300 aircraft worth $17 billion (some of which were options). Deliveries of these aircraft took place after the Gulf War and subsequent world-wide economic recession (and in mid-1991 they still had 376 firm orders outstanding). At the end of 1991, GPA had 392 aircraft in its fleet, which were leased to 100 airlines in 47 countries. The group's annual revenues grew from $360 million in 1986/1987 to more than $2 billion in 1991/1992, when they recorded a net profit of $268 million. However, the financial strain imposed by falling lease rates and

---

13 *AirFinance Journal*, (1994) *Guide to Export Credits*, p. 32.

the lack of customers for some aircraft (22 aircraft were in storage in 1992) led to the collapse of GPA in 1993. This was after repeated attempts to raise new equity finance. Commenting on the Group's downfall, the *Financial Times* stated that 'rarely can so much have been borrowed by so few, on the basis of so insubstantial a balance sheet'.[14]

The company that came to GPA's rescue in 1993 was the aircraft leasing arm of General Electric of the US, or GE Capital Aviation Services (GECAS). GE had acquired 22.7 per cent of GPA in 1983, and having tried to buy control, sold almost all its stake in 1986 for a profit of almost \$40 million.[15] When GPA's \$1 billion stock offering failed in 1992, GE purchased an 85 per cent interest in 45 of GPA's stage 3 aircraft for \$1.35 billion. Once the collapse came in 1993, it was the obvious rescuer. Under the rescue agreement, GECAS was established to manage the GPA's aircraft under a 15-year contract for a fee paid by GPA. GPA remained as a separate company, retaining ownership of just over 400 aircraft at the end of 1993 (many of these have since been removed from their balance sheet through securitisation or sale). GE had an option to acquire 67 per cent of GPA for between \$110 million and \$165 million, which was eventually exercised. GECAS is part of the equipment management division of GE Capital Services; the division as a whole generated \$14.7 billion in revenues in 2000.

The next largest operating lessor in terms of owned aircraft value after GECAS and ILFC, was Aviation Capital Group, owned by a major US life insurance company (Pacific Life), followed by Boeing Capital. AWAS, which was number three in the mid-1990*s*, was originally owned by the Ansett/Murdoch group, but they were eventually sold to Morgan Stanley, and in 2001 were again up for sale. Many of the remaining firms have Japanese shareholders, such as Orix which acquired a portfolio solely of A320 aircraft, but has recently added Boeing 737s to their fleet.

The average number of aircraft placed with each airline is between 3 and 4 for most of the larger lessors. This strikes a happy medium between putting all their eggs in one basket, and avoiding the higher operating costs which come from dealing with too many different airlines.

Aircraft manufacturers with largish leasing subsidiaries were Boeing Capital (349 aircraft), Airbus Asset Management (56 aircraft) and BAE Systems (267 aircraft, but mostly small jets or turbo-props). Neither of the two major manufacturers market their leasing arms very proactively, since this would compete with their major lessor customers.

Many of the lessors are owned by banks: In 2001, Westdeutsche-Landesbank made an offer for Boullioun Aviation (later sold to Aviation Capital), while Morgan Stanley bought Ansett Aviation.

---

14 *Financial Times*, (13 May 1993) p. 24.
15 Feldman, J. (1993), The Eagle Has Landed, *Air Transport World*, December, p. 44.

Table 5.3   Top 10 operating lessors and their fleets – end 2005

	Owned jet aircraft	Value of owned jetfleet (US$ million)	Managed aircraft
GECAS	1,301	23,986	3,309
ILFC	911	27,176	719
Aviation Capital Group	222	4,471	606
Boeing Capital	349	4,446	81
RBS Aviation	138	3,508	
Babcock & Brown	156	3,337	2,689
AerCap (former debís)	245	3,069	896
GATX Capital	139	3,009	289
AWAS	156	2,559	8
Total	6,066	100,681	12,510

Source: Airline Business, February 2006

Airlines have mostly withdrawn from a major role in operating leases. Ansett was uncoupled from Ansett Aviation (which changed its name to AWAS), and Swissair had to withdraw from its joint venture with GATX (Flightlease). Singapore Airlines and the Singapore government has a joint venture with Boullioun Aviation (SALE), focusing on the Asian and Chinese markets, although it was suggested that this might be sold through an IPO.

It can be seen from Table 5.3 that ILFC's average aircraft value is significantly higher than that of GECAS. This is because ILFC has a higher percentage of wide body aircraft, and no turbo-props compared to 21 owned by GECAS. Operating lessors have occasionally acquired equity capital of customer airlines as part of a lease deal. For example, ILFC had small stakes in Air Liberté, Air New Zealand and American Trans Air.

5.3.4   Governmental Financing Organisations

International Bank for Reconstruction and Development (IBRD)   The IBRD or World Bank has financed both airport and airline projects in the past. More recent funding has gone towards privatisation studies, but it has also sponsored a study into the feasibility of establishing a multinational airline in Southern Africa (through the Southern Africa Development Coordination Council), as well as a study of the West African airline, TAGB Air Bissau. Cumulative lending to the air transport sector up to the end of June 1993 amounted to US$299 million out of total transport sector lending of $33,604 million and total lending of $235.2 billion.[16] Thus, although transport accounted for 14.3 per cent of total lending, mostly on roads, air transport was under 1 per cent of transport lending.

---

16 World Bank Development Report, 1994.

A large part of the air transport lending went to Latin America and the Caribbean (73 per cent) and Africa (20 per cent). Much of the lending in Latin America, however, was for airport projects, including a study on the privatisation of Argentina's airports.

In 2006, The World Bank's private funding arm, The International Finance Corporation (IFC), financed the spares holding of Brazilian LCC, Gol (US$50 million), which has previously benefited from US$40 million of funding from its government development bank. The IFC also provided the Mexican LCC start-up in 2006 with a US$30 million credit facility to finance its purchase of A320 aircraft, as well as a $10 million loan for working capital.

European Investment Bank (EIB)   One source of funds for airlines (and airports) is the European Investment Bank. This was created by the Treaty of Rome establishing the European Economic Community, in January 1958. The bank's mission is to contribute to the European Union's balanced development. It is an autonomous public institution and operates on a non profit-making basis.

Table 5.4   Examples of European Investment Bank lending to airlines

Airline	€ million	Aircraft type
Iberia (1997)	158.2	A340s
Egyptair (1997)	75.0	A321s
Austrian Airlines (1999)	46.5	A320s
Aer Lingus (2004)	166.0	A320s

The EIB grants long-term loans or guarantees to the public and private sectors for investments which help the economic development of structurally weak regions. These are either made directly or through financial institutions. Loans normally cover up to 50 per cent of the gross investment cost of a project, supplementing the borrower's own funds and credits from other sources.

The EIB lending is on a project rather than asset basis, and is generally for aircraft acquisition. The cost of loans tends to be low, and the term relatively long. The typical loan term for aircraft has been between 12 and 18 years, significantly longer than commercial bank borrowing. Their airport lending is even longer term. European airline borrowers originally had to operate the aircraft only within the European Union to qualify for loans at small margins over LIBOR, such as the BF 3.6 billion loan for Sabena's 23 RJ70 regional aircraft, but the EIB later financed B747-400s for both BA and KLM. Its airline lending from the beginning of 1990 to the end of 2001 totalled €5,370 million, 64.5 per cent of which was to large or second rank EU flag carriers. A total of 31 airlines benefited, only two of which were based outside the EU.[17]

---

17 European Investment Bank (2004) *Evaluation of EIB Financing of airlines: A synthesis report.*

The European Bank for Reconstruction and Development (EBRD)   The EBRD
was established by the governments of Europe and North America after the break
up of the Soviet Union to help with economic restructuring in the former eastern
bloc countries. Its role is similar to The World Bank (IBRD), but specialising in the
CIS and Eastern European countries. The European Commission also significantly
increased its lending to these countries, through its PHARE and TACIS programmes
for Eastern Europe and the CIS countries respectively (although their combined
lending to the air transport industry amounted to less than one per cent of total
lending in the first half of the 1990s).

In 1992, the EBRD invested ECU20.8 million towards a fleet replacement and
modernisation programme for the Czech national airline, CSA. The aim of this
finance was to support the privatisation process by catalysing investment from Air
France and mediating between the two partners in the project. EBRD took a 20 per
cent share in the airline and Air France 40 per cent, although the latter subsequently
pulled out and sold its share back to the Czech Government. More recent equity
finance deals are described in the next chapter. In 2006, the EBRD also helped a
Russian start-up airline, VIM Airlines, finance 12 used B757-200s through the issue
of a US$92m asset-backed senior secured loan, just under half of which was funded
by participating banks and $51.5 million by the EBRD itself. In the same year EBRD
planned to provide $20 million in funding for a Russian start-up LCC (Sky Express),
part of which would be equity along with private investors.

Otherwise, the EBRD tends to focus on project lending to airports, privatisation
studies, and technical assistance and institutional support to air transport in general.
Its total lending to airlines, airports and ATC authorities in the early 1990s only
amounted to some 2 per cent of its total lending.

International Civil Aviation Organization (ICAO)   ICAO plays a major role in air
transport training programmes and technical assistance, but does not have the funding
capability to lend or give grants for capital investment. In fact, its programmes
are largely financed from the United Nations Development Programme (UNDP)
resources. Furthermore, ICAO tends to support projects for aviation authorities
or airports, rather than airlines. Airline training and some technical assistance is
provided through the airlines' own trade association, the International Air Transport
Association (IATA).

Other development banks   Development banks such as the, the Asian Development
Bank and the African Development Bank have usually only financed airport projects.
They have, however, sometimes funded airline studies or transport sector studies
that have included airlines.[18] One exception to this, however, is the Caribbean
Development Bank, which is a shareholder in the regional airline, LIÂT, and has
played a major role in that airline's finances.

---

18 For example, Asian Development Bank's technical assistance to the Solomon Islands.

Appendix 5.1 Term Loan Repayment, Book Profit and Manufacturers' Prepayments

a) Calculation of Term Loan Repayment Amount

The repayment amount can be calculated from the following formula:

$$0 = PV + (1 + i.s)(PMT) \left\{ \frac{1-(1+i)^{-n}}{i} \right\}$$

where: PV $\quad = \quad$ Present value of the loan

$\quad\quad$ i $\quad\quad = \quad$ Periodic interest rate (decimal form)

$\quad\quad$ n $\quad\quad = \quad$ Number of compounding periods

$\quad\quad$ s $\quad\quad = \quad$ Payment factors (0 for arrears/1 for advance)

$\quad\quad$ PMT $\quad = \quad$ Periodic payment

If an airline borrows US$10 million at 10 per cent interest and is required to repay the loan over 10 years, with repayments annually in arrears:

i.e., $\quad$ PV $\quad\quad = \quad$ $10,000,000

$\quad\quad$ i $\quad\quad\quad = \quad$ 0.1

$\quad\quad$ n $\quad\quad\quad = \quad$ 10

$\quad\quad$ s $\quad\quad\quad = \quad$ 0

From above formula, the periodic payment would be US$1,627,454 annually in arrears throughout the loan term. A lower payment of US$1,479,400 would be required if paid in advance (*i.e.*, with $s = 1$).

The airline will also pay for the preparation of the loan documents, and the bank commitment fees. There may be other conditions such as debt/equity ceilings or minimum net working capital levels. A common practice is to amortise the loan by making periodic payments to reduce the loan balance:

Loan amount $\quad = \quad$ US$10 million

Interest rate $\quad = \quad$ 10 per cent a year

Loan term $\quad\quad = \quad$ 10 years

Repayment $\quad\quad = \quad$ US$1,627,454 annually in arrears

In US$ thousands

Year	Annual interest	Principal repayment	Year end balance
1	1,000.00	627.45	9,372.55
2	937.26	690.19	8,682.36
3	868.24	759.21	7,923.15
4	792.32	835.13	7,088.02
5	708.80	918.65	6,169.37
6	616.94	1,010.51	5,158.86
7	515.89	1,111.56	4,047.30
8	404.73	1,222.72	2,824.58
9	282.46	1,344.99	1,479.59
10	147.96	1,479.49	0
Total	6,274.54	10,000.00	

Since interest is deductible for tax purposes, it is important to separate this out from the repayment of principal in the periodic payments.

b) Calculating Book Profit

The airline borrows US$10 million to acquire an aircraft which is then depreciated over 15 years to 10 per cent residual value. After five years years the airline decides to sell the aircraft for its market value of US$8 million. What is the book profit realised, and what is the cash flow after repayment of the outstanding loan balance?

Annual Depreciation = ($10,000,000 −$1,000,000) ÷ 15 = $600,000

Depreciated value at year end:

Year	*Value ($000)*
	9,400
1	
	8,800
2	
	8,200
3	
	7,600
4	
	7,000
5	

Book profit	=	Sale price less depreciated value
	=	$8,000,000 −$7,000,000 = $1,000,000
Cash flow	=	Sale Price less loan outstanding
	=	$8,000,000 −$6,169,370 = $1,830,630

c)   Effect of Prepayments to Manufacturers

The airline is required to make the following prepayments totalling 33 per cent of the aircraft price (probably the upper limit of what the manufacturer requires):

- 5 per cent at contract signature, 30 months before aircraft delivery.
- 5 per cent at quarterly intervals between 12 and 24 months before delivery.
- 3 per cent 9 months before delivery.

What is the effect of these prepayments on aircraft price if the prevailing interest rate is 10 per cent?

The aircraft price quoted is US$10 million, estimated at date of delivery (including manufacturer's escalation). If the airline had no prepayment obligation, these payments could have been invested at 10 per cent a year which would have amounted to $3.867 million, rather than the 33 per cent of aircraft price or $3.3 million. Thus, the effect of the prepayment schedule is to raise the cost of the aircraft by $0.567 million, or by 5.7 per cent.

Chapter 6

Equity Finance

Equity finance is one of the two main forms of long-term borrowing discussed in the previous chapter. It will be addressed in more detail here. It consists of various classes of shares which are issued by the airline in return for a consideration or price. They may be subsequently bought and sold, usually through a stock exchange.

A new issue of shares can either be offered to the public or placed with financial institutions. A prospectus will be issued, showing past financial performance and short-term prospects. The issue will need to be underwritten to ensure success, and this is done by obtaining commitments from several financial institutions to take a given number of shares at a substantial discount in return for a fee. For a more risky start-up airline, a venture capital firm might be invited to take an initial stake. This will be explored more below.

6.1   Share Issues

Various classes of share may be issued by a company to raise money for the business. The holder of the share has various rights, the main usually being:

- the right to a dividend, if one has been declared;
- the right to vote at various meetings and by post;
- the right to a share of the assets if and when a liquidation takes place (although they would only be paid after all the other classes with claims on the assets had first been paid).

The rights of shareholders are normally described in the Articles of Association reflected in the company laws of the country in which it is based. In some countries (such as China and Russia), company law is less well developed and shareholders need to rely on government agencies to enforce their rights, rather than the law courts.

The airline's balance sheet will show the nominal value of the shares issued, together with any premiums paid on subscription. BA's nominal value for each ordinary share is 25p, but this has little practical significance. Both these will appear under shareholders' or stockholders' equity, which will also include any revaluation surpluses or deficits, other reserves and retained profits and losses from previous years.

The different classes of ordinary share will be shown separately under shareholders' equity. For example, China Southern Airlines has three classes: domestic shares held by the Chinese Government (2.2 billion), 'H' shares listed overseas and held by foreign nationals (1.17 billion) and 'A' shares which were issued in 2003 to private Chinese shareholders (1 billion).

Companies may issue special classes of shares either to thwart a hostile take-over or restrict the ownership to nationals of its country. Air transport is especially dependent on the latter, and foreign ownership restrictions will be discussed below.

Singapore Airlines had two classes of ordinary shares – SIA200 and Foreign – each with a separate stock market listing. In 1999, it decided to merge the two and issue one non-tradable special share to the Ministry of Finance. The vote attached to this share was required to approve certain resolutions, allowing the Singapore government effectively to block certain strategic changes to the airline, such as acquisition by foreign interests. In addition the airline created 3,000 million non-tradable redeemable preference shares with full voting rights: these would be issued to Singapore nationals in the event of any threat to their Air Services Agreements from foreign ownership.

There are a large number of conditions and requirements for listing shares or securities on a stock market. These are more onerous for the major ones such as the London Stock Exchange (LSE) or the New York Stock Exchange (NYSE).

Many non-US companies prefer to obtain a listing in the US by issuing American Depositary Shares (ADSs), which give the holder a claim on a given number of ordinary shares held outside the US. An American Depositary Receipt (ADR) is a certificate of ownership of such shares, and the ADR is often used to describe both the certificate and the shares themselves. The advantages of issuing an ADS include:

- Access to the world's largest capital market;
- Ease of trading and settlement;
- The ability to denominate the shares in local currency and at appropriate price level for US investors (the Depositary Receipt ratio);
- Easier stock/option allocation to US employees.

SEC reporting requirements are less onerous for ADSs than for US companies: annual results are filed on Form 20-F up to six months after the close of the financial year, compared to US companies need to file the 10-K form up to 90 days from their close. No quarterly reports need to be filed. More importantly, the 20-F can be produced using the accounting standards of the home country, with only a reconciliation to US GAAP.[1] The 10-K report needs to be prepared in accordance with US GAAP. However, Some foreign firms are unhappy with the more onerous regulatory burdens placed on foreign companies using ADRs resulting from the Sarbanes-Oxley Act of 2002. While not all the requirements of the Act apply, some such as the personal liability of the CEO and Finance Director may deter some foreign firms from listing in the US. It should be added that the ADR allows listing on all US stock exchanges, and the Over-the-Counter market. No 20-F reporting is needed for the latter, but the ADS gets less exposure to US investors.

---

1   *Depositary receipts Information Guide*, Citigroup website, July 2006.

BA is one example of an airline that has issued ADSs that have been traded on the NYSE for many years. Each of its ADSs is equivalent to 10 ordinary shares, while China Southern's more recently issued ADS can be converted into 50 of their 'H' class of shares. Arbitrage keeps the prices of ADRs (quoted in US$) and underlying foreign shares (quoted in non-US currencies), converted at current market exchange rates, essentially equal.

Capital can be raised from existing shareholders through a rights issue, where the owner of each share has the right to subscribe to a given number of new shares in proportion to their existing holdings, by a given ratio, say, one new share for every three shares held. A rights issue will need to be priced at a discount to the current share price of up to 15 per cent, which is why the rights have a value in themselves even before they are fully paid up. New shares can also be issued in the form of a free distribution of the company's reserves (accumulated from previous years' profits) by a scrip or bonus issue, but this will not raise any new capital.

An example of a rights issue was Lufthansa's issue of one new share for five existing ones in June 2005. The issue was 99.82 per cent subscribed at the offer price of €9.85, raising €752 million for the airline. The AMR Corporation also raised $223 million in November 2005 through the issue of 13 million new shares at around $17 per share, capitalising on the doubling of their share price over the year.

6.2   Equity Finance for Start-up Airline

Smaller or start-up airlines with no access to more conventional sources of capital often turn to venture capital companies. These firms are looking for a large potential capital gain commensurate with the high risk. Most start-up airline business plans are now based on the low cost model, although there are also some business class only, regional and charter start-ups. A typical scenario might be the venture capital firm taking an equity stake at the outset or after an initial proving period. If the airline were successful, the firm would seek to sell its shares a few years after launch, either through acquisition by a larger airline, or by way of a public share issue (Initial Public Offering or IPO). This would give the venture capitalist an *exit* route to realise their capital gain.

Examples of earlier venture capital firms are the US west coast specialists, Hambrecht and Quist (which has financed People Express in the US, the short-lived Scottish airline, *Highland Express*, and more recently Vanguard Airlines and Ryanair), and New Court Securities, an offshoot of Rothschilds, which lent to Federal Express. The large banks now also have their venture capital arms, notably Citicorp Venture Capital, which lent $600,000 to People Express,[2] and NatWest Venture Capital, who have financed British World Airlines. There are many more such firms in the US, with a few specialising solely in airline ventures. George Soros and Chase Capital were the original backers of JetBlue, the former the venture capital arm of a retail

2   Wells, A. and Wensveen, J. (2004), *Air Transportation: a Management Perspective*, fifth edn, Wadsworth.

bank. In Europe, banks are becoming more active in this area, but are still reluctant to subscribe equity to the airline industry.

One of the few exceptions is 3i, the venture capital company jointly owned by UK clearing (retail) banks. They had an equity stake in British Caledonian some years ago, and more recently in the UK airlines Gill Airways and CityFlyer Express. Both of the last two have been sold, Gill to its management and CityFlyer to British Airways. In 2001, 3i took a majority stake in the British Airways low cost airline 'Go', together with 20 per cent from Barclays Bank, 4 per cent from its chief executive and 18.5 per cent from staff. Another venture capital firm, Elektra Partners was originally one of the bidders, as was the Carlyle Group. BA received $112.7 million in cash and $28.1 million in loan notes, and would receive a further $14 million if 3i decided to sell the airline within the next five years years. The intention was to float the airline with an IPO by 2003 but the airline was sold to easyJet and BA collected its bonus. According to KPMG,[3] venture capitalists generally require:

* A return of around 30 per cent a year over three years.
* An *exit* route for their investment in around three years' time, through an IPO or placing.
* Confidence in management and business plan.
* 65-80 per cent of the equity, preferably with management having the rest.

The very high rate of return required is to compensate for the investments made by venture capitalists that fail. Management are left to run the business, in spite of having a minority of shares. The level of profits required to satisfy the high rate of return demanded can be reduced if a significant amount of debt capital can be raised.

Table 6.1   Venture capital interests in LCC/start-up airlines, early 2000s

Airline	Investor	% equity
Gol (Brazil)	AIG (ILFC)	20
SkyEurope (Slovak)	Euroventures Danube*	72
Spirit Airlines (US)	Oaktree Capital	51
Tiger Air (Singapore)	Indigo Partners	24
Wizz Air (Hungary)	Indigo Partners	*n/a*
Vueling (Spain)	Apax partners	40

* formed by the European Bank (EBRD), EU/EBRD SME Finance and ABN AMRO

Spirit Airlines, based in Fort Lauderdale, is said to be the largest privately owned airline in the US, with 4.7 million passengers in 2005. Its backer, Oaktree Capital Management is the fund management arm of Indigo Partners.

---

3   Meldrun, A., (2001), *Financing start-up airlines: private equity*, presentation to Airline Finance course at Cranfield University, 1 March.

One publicly owned bank, the European Bank for Reconstruction and Development (EBRD) has taken small equity stakes in airlines in Eastern Europe and the CIS countries. These have been designed to encourage other private sources of capital to invest in airlines after the collapse of the Soviet bloc. Their stake in SkyEurope (Table 6.1) was sold at the subsequent IPO discussed below, while the EBRD still retains a 9.93 per cent stake in majority government-owned Ukraine International Airlines, together with 22.5 per cent held by Austrian Airlines (see Table 6.7).

Other LCCs have had a large part of their equity funding provided by individuals or families: the Ryan family founded Ryanair and the Haji-Ioannou family easyJet. The latter still control the airline, whereas the Ryan family have only retained a minority interest in Ryanair.

The Brazilian LCC 'Gol' divides its shares into ordinary and preferred; the preferred began trading on the Sao Paulo Stock Exchange in June 2004. They are also traded on the New York Stock Exchange as ADRs, originally with one ADR equivalent to one preferred share, changing to one ADR to two preferred shares in December 2005. The average daily trading volume in these shares in December 2005 was R$1,783 million (US$783 million) in Sao Paulo and US$55,168 million in New York. Only 26.4 per cent of the voting share capital was publicly held (and could thus be foreign owned) at end December 2005. This example shows how it is possible to tap the large US market by combining a listing there with one on a relatively small exchange in the home country.

6.3 Foreign Ownership Limits

Air Services Agreements (ASAs) usually have a clause that requires designated airlines to be effectively controlled by nationals of that country. If that clause is contravened, the other country has the right to refuse designation and thus remove the airline's air traffic rights. This could be a problem at the time of privatisation, since the airline's shares will change from government (nationally owned) to private hands, the latter potentially being foreign owned. This will be addressed in the next chapter, but the problem may also arise in connection with airlines that are in private (non-government) ownership.

Given the very large US capital market, it is easy to see foreign ownership rise substantially, either through an IPO or subsequent issues or market purchases. The question is what constitutes *substantially owned and effectively controlled* by a country's nationals?

The US limits foreign control to 25 per cent of the voting equity in contrast to the EU's 49 per cent. The EU were pressing for a relaxation in the US limit as part of their 2005/2006 Air Services Agreement (ASA) negotiations, and the US Department of Transportation were awaiting comments on a draft proposal in 2006 which would introduce minor changes to the definition of control. Limits for a selection of other countries ranged from only 20 per cent for Brazil to 49 per cent for Australia (which allowed 100 per cent foreign ownership of its domestic airlines) and 50 per cent for

Korea.[4] Some countries had relaxed the limits between 1998 and 2000, although still keeping them below 50 per cent.

Some airlines, such as Thai, Air New Zealand and AeroMexico, have 'A' and 'B' shares, with the 'B' or foreign shares only purchasable by foreign nationals. This is one way to avoid exceeding the share ownership limits for ASA purposes.

In December 2005, 38 per cent of BA's issued share capital was held outside the UK, with just under half of these held in the US (see more on this in the next chapter).[5]

Ryanair took steps in June 2001 to limit the share of its stock held by non-EU investors. The airline instructed its ADS depositary bank to suspend the issue of new ADSs until further notice.[6] At end June 2005, non-EU nationals held 46.2 per cent of Ryanair voting stock, and this suspension was still in force in September 2006.

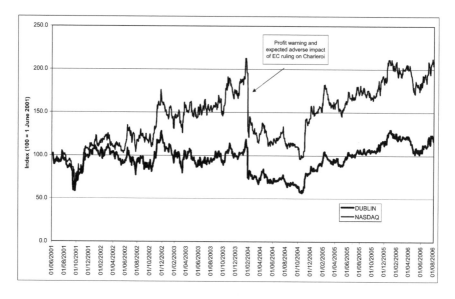

Figure 6.1   Ryanair (Dublin) *vs* Nasdaq (ADR) share price

(Indexed on 1 June 2001)

Figure 6.1 shows the effect of the ADS restriction, the two prices drifting apart between 2002 and 2004. It also shows how the sudden release of bad news can affect the share price: in this case a profit warning combined with the indication of an adverse EU ruling to come. The EU ruling would mean repaying some support that it had received from airports, and a generally less favourable airport charges environment in the future.

4   Chang, Y-C *et al.* (2004),, The evolution of airline ownership and control provisions, *Journal of Air Transport Management* 10, 161–72.

5   British Airways Fact Book, (2006), www.bashares.com under 'Financial Information'.

6   *Ryanair 20F Annual Report*, 2004/2005, p. 18.

6.4   Share Trading and Stock Market Listings

Airlines have a large choice of world stock markets on which to list their shares, though they are first likely to choose their home market where they are best known. By far the largest in terms of domestic market capitalisation is the New York Stock Exchange (NYSE) at almost US$14,000 billion at May 2006. Next was Tokyo with over $4 billion, Nasdaq with $3,559 billion, and then London, Euronext (Amsterdam, Paris, Brussels and Lisbon) and Osaka each with just over $3,000 billion.[7] Nasdaq ranks second in terms of value traded, and the Deutsche Börse replaces Osaka in fifth place.

Amongst the 'emerging economies,' the South Korean stock market turnover was around $650 billion, with Russia, India, Brazil, China and Hong Kong all totalling around $600 billion. China includes the Shanghai and Shenzhen exchanges.[8]

Some of the larger exchanges have their main market and a somewhat less regulated one for smaller companies and start-ups. For example, the London Stock Exchange (LSE) launched its Alternative Investment Market (AIM) in 1995 and by 2006 it had attracted around 1,500 companies. Lighter regulation means that it is slightly more risky than LSE's main market.

The NYSE had 449 foreign firms listed in May 2006 compared to 1,732 domestic companies. Nasdaq had a total of 3,151 firms of which 328 were foreign. London had 333 foreign and 2,856 domestic. In Asia, Singapore had the highest share of foreign firms (224 out of a total of 689).

Turnover of shares varies considerably between exchanges. This is measured as daily turnover divided by market capitalisation, or 'share turnover velocity'. Nasdaq was highest with 261 per cent in May 2006, followed by Shenzhen in China with 186 per cent. London, Euronext and NYSE were both between 110 and 120 per cent. Tokyo's 132 per cent contrasts with Osaka's 9 per cent, while Hong Kong (58 per cent) was much lower than Shanghai (120 per cent).

The above exchanges now accommodate electronic trading, for example through Deutsche Börse's XETRA. A growing volume of dealing is also taking place outside the exchanges: large brokers and investment banks can deal directly using alternative trading systems; 'over the counter' or OTC trades can take place using only brokers as intermediaries; and new institutions have recently emerged in the US such as Liquidnet, handling large blocks of shares.

Trading is becoming dominated by hedge funds, estimated to account of around 40 per cent of volume in the US. The US pre-eminence described above can no longer be taken for granted, with a large number of IPOs moving from America to Europe and Asia, mainly due to the requirements of the Sarbanes-Oxley Act.[9]

Any issue of equity capital will be more attractive if the shares offered are or subsequently quoted on one or more stock exchanges. Having a quotation in more than one market increases the ease of trading by potential investors, but also adds to the legal and accounting requirements, which may become expensive. Stock markets such as Nasdaq in the US and Europe, and easdaq in Europe were introduced as a cheaper way to obtain a market quote, without such onerous requirements, although the US Sarbanes-Oxley law affects all US based trading.

---

7   From World Federation of Exchanges. Available at: www.world-exchanges.org.

8   *The Economist*, (July 2006), p. 17.

9   *The Economist*, (May 2006) p. 25.

**Table 6.2   International passenger airlines with stock market listings
               (Only those in top 50 by total revenues in 2005)**

Airline	Exchange(s)	Share Price[1] US$	Market Capitalisation[1] US$ Million
Europe/Africa:			
Aeroflot	Russian Trading	1.85	2,077
Air France-KLM	Paris, Amsterdam, NYSE	24.54	6,611
Alitalia	Milan	1.08	1,498
Austrian Airlines	Vienna, Frankfurt	8.14	277
British Airways	London, NYSE	7.24	8,190
easyJet	London, Frankfurt	8.16	3,315
Finnair	Helsinki	13.36	1,178
Iberia	Madrid, Frankfurt	2.43	2,303
Lufthansa	German exchanges,[2] Amex	18.33	8,395
Ryanair	Dublin, London, Frankfurt, Nasdaq	10.05	7,735
SAS	Stockholm, Oslo, Copenhagen	10.22	1,681
Turkish	Istanbul	3.54	620
Americas:			
Alaska Air	NYSE	37.23	1,463
American (AMR)	NYSE	22.49	4,259
Continental 'B'	NYSE	27.34	2,445
Delta Air Lines	Frankfurt (OTC)	0.67	132
JetBlue	Nasdaq	10.82	1,899
North-west	*n/a*(OTC)	0.57	49
Skywest	Nasdaq	23.57	1,501
Southwest	NYSE	18.15	14,267
United Airlines	Nasdaq	26.99	2,659
US Airways Group	NYSE (from September 2005)	47.99	4,134
ACE Aviation	Toronto	25.87	2,053
Concorcio AeroMexico	Mexico City	0.25	247
LAN Airlines	Santiago, NYSE	6.21	1,979
tam	Sao Paulo, NYSE	22.80	1,363
Asia/Pacific:			
Air China	Hong Kong, NYSE	0.39	1,245
Air New Zealand	NZSX and Australian	0.71	709
All Nippon Air	Tokyo, London, Frankfurt	3.73	7,282
Cathay Pacific	Hong Kong, London, Frankfurt	1.79	6,056
China Airlines	Taiwan	0.44	1,590
China Eastern A	Shanghai, Hong Kong, NYSE	0.15	232
China Southern H/A	Shanghai, Hong Kong, NYSE	0.23	264
EVA Air	Taiwan	0.39	1,440
Japan Airlines	Tokyo, Frankfurt, London	1.85	4,974
Korean Air	Seoul	32.50	2,317
Malaysia Airways	Kuala Lumpur	0.76	955
Qantas Airways	Sydney, Frankfurt	2.37	4,634
Singapore Airlines	Singapore, Frankfurt	8.36	10,255
Thai Airways	Bangkok, Frankfurt	1.04	1,772

1. At 28 July 2006; quote based on first exchange listed
2. Frankfurt, Stuttgart, Munich, Hanover, Düsseldorf, Berlin/Bremen and Hamburg

Table 6.2 gives the majority of airlines which have quotations, as well as some trading. For the ones listed, the amount of daily trading will vary considerably from, say, BA with an average of 10.6 million shares traded per day over 2005/2006 (or 1 per cent of the shares issued), compared to majority government owned Finnair, which had only 116,000 shares traded on average, or 0.1 per cent of shares issued. For the US carrier, Southwest, the figures were 2.7 million/day, and 0.3 per cent respectively.

In Table 6.2, only those airlines in the top 50 by total revenues have been considered. The only three airlines in the top 30 that did not have a listing were Emirates, Saudi Arabian and Virgin Atlantic.[10] The first two were 100 per cent government owned. In terms of market capitalisation, Southwest Airlines is by far the largest US airline, while Singapore Airlines is also well ahead of the next largest Asia/Pacific carrier.

In Europe, Lufthansa, BA, Air France-KLM and Ryanair are the leaders, their ranking sensitive to small share price movements. The important point, however, is that there are no global giants partly because of the restrictions on trans-national ownership. Thus, the largest airline's capitalisation ($14 billion) is dwarfed by banks such as Citigroup (around $200 billion) or oil company Exxon's $360 billion.

Stock price indices are constructed by selecting stocks and weighting their price movements by capitalisation. These are to give a general idea how stocks in a particular country or sector are moving, but it is also possible to buy a derivative security that is based on these index changes to get a diversified portfolio. The major world indices are shown in the table below.

Table 6.3   Major world stock indices

Index	Exchange	No. of stocks	Airlines included
Dow Jones Industrial Average	NYSE	50	None
Nasdaq Composite	Nasdaq	3,163	UAL, Ryanair, JetBlue*
S&P 500	Major US	500	Southwest
FTSE 100	London	100	British Airways
Dax	Frankfurt	40	Lufthansa
CAC 40	Paris	40	None
Nikkei average	Tokyo	225	Japan Airlines, ANA
Hang Seng	Hong Kong	33	Cathay Pacific

* And a number of US commuter airlines such as Skywest and Mesa.

The FTSE 100 is the top 100 shares traded on the London exchange in terms of market capitalisation. BA is the only airline included, although there are others listed

---

10 Virgin Atlantic is 49 per cent owned by Singapore Airlines and 51 per cent by the Virgin Group, which used to be listed on the London Stock Exchange, but Sir Richard Branson bought out the public shareholders and de-listed the group.

on the exchange. In 2005, easyJet set its managers the target of becoming part of the FTSE 100 for at least six months before the end of September 2008. If this is achieved they will qualify for a bonus in shares equivalent to their annual salary, as long as they stay with the airline for another 3½ years. Some of the smaller country indices also include airlines, such as Iberia in the Madrid index. Ryanair is the only foreign airline included in a major US index.

Various composite airline indices have been developed and are quoted by such firms as Reuters, Bloomberg and Yahoo Finance. The American Stock Exchange has an airline index that is now entirely made up of US airlines (although it used to include one foreign airline, KLM). Many of the US majors were not in this index in 2006 due to being in, or recently out of, Chapter 11.

Table 6.4   AMEX Airline Index (XAL), July 2006

Airline	Symbol	% Weighting
JetBlue Airways	JBLU	12.45
Continental Airlines 'B'	cal	11.73
Expressjet Holdings	XJT	11.14
Southwest Airlines	luv	10.37
AMR Corp.	AMR	10.10
Alaska Air	ALK	9.01
Skywest Inc.	SKYW	8.97
Frontier Airlines	FRNT	8.91
Mesa Air Group	MESA	8.69
Airtran Holdings	AAI	8.62

Source: American Stock Exchange

The London Exchange includes airlines in their 'travel and tourism' index, but in the US, Dow Jones publishes the DJ US Airline index that includes eight US airlines. Morgan Stanley Capital International (MSCI) publishes a large number of stock indices based on regions, countries and industries, including a number of ones dedicated to airlines. The MSCI Europe Airlines Index has been published since 1995 and includes Lufthansa, British Airways, Air France (now Air France-KLM), SAS and Iberia. Their World Airline Index included 28 international airlines in 2006, with only Southwest Airlines from the US.

Some airlines link executive remuneration to their share price performance, in terms of total shareholder return (including both share price movements and dividends paid) relative to a market index. Qantas granted share options to senior executives subject to its share price outperforming both the ASX 200 index and a basket of global airlines which then included Air Canada, Air New Zealand, the AMR Corp., BA, Cathay Pacific, Delta Airlines, Japan Airlines, KLM, Lufthansa, Northwest, Singapore Airlines and UAL. The plan was suspended in 2002, although their 2005 Annual Report included a graph of the MSCI World Airline Index.

Table 6.5   Constituent airlines of the MSCI world airline index (July 2006)

ACE Aviation	China Southern 'H'	Malaysia Airlines
Air China	EVA Airways	Qantas
Air France-KLM	Gol (Brazil)	Ryanair
Air Asia	Iberia	SAS
All Nippon	Japan Airlines	Singapore
Asiana (Korea)	Jet Airways (India)	Southwest
British Airways	Korean Air	TAM (Brazil)
Cathay Pacific	Cathay Pacific	Thai Airways
China Airlines	Lan (Chile)	Turkish
China Eastern 'H'	Lufthansa	

From 1996, BA had a similar long-term incentive arrangement for senior executives, which was discontinued in 2004. Half of the incentive was linked to an operating margin target and half to a total shareholder return target of BA shares against the FTSE 100 index. In 2005, the scheme was changed, keeping the two independent benchmarks: operating margin and total shareholder returns. The index target was changed from the FTSE 100 index to a basket of 20 airlines against which BA competed. The award of 25 per cent of the shares would only be triggered if BA's total shareholder returns reached the median of the 20 airline group performance. A sliding scale then applied until the full award is made when BA's returns are at or above the upper quintile (or top 20 per cent) of the airline group. The scheme was to run over a three-year period.

Table 6.6   British Airways@ Performance Share Plan comparator airlines*

ACE Aviation (Air Canada)	Iberia
Air France-KLM	Lufthansa
Air New Zealand	Northwest Airlines
Alitalia	Qantas Airways
All Nippon Airways	Ryanair
American Airlines	SAS
Cathay Pacific Airways	Singapore Airlines
Continental Airlines	Southwest Airlines
Delta Airlines	United Airlines
easyJet	US Airways

* used in 2005/2006 award (*Source*: BA Annual Report 2005/2006)

A variation of the above was applied by Austrian Airlines in 2005, with awards made if the Austrian Airline shareholder returns outperformed the MSCI Europe Airline Index (described above) by at least 3 per cent over a three-year period.

6.5   Initial Public Offering (IPO)

An Initial Public Offering is the sale of shares to the public for the first time, usually before a stock exchange listing. The shares could then be traded in the secondary market. The process is often a means for the controlling and possibly founding shareholders, which may be those who launched the business together with any venture capital firms, selling all or part of their stakes. New shares may also be issued by the airline at the same time to raise fresh capital for investment in aircraft. For example, 82.5 per cent of the Indian airline, Jet Airways, IPO consisted of new shares, the remainder coming from Tail Winds, a company owned by their founder, Naresh Goyal. The IPO will involve the preparation of a prospectus containing detailed information on the company, including its latest audited accounts and perhaps a profit forecast. It will be publicised through the press (if it is to be offered to the general public) and brokers, and applications sought for a certain number of shares at a fixed price (or a narrow price range).

The IPO will normally be priced at a level that ensures that all the shares will be subscribed. If not, one or more investment bank will underwrite the issue: agree to take the shares that are not taken up at a preferential price or for a commission.[11] Sometimes, the price is adjusted downwards following feedback from the market via the lead manager of the issue (investment bank). This may be because of events that negatively affect the market in general, or factors specific to the industry and company. An example of this was the IPO of the fast expanding Indian airline, Air Deccan, in 2006. An initial price range for the shares of Rs300-325 was suggested by the airline, but their advisers eventually persuaded them that Rs150-175 was more realistic. The shares were finally offered at Rs148, but the shares dropped to Rs98 on the opening day of trading on the Mumbai Stock Exchange, largely because of factors affecting the Indian market in general. They drifted lower to Rs85 over the next month.[12] This is an example of both over-optimistic pricing (the airline was trading at a loss), and a severe change of market sentiment too late to withdraw the issue.

IPOs are often marketed to the general public and financial institutions separately, each being allocated a given number of shares. The price per share may be determined in advance and bids sought at that fixed price. However, the prospectus may indicate a price range with bids sought above the bottom of that range. The public are then asked to submit their bids in a monetary amount, the number of shares they receive then depending on the final price. The final price is decided following the results of a 'book building' phase, involving the lead investment bank adviser consulting financial institutions about demand for the shares and bid price intentions. Once the book is closed, the price will be decided (there could be two prices: one for the institutions and one for the public). In cases where the issue is oversubscribed, bids will be scaled down *pro rata*, with public and institutional allocations often dealt

---

11   Underwriting discounts and commissions totalled US$1.89 per share for the jetBlue IPO, or 7 per cent of the issue price (from *JetBlue Prospectus*, 11 April 2002).

12   Air Deccan: IPO Struggle Reflects Indian Overcapacity Worries, *Aviation Strategy*, (June 2006).

with separately. Over-subscription may also trigger a 'greenshoe' option whereby additional shares may be sold for a short period after trading in the shares starts. Where a small number of founder shareholders retain a large stake after the IPO, they may sign an agreement not to sell any of their holding for a specified 'lock up' period, usually between six months to one year.

Table 6.7 shows the mixed fortunes of some of the airline IPOs between 2000 and 2005. One significant IPO not included in the table was by Ryanair: this occurred in 1997 at a price equivalent to €2.48, allowing the Ryan family to reduce significantly their holding and for a listing to be obtained in Ireland and New York. New shares were also issued to raise finance for the airline. This was a fixed price offer but with an over-allotment option to increase the shares sold by 10 per cent (which was in fact exercised).

Table 6.7   Airline IPOs taking place between 2000 and 2006*

Airline	Date	Listing	Issue price	Raised	Times over-sub-scribed	July 2006 price	July 2006 *vs* issue price ± per cent
easyJet	Nov-2000	London	310p	£224.6 million	10	442p	42.6
JetBlue	Apr-2002	New York	US$27	US$158.4 million	26	US$11	− 59.3
Virgin Blue	Dec-2003	Australia	A$2.25	A$666	10	A$1.67	− 25.8
Norwegian	Dec-2003	Oslo	NKr27-33	NKr250	7	NKr 92.25	179.5
Gol	Jun-2004	Brazil/US	US$8.5	US$280 million	*n/a*	US$32.66	284.2
Air Asia	Nov-2004	Kuala Lumpur	RM 1.1625	RM717 million	*n/a*	RM 1.28	9.9
Jet Airways	Feb-2005	Mumbai	Rs 1,100	Rs 18,997 million	16.2	Rp 513.5	− 53.3
TAM	Jun-2005	Brazil/US	R$18	US$257 million	*n/a*	R$58.94	227.4
SkyEurope	Sep-2005	Vienna, Warsaw	€6	€78 million	'several'	€1.72	− 71.3
Eurofly	Dec-2005	Milan	€6.41	€40.32 million	*n/a*	€2.41	− 62.4
Air Berlin	May-2006	Frankfurt	€12	€510 million	*n/a*	€10.19	− 15.1
Silverjet	May-2006	London	112p	£33.6 million	*n/a*	115p	2.7
Deccan Aviation	Jun-2006	Mumbai	Rs 148	US$79	1.23	Rs 75.25	− 49.2

* IPOs that were part of airline privatisations are discussed in the next chapter

The issue prices shown above may have followed the publication of a price range: for example, Jet Airways issued a price range of Rs950 to Rs1,125 before deciding on Rs1,100. The share prices of the two Brazilian airlines in the above table, TAM and Gol, have done extremely well since the IPO, partly due to the collapse of the country's national flag carrier, Varig. The Indian carriers, Jet Airways and Deccan, suffered from the general decline in the Indian stock market, although the former was operating at a loss at the time of floatation. Similarly, Air Berlin, Eurofly and SkyJet were loss making at the time of the offer, and did not provide a profit forecast, rather promises of profits to come. JetBlue were offered at US$27 (or US$8 to take into account the later stock split) in April 2002 ending their first day's trading (when 48 million shares changed hands) at $45 (adjusted to $13.33), falling to a low of $8.93 in October 2002 and then climbing to a high of $31.23 exactly one year later. They subsequently declined as a result of worsening financial results and a more competitive operating environment.

The IPOs shown above varied in their marketing strategy: Jet Airways offered 60 per cent of its issue to financial institutions in contrast to Norwegian offering only 20 per cent. One start-up, Silverjet, managed to raise over £30 million in equity before it had even applied for Air Operator's Certificate (AOC) from the UK Civil Aviation Authority. By August 2006, easyJet's highest share price reached 57 per cent above the issue price and Air Asia 67 per cent ; on the other hand, Virgin Blue only climbed 16 per cent above its issue price and SkyEurope 6 per cent higher. Air Berlin had not risen above its initial offer price, neither had Eurofly.

6.6 Mergers and Cross-Investment

Airlines are normally prevented from acquiring a majority of airlines in other countries because of Air Services Agreement (ASA) restrictions on foreign ownership. However, it is possible, as will be explained in the next section. An airline taking a majority stake in another airline in its own country is much easier, and has usually taken the form of a financial link with a commuter or feeder airline (*e.g.*, Northwest 27.8 per cent in Mesaba Air, or Air France's 100 per cent stake in Régional Airlines). An airline might also set up a subsidiary airline to operate as a low cost or charter carrier.

Taking a minority stake is possible, and has mostly been to cement a strategic alliance (*e.g.*, British Airways and American Airlines in Iberia), or as a strategic partner in an airline privatisation (British Airways in Qantas). The Ryan family discussed selling 25 per cent of Ryanair to BA in 1995 to raise money for expansion, but BA wanted 49 per cent and an option to take full control. The deal fell through, and the following year the 25 per cent was sold to David Bonderman's Texas Pacific Group, after he decided to withdraw from Richard Branson's low cost airline venture in Belgium (later to become Virgin Express).[13]

---

13 Creaton, S. (2004) *Ryanair: How a Small Irish Airline Conquered Europe*, Aurum Press.

Table 6.8 shows the more significant investments in other airlines. Most of these are connected with a privatisation or strategic alliance. Virgin Atlantic's investment in Nigeria followed the failure of the country's national airline. Both the Air France-KLM investment and that of AMR/BA were relatively small but intended to cement a strategic alliance. The former maintained its 2 per cent share in Alitalia by subscribing to the December 2005 rights issue.

Icelandair's parent, FL Group, had also invested in a sizeable stake of easyJet (16.9 per cent) that it had gradually acquired in the open market since October 2004. This was sold in April 2006 for €325 million, giving them a profit of €140 million.[14] FL Group also acquired 100 per cent of Sterling Airways of Denmark (recently merged with another Danish airline, Maersk Air) for US$242 million in early 2006, followed by a 10 per cent stake in Finnair.

Table 6.8   Major airline cross-border investments in other airlines (June 2006)

Airline owner	Airline owned	% Share
ACE Aviation	US Airways	6.00
American Airlines	Iberia	1.00
Air France-KLM	Alitalia	6.00
Austrian Airlines	Slovak Airlines	62.00
Austrian Airlines	Ukraine International	22.50
British Airways	Iberia	10.00
Lufthansa	BMI	30.00
SAS	BMI	20.00
Virgin Atlantic	Virgin Nigeria	49.00
Air China*	Cathay Pacific	10.16
Cathay Pacific	Air China	20.00
Emirates	SriLankan Airlines	43.63
Qantas	Air Pacific	46.30
Singapore Airlines	Virgin Atlantic	49.00
South African	Air Tanzania	49.00

* An additional 7.34 per cent of Cathay Pacific held via its 100 per cent holding in CNAC

A number of investments have recently been reversed: BA sold the 18 per cent of shares it had remaining in Qantas after taking 25 per cent before the latter's privatisation. Singapore Airlines took a loss of S$45.7 million from its 25 per cent of Air New Zealand after its collapse. Continental Airlines sold its 43.5 per cent stake in the Panamanian national airline, copa, through an IPO that was offered at US$15-17; in spite of its legacy flag carrier origins, the offer was oversubscribed and trading started at $24.

---

14 FL Group Sells Entire easyJet Holding, *Victoria Moores in Air Transport Intelligence News*, (April 2006) 5.

Two cross-border airline mergers have occurred in Europe between 2004 and 2005: Air France and KLM, and Lufthansa and Swiss. With moves towards substituting EU for national controls in EU ASAs, mergers between EU carriers should become easier than in other world regions. However, there were still major obstacles in both cases.

Air France-KLM

The acquisition of KLM by Air France was announced in September 2003, and was completed around the middle of 2004. The deal involved compensating the KLM shareholders with Air France stock, and resulted in the French Government share of Air France dropping below 50 per cent. It is thus the last phase of Air France's privatisation and will be discussed in the next chapter.

Lufthansa-Swiss

The acquisition of Swiss by Lufthansa announced in March 2005 did not involve government majority ownership, with only 20.2 per cent of Swiss shares held by the Swiss Federal government. The deal was approved by both the European Commission and the US anti-trust authorities in early June 2005. A Swiss-domiciled company, AirTrust, gradually acquired all the shares of Swiss, offering CHF8.96 per share for the remaining minorities. In addition to a total of €47 million, former Swiss shareholders also received a 'debtor warrant' or 'out-performance option' that would give them up to a further total of up to CHF390 million subject to the Lufthansa share price outperforming an index of competitor airline share prices by 50 per cent in steps over a three-year period to 2008. The pay-out doubles for every 10 per cent that Lufthansa out-performed the competitor index, up to the maximum over the period 21 March 2005–20 March 2008. Thus, depending on the future exchange rate, the acquisition will cost Lufthansa between €45 million and around €300 million. The competitor airline index consisted of BA (40 per cent), Air France-KLM (40 per cent) and Iberia (20 per cent).

Chapter 7

Airline Privatisation

The trend towards the privatisation of government owned assets gathered pace during the 1980s, as part of overall economic programmes introduced by more capitalist governments. This was encouraged by aid agencies such as The World Bank, the Asian Development Bank and the European Bank for Reconstruction and Development. Policies pursued by the latter became increasingly influenced by the USA, their major donor country.

The justification for privatisation was both strategic and financial. Strategic reasons encompassed:

- Reducing the involvement of the state in the provision of goods and services.
- The promotion of economic efficiency.
- The generation of benefits for consumers.
- The promotion of an enterprise culture.
- The achievement of wider share ownership.

Of equal, or even greater, importance were often the financial reasons: governments welcomed these sources of cash with which to reduce their budget deficits, allow room for reducing taxes, or shift the financial burden to the private sector. However, it is not entirely obvious that an airline would be a financial burden, once it had been prepared for privatisation. Furthermore, while these policies may have looked attractive in the short-term, they might, in some cases, have resulted in fire sales of quality assets at low prices which effectively transferred wealth from the population as a whole to those who were lucky enough to be allocated shares in the newly privatised company.

This chapter focuses on the financial aspects of airline privatisation. Equally important, but beyond the scope of this book, are the economic aspects and the preparation before privatisation. This is discussed in some depth by Doganis, with particular reference to Olympic Airways, an airline which he chaired during its preparation period.[1]

The average government stake in the largest 25 international airlines was 28 per cent in 1996, 19 per cent in 2001 and 16 per cent in 2005 (ranked and weighted by international RTKs in each year). This reduction was caused by the governments of Germany, France, Italy, Spain and the Netherlands all reducing significantly their shareholdings, offset to a small extent by the Malaysian Government re-nationalising

---

1 Doganis, R. (2001), *The Airline Business In The 21st Century*, Routledge, see Chapter 8.

Malaysia Airlines. This compares with an average of 59 per cent for the next 25 largest international airlines in 2001 (up from 51 per cent in 1996).

The trend towards airline privatisation began over the period before 1996, but was mainly in these top 25 airlines: this is evident from the reduction in average government stake for these airlines from 48 per cent in the early 1980s, with the privatisation of British Airways, JAL, KLM, Qantas, Malaysian and Air Canada.

Table 7.1   Government shareholdings (per cent) in top 20 international airlines, 2005

		International RTKs (million)	% government owned
1	Lufthansa	18,710	0.0
2	Singapore Airlines	15,447	56.4
3	Air France*	15,200	0.0
4	British Airways	14,528	0.0
5	Korean Air	13,449	0.0
6	Cathay Pacific	12,809	0.0
7	KLM*	11,672	0.0
8	Japan Airlines	10,574	0.0
9	Emirates	9,894	100.0
10	American Airlines	9,582	0.0
11	United Airlines	9,193	0.0
12	China Airlines	8,896	70.1
13	Qantas	7,563	0.0
14	EVA Air	7,336	0.0
15	NortwestNorth-west Airlines	7,297	0.0
16	Malaysian Airline System	6,457	69.3
17	Thai Airways	6,298	54.0
18	Federal Express	5,695	0.0
19	Air Canada	5,588	0.0
20	Delta Air Lines	5,350	0.0

* full merger agreed

Source: IATA WATS 2006 for 2005 RTK weights and airline annual reports

Since 1996, the privatisation process has been completed for some of the top 25, with others such as Iberia and Air France added to the list. However, little progress has taken place amongst the next 25 largest, with the average government share in fact increasing. This was because of the entry into the top 50 of state owned airlines such as China Eastern, and the disappearance of part privately owned Finnair. Boeing estimated that, among the top 25 airlines, the share of total capacity offered by government controlled airlines has fallen in the past 20 years from 38 per cent to 10 per cent.[2]

---

2   Boeing, (2001), Current market outlook 2001.

British Airways is one of the early examples of a total privatisation. Before the airline could be privatised, it had to go through a radical shake-up, resulting in drastic staff cuts, axing unprofitable routes and disposing of loss-making subsidiaries.

Privatisation can involve the sale of a minority government stake to the private sector (as in the case of Finnair), the sale of a majority in a number of stages (*e.g.*, Lufthansa) or in one stage (*e.g.*, Kenya Airways), or an outright sale of a 100 per cent government shareholding (*e.g.*, British Airways). Examples of each of these paths are discussed in more detail below.

Methods of privatisation are one or a combination of the following:

- Flotation (public subscription).
- Private placement (a number of different private investors).
- Trade sale (one large investor which also operates in the same or related industry).
- Employee or management buy-out.

A flotation is only possible where there is a strong domestic equity market (with good volume trading in a number of different companies and industry sectors), and the local stock market regulations can be complied with by the airline. Success will depend on the airline having a good track record (at least two or three years' of profitable trading), and an appropriate capital and issue structure. Iberia's privatisation was repeatedly postponed in the early 1990s because it had not been profitable and needed more time to restructure.

7.1 Full Privatisation through Flotation – British Airways

The conservative government of Margaret Thatcher was elected in 1979 with a programme which included the privatisation of many of the state owned firms. British Airways was one of the first candidates for this process, and John King was appointed as its chairman in 1980 with the task of preparing the airline for privatisation.

Most airlines had suffered badly as a result of the economic recession of the early 1980s. In 1981/1982, British Airways were technically insolvent,[3] with long-term debts of over £1 billion and negative equity of almost £200 million. The privately owned Laker Airways was in a similar position in that year. A snapshot of the two British airlines at end March 1981 and 1982 is shown in Table 7.2.

Apart from their contrasting ownership, a major factor in BA's subsequent recovery, and Laker Airways' 1982 bankruptcy was the sterling/US$ exchange rate: the strengthening of sterling before 1981 had an adverse effect on the national flag carrier, but had the opposite effect on Laker, which had low foreign exchange revenues relative to its foreign exchange costs. The dramatic weakening of sterling

---

3   Gordon Dunlop, BA's Finance Director stated in 1982 that had the airline been in the private sector it would have gone through the bankruptcy courts, Reed, Arthur, (1990), *Airline: the inside story of British Airways*, p. 47.

against the dollar after 1982 helped BA's recovery, while sealing the fate of Laker Airways.

Table 7.2   British Airways' and Laker Airways' liabilities

£ million	British Airways		Laker Airways	
	1980/1981	1981/1982	1980/1981	1981/1982
Current liabilities	594	751	38	24
Long-term debt	739	1,074	177	226
Shareholders' funds	350	− 192	25	− 20
Total liabilities	1,683	1,633	240	230

The exchange rate, however, was only one factor in BA's recovery. The new management team introduced a radical restructuring of the airline, which involved the reduction in staff numbers from just under 54,000 in 1980/1981 to 36,000 in 1983/1984. The measures taken to prepare the airline for privatisation are well documented,[4] the overall outcome being the reduction in long-term debt to £626 million by the end of March 1985, and a return to a positive figure for shareholders' funds of £287 million. Helped by further growth in the world economies, the balance sheet was in even better shape by the time the privatisation prospectus was issued in January 1987 (long-term debt down to £316 million and shareholders' funds standing at £620 million at end September 1986).

The method of valuation for a share issue such as this was described in the previous chapter. Early on in the UK privatisation programme, the government set a higher priority on making the issue a success with small investors, and were thus erring on the low side in determining the price at which the shares were to be sold. They later faced a substantial amount of criticism in selling state assets too cheaply, so that other mechanisms for flotation were used for subsequent privatisation issues which did not command such high premiums in early trading.

The prospectus was issued in January 1987, and contained much information on the airline, the industry environment and outlook, as well as the procedures for application for shares, and arrangements for employees and airline pensioners.[5]

Table 7.3 summarises the key ratios predicted in the prospectus for the financial year 1986/1987, and compares these with the actual outcome which was published in May of the same year. The prospective *P/E* ratio was considerably below the UK market average of 14, and the prospective dividend yield compared favourably with the equity market average of 4.2 per cent.

---

4   Ashworth, M. and Forsythe, P., (1984), *Civil aviation policy and the privatisation of British Airways*, Institute for Fiscal Studies.

5   British Airways, (1987), *Offer for sale on behalf of the Secretary of State for Transport*, Hill Samuel & Co. Ltd., January.

Table 7.3   British Airways privatisation factsheet (1987)

	Prospectus	Outcome
Issue price per share	£1.25	£1.68–£1.78[1]
Market capitalisation	£900 million	£1.21-1.28 billion[1]
Forecast profits for 1986/1987	£145 million	£162 m[2]
Prospective P/E	× 6.3	
(Based on 1986/1987 pre-tax profit)		
Historic P/E	× 4.7	× 5.3[3]
(Based on 1985/1986 pre-tax profit)		
Net dividend yield	3.2%	2.3%[3]
Dividend cover	× 3.3	× 4.9
Net tangible assets per share	£0.86	£0.84

1. Price range on first day's trading
2. Actual pre-tax profit for the financial year 1986/1987
3. Based on the market price per ordinary share of 181p on 31 March 1987

A further inducement to subscribe to the offer was given in the form of a loyalty bonus. Individuals obtaining shares under the offer would be eligible to receive one additional free share for every 10 shares held continuously until the end of February 1990, or for three years. This was to dissuade individuals from taking their profit early on, and thus to support the government's policy of a shareholding society.

To provide some incentive for BA staff, a number of arrangements were made for the distribution of both free and paid shares:

- The free offer of 76 shares for each BA employee.
- The matching offer of two free shares for each share employees purchased at the offer price (for up to 120 paid shares).
- The priority offer, whereby BA employees would receive priority for any further applications, subject to any scaling down that might occur.
- The discount offer under which 1,600 shares applied for by BA staff under the above priority offer could be purchased at a 10 per cent discount.

The share offer was 11 times oversubscribed, reflecting both the attractive offer price and the considerable advertising effort undertaken by the government. This meant that applications had to be scaled down, and the employee scheme had the effect of making a substantial bonus payment to them of just under £30 million (62 million shares multiplied by a first day average premium of 48 pence).

Only around 4 per cent of shares were held by employees by 1996, with two-thirds of the airline's staff holding shares. A profit sharing scheme was first introduced in 1983/1984 whereby, if profits exceeded a certain target, all eligible (UK based) employees would receive a given number of weeks' additional salary as a bonus. This could be taken in cash or used by trustees to buy shares in the airline on behalf of the employees (an incentive to take shares was introduced in 1996 in the form of a 20 per cent increase in value of the bonus taken as shares). The bonus amounted to

£94 million in 1995/1996, or one week's basic pay for every eligible staff member for every £100 million in pre-tax profits earned over a target of £269 million.[6]

Table 7.4   Initial post-privatisation British Airways share distribution

Shareholder category	Share %
Employees	8.6
UK public (individuals)	35.4
UK institutions	36.1
Overseas	17.2
Loyalty bonus retention	2.7
Total	100.0

Around 20 per cent of the total offer of 720 million BA shares was made under a separate overseas offer in the USA, Canada, Japan and Switzerland. An application was made to list the shares on the New York Stock Exchange, in addition to the London exchange, and it was intended to obtain a listing on the Toronto exchange at a later date. These listings would clearly increase the attraction of the shares to foreign investors, but, on the other hand there would be problems if too large a proportion of shares were held by foreign nationals.

This is because air services agreements, which give the airline its right to operate international routes, require that the airlines designated by the UK Government are *substantially owned and effectively controlled* by UK nationals. The implication of this clause for the exact percentage of foreign owned shares allowed is subject to interpretation. Substantial ownership implies foreign ownership of perhaps 50 per cent and over, but effective control might be exercised if one foreign corporation or individual held, say 25–30 per cent of the issued share capital, and the remainder of shares were widely distributed among a large number of entities. No maximum percentage was stated in the prospectus, but in the event of BA's traffic rights being removed or reduced as a result of this clause in the air services agreement, a mechanism was introduced to refuse to register the shares which caused such a situation (a nationality declaration is required for shares to be registered in any new owner's name).

In practice, BA's foreign ownership has reached 41 per cent in 1992 without any problems for traffic rights, and without the need to refuse registration. The level subsequently fell to 26 per cent in March 1993, was 35 per cent at year ends 1994 and 1995, 27 per cent at the end of March 1996, rising to 43 per cent in early 2001 (of which around three-quarters are held in the US) and back to 38 per cent at end December 2005, with only half of these held in the US. This compares with the initial US allocation of just over 17 per cent.

BA has outperformed its home market following privatisation (see Figure 7.1), especially in the period after the effects of the Gulf War had been fully digested.

---

6   *British Airways News*, (24 May 1996).

However, since 1997, the airline has faced considerable problems, and its performance declined in relation to the UK market and other airlines.

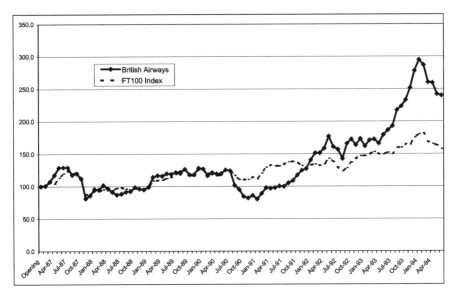

Figure 7.1   British Airways share price *trend vs UK* market

7.2   Full Privatisation through Trade Sale and Flotation – Qantas

The privatisation of Qantas Airways Ltd was achieved by taking a number of steps. First, the airline was merged with one of the two major domestic airlines, Australian Airlines, in September 1992. This was to give it control over domestic feeder services, as well as to improve crew, aircraft and overall productivity. Next, in March 1993, a trade sale was made of 25 per cent of the share capital to an international airline that could give the airline a stronger presence in international markets. This was done by tender, and BA's bid of A$666 million was successful against the only other contender that could realistically be considered, Singapore Airlines.

At the same time, BA also entered into a 10-year commercial agreement with Qantas, thus cementing a strategic alliance between the two airlines. The final step was the sale of the remaining 75 per cent of the shares in Qantas, which were held by the Commonwealth (government) of Australia. This was done through an offer of 750 million shares to both the public and institutions. The price of the issue was determined by tenders from the institutions, with the final price being set at A$2.00. The price of public offer was then set at 10 per cent below the institutional price, or A$1.90. Thus, the total issue was valued at A$1.45 billion.[7] The issue was 2.5 times oversubscribed at the bottom end of the price range and 2.2 times oversubscribed at the institutional final price of A$2 (individual subscriptions were allocated in full).

7   Qantas Airways Limited (1995), *Offering Memorandum*, 22nd June.

Table 7.5   Qantas Airways' post-offer share distribution

Shareholder category	Share %
Australian individuals and employees	27
Australian institutions	27
Foreign institutions	20
British Airways plc	25
Loyalty bonus retention	1
Total	100

Source: SBC Warburg

The 20 per cent foreign institutional demand was principally from the US and UK/ Europe, with 47 per cent and 43 per cent respectively, leaving only 10 per cent from Asian investors.

As with the BA issue, it was necessary to limit foreign ownership in the airline. The government passed the Qantas Sale Act to ensure that Qantas remained an Australian airline. In the act, the total amount of foreign ownership was limited to 49 per cent of the shares. To enforce this restriction, the directors of the airline have powers to remove the voting rights of a share, to require the disposal of shares and to transfer shares which exceed the limit.

In the days following the issue, foreign investors pushed their share up from the 45 per cent at allocation (see table above) to the maximum 49 per cent allowed. To satisfy foreign demand, which was running at a higher level than the shares available, finance houses issued derivatives which shadowed the Qantas share price and dividend distribution, but which did not give the holder any claims on Qantas assets or any votes. Air New Zealand's privatisation contained similar foreign ownership limits: 49 per cent overall, 25 per cent from any one airline, and 35 per cent from any group of airlines.

Table 7.6   Qantas Airways privatisation factsheet (1995)

	Prospectus	Outcome
Issue price per share	A$ 1.90 – A$2.00	A$2.15[1]
Market capitalisation	A$1.9-2.0 billion	A$ 2.15 billion[1]
Forecast profit after tax:		
1995/1996 (to end June)	A$ 237 million	A$ 247 million
Prospective P/E (1994/1995)	× 11.1	
(Based on A$2 issue price)		
Prospective P/E (19951996)	× 8.5	
(Based on A$2 issue price)		
Historic P/E (1993/1994)	× 12.8	
Dividend yield (1995/1996)	6.5 per cent	
Net tangible assets per share	A$ 2.27	

1. Highest price on first day's trading

Each employee was given free shares with a total value of A$500 at the then market price. During the financial year 1996/1997, a similar free distribution would be made to employees, subject to a performance target for the year ending 30 June 1995 being met.

The shares opened at A$2.15, giving individual investors a 13 per cent day one premium. The shares moved ahead to almost A$2.30 over the next few months. After a good start, Qantas has underperformed compared to its home market in the two years years following privatisation (see Figure 7.2).

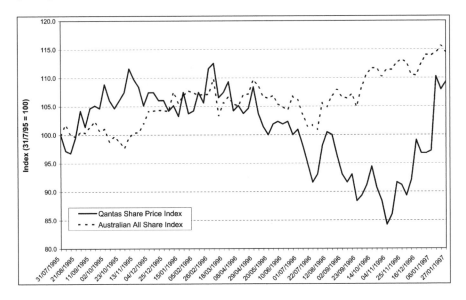

Figure 7.2   Qantas Airways share price trend *vs* Australian market

Subsequently BA's 25 per cent stake was diluted to 18.25 per cent as a result of not taking up their allotment in a rights issue. They finally sold their remaining shares by placing them with institutions in 2004. By then this was no longer seen as a necessary strategic investment and BA's major concern was to reduce its long-term debt. The sale raised A$1.1 billion (around £430 million).[8] This gave them a book profit of 165 per cent, aside from the dividends received each year and the benefits from the alliance.

7.3   Gradual Privatisation – Lufthansa

Lufthansa has had private shareholders and its shares have been traded on the Frankfurt market for many years. The Federal government's stake fluctuated between 72 per cent and 85 per cent over the years 1953–1987, when it declined to 65 per cent. In 1989, however, the German Government took the first step in

---

8   British Airways Press Release, (9 September 2004).

pursuit of their policy of eventual privatisation of the airline. In the autumn of 1989, Lufthansa issued DM304 million worth of shares (nominal value), and the Federal Government and other state entities (the Federal Railways and the Kreditanstallt für Wiederaufbau) did not subscribe to the issue. This resulted in the government share falling from around 60 to 52 per cent.

Further progress towards privatisation was halted first by the serious financial consequences of the Gulf War recession, and second by the staff pensions problem. Lufthansa employees were covered by the government backed supplemental pension fund (VBL), and the fund's constitution would have resulted in the loss of pension rights if the government's share in the airline were to drop below 50 per cent. Lufthansa did not have the financial resources to fund these benefits themselves.

The issue was finally resolved in 1994, when the Federal government agreed to provide DM1.567 billion to maintain the pension benefits of existing staff, following Lufthansa's withdrawal from VBL. The airline would fund a separate pension plan for new staff themselves. The withdrawal took place at the end of December 1994.

Once the pensions problem had been resolved, the way was clear for the government to reduce their take to below 50 per cent. This occurred in October 1994, with a share issue of DM1.2 billion not taken up by the government, and a placement of 2 million shares held by the Federal government with institutions.

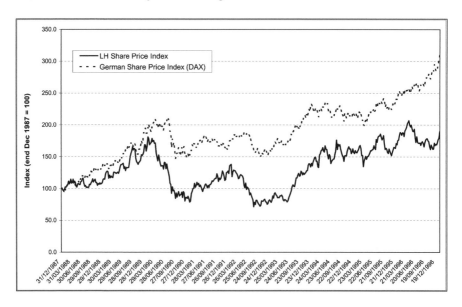

Figure 7.3   Lufthansa share price trend *vs* the German market

During the 1995 financial year, Lufthansa bought 105,531 of its own shares in the market, representing 0.28 per cent of its nominal share capital. The shares were offered to employees of the various companies in the group between August and December 1995 as part share in the profits earned in 1995.[9]

---

9   Deutsche Lufthansa (1995), *Annual Report*.

One final problem relating to Lufthansa's privatisation was solved in 1999. Most shares in German companies are 'bearer,' rather than registered in the shareholder's name. Bearer shares are similar to banknotes in that their owners are not known and cannot be traced. Dividends have thus to be claimed by holders, since payments cannot be sent to known holders. It is thus impossible to know who is holding the shares. This becomes a problem once the government only holds a minority of the shares, since many of Germany's air services agreements with other non-EU countries require their designated airline to be wholly owned and controlled by German nationals.

Table 7.7   Lufthansa shareholding – 1996 and 1997

Shareholder	January 1996 %	January 1997 %
Federal Republic of Germany	35.68	—
Kreditanstallt für Wiederaufbau*	1.82	37.50
Deutsche Postbank and Deutsche Bahn	1.38	1.38
State of North Rhine-Westfalia	1.77	1.77
Munich Air Transport Securities Company (MGL)	10.05	10.05
Total above known German shareholders	50.70	50.70
Other shareholders	49.30	49.30
Total	100.00	100.00

* 100 per cent owned by the Federal Republic of Germany

The group of state companies and institutions that, following full privatisation, had agreed to retain their holdings to ensure majority German ownership (see Table 7.7), no longer needed to do so. In 2001, 62 per cent of the airline's shares were held by German nationals, with a further 14 per cent held by UK nationals, and another 4 per cent and 3 per cent held in Luxembourg and Belgium respectively. By the end of 2005, 79 per cent of their shares were owned by German nationals, and only 5 per cent US nationals.

However, Lufthansa reported that in August 2006 the share of foreign investors in their share capital had reached 40.29 per cent, or above the threshold level when it is authorised to buy back its own shares. It added that it did not need to do so because it did not see a threat of excessive foreign control.[10]

7.4   Partial Privatisation – Kenya Airways

As with Qantas, the Kenya Airways privatisation involved both a trade sale and a public offering of shares. The trade sale took place in December 1995, with KLM acquiring 26 per cent of the shares of the airline for US$26 million in cash and the provision of various services to the value of US$3 million. This followed a period

---

10 *Deutsche Lufthansa*, Corporate Communications, Press Release, (3 August 2006).

of restructuring and rationalisation under a management contract with Speedwing Consulting, which is owned by British Airways, following an unsatisfactory relationship with Swissair.

The public offering took place in March 1996, with a flotation of 34 per cent of the company's shares on the Nairobi stock exchange, as well as an international sale of a further 14 per cent of shares, with 3 per cent allocated to employees. This left the Kenyan Government with a minority stake of 23 per cent of the issued share capital, and limited foreign ownership to a maximum of 40 per cent.[11]

The shares were offered at KShs 11.25 (or around 20 US cents) per share to international investors. This compared with the cash price KLM paid of about 22 cents per share.

It should be noted that the net financial charge disappeared in 1995/1996, and was replaced by net financial income. This was partly because of a US$7 million foreign exchange gain, but also resulted from the government having previously swapped US$33.1 million of long-term debt into equity. At the same time, the airline had built up cash and bank balances to US$52.5 million by the end of September 1995.

Table 7.8   Kenya Airways' pre-privatisation financial data

	1993/1994 (12 months)	1994/1995 (12 months)	1995/1996 (6 months)
Total revenues (US$ million)	168.7	172.7	90.4
Total costs (US$ million)	n/a	141.4	73.3
Operating profit (US$ million)	n/a	31.3	17.1
Net financial income (US$ million)	n/a	(14.4)	2.8
After-tax profit (US$ million)	n/a	29.3	13.6
Passenger yield (US cents per RPK)	7.1	7.4	7.9
Passenger load factor (%)	69.6	68.9	67.7

Source: Kenya Airways Initial Public Offer Document, Citibank, March 1996

No profit forecast was included in the prospectus. On the pessimistic assumption that the audited results for the six-month period in 1995/1996 (which covered the more profitable summer season) could only be maintained, then earnings per share would have been KShs 1.56, and the price-earnings ratio of 7.2 at the issue price of KShs 11.25 a share. This compared with the average *P/E* ratio of 12.4 for the Kenyan market as a whole in 1995. Net assets per share amounted to just over KShs 5 at the end of September 1995, compared to the issue price of KShs 11.25 per share.

---

11 Kenya Airways, *Initial Public Offer Document*, Citibank (March,1996).

Table 7.9   **Kenya Airways' post-privatisation results***

	1994/1995	1995/1996	per cent change
Total revenues (US$ million)	170.5	181.3	+ 6.3
Total costs (US$ million)	105.8	112.8	+ 6.7
Operating profit (US$ million)	64.7	68.5	+ 5.9
Net profit (US$ million)	40.7	25.6	− 37.1
Passengers (000)	754	743	− 1.3
Passenger-kms (million)	1,737	1,757	+ 1.2
Passenger yield(US cents/RPK)	8.2	8.7	+ 6.1
Passenger load factor (%)	68.9	66.8	− 2.1pts
No. of employees	2,365	2,339	− 1.1

* Financial year ended 31 March (released after public offering)
Source: Air Transport World, December 1996, from Kenya Airways Annual Report

The March 1996 prospectus warned potential investors that the Nairobi stock exchange is smaller and more volatile than most US or European exchanges.[12] The exchange's index of 52 listed shares (the NSE Index) had increased by 115 per cent in 1993 and by 81 per cent in 1994, followed by a fall of 24 per cent in 1995 (to which foreign investors would need to add an allowance for currency movements). It had also experienced some delays in settlement, so holders of shares that wished to sell them on this exchange would have to wait some time before receiving payment. Investors were also warned of differences in Kenyan accounting standards and principles compared to those in the UK and US, although these did not appear very significant.

The historical figures for the financial year 1994/1995 in Table 7.9 are not identical to those in Table 7.8, which may be due to the exchange rate used for the translation into US dollars. However, the net profit for the year was almost double the position after six months, giving a historical *P/E* ratio of only 3.8 at the issue price. Even though demand was reported to be twice the number of shares available,[13] the share price fell immediately once trading started, and by October 1996 the shares were quoted at KShs 9.5, or *a P/E* ratio of 4.5. By the end of 1996, the price had fallen to KShs 8.4.

The airline's results for the remainder of the decade were positive, with the net result reaching US$40 million in 1999/2000 before falling back to US$17.5 million in 2000/2001.

The KLM co-operation agreement envisaged Nairobi being the hub for KLM's services to Sub-Saharan Africa. From March 1997, KLM would stop flying to all points below Kenya, except for South Africa which is regarded as a key KLM market. Kenya Airways would connect to KLM's Nairobi–Amsterdam flights from 11 African points. The agreement also covered a comprehensive alliance which

---

12 The exchange's 1996 turnover was only $60 million, compared to almost $100 billion for the Johannesburg exchange.

13 KLM (1995/1996), *Annual Report and Accounts*.

would include code-sharing, route and systems integration, fare coordination, shared sales and ground resources and joint purchasing.

The KLM shareholders agreement contained a provision to protect KLM's interest at 26 per cent of the issued share capital. KLM would appoint two board directors and nominate candidates for the positions of managing director and finance director for approval by the 11 member board. They agreed not to dispose of any of their shares for at least five years, but Kenya Airways would require the prior approval from KLM if it wished to make any major strategic decisions or changes. In 2006, Air France-KLM still retained 26 per cent in the airline, with the Kenya government holding 23 per cent.

7.5   Full Privatisation and Trade Sale – Iberia

The privatisation of the Spanish national carrier, Iberia, was originally contemplated in the mid-1990s, but only in November 1999 did it look like becoming reality. However, it was postponed until the following year owing to global equity turbulence and continuing problems with Aerolineas Argentinas, and yet again to 2001 because of the impending national elections.

The market value was fixed at US$2.73 billion, down 22 per cent from the November 1999 valuation. A trade sale was completed with British Airways, who took 9 per cent of the total equity, and American Airlines who took 1 per cent. BA's share entitled them to two members of the board. Private institutions then took 30 per cent of the shares with the employees taking a further 6 per cent. All the private institutions were Spanish – Caja Madrid, BBV Bank, El Corte Ingles, Logistica and Ahorro Corp. – so the likelihood of foreign control was minimised.

A public offer was made for the other 53.9 per cent of the shares in March 2001: 492 million shares were offered at €1.19, with a price range of €1.12-1.20 on the first day of trading. Up to the beginning of September 2001 it traded between €1.15 and €1.19.

The Spanish Government retains a 'Golden Share' for at least five years years from the date of the sale, with an option to extend this for a further two years years. This gave them a veto over any major change of objectives, merger or voluntary liquidation.

To prevent more than 25 per cent of the voting control of Iberia falling into non-Spanish hands, the law allows for the board of directors to purchase foreign owned shares to rectify the situation. The directors may also suspend the voting rights of such shares until such time as the re-purchase has taken place.

7.6   Gradual Privatisation and Acquisition – Air France

Air France was partially privatised in February 1999, with a track record of only 18 months of profitable trading. A public offer was carried out (flotation) in February 1999: around half to the French public and remainder to institutions in France and abroad. The French public offer totalled approximately 13.5 million shares, and the international offer to institutions around 21.2 million shares. The offer price was fixed at €14 and the public offer was 10 times oversubscribed. None of the net proceeds of the sale went to the Air France Group.

At the offer price, Air France was floated on *a P/E* ratio of 35.5 based on earnings to the end of March 1999, and 14.2 on forecast earnings to end March 2000.

Ownership at the end of March 1999 was: the state 73.4 per cent, employees 0.8 per cent, and the public: 25.8 per cent. Employees were offered shares on terms preferential to those offered to the public, and by end March 2000 they had increased their share in the airline to 10.9 per cent, with the public/free float at 31.7 per cent and the state down to 56.8 per cent. Two schemes were available, the Aéromixt and the Aérodispo options. Under the former, employees could purchase shares at a 20 per cent discount from the French public offer price, but they would be prohibited from selling or transferring them for two years years. After that time they would be entitled to one free share for one purchased share up to a limit of €609.80, and one for four above that limit. Under the latter scheme, there was no discount on the price, but holders would be entitled to one free share for every three held after only one year.

The share price ranged from €14-18 on the opening day and by the 22 February 2000 was €15.30, following a high of €21.52. Figure 7.4 shows this trend in index form against the French index of major shares. It also shows the pre-privatisation trend, including the big jump in the second quarter of 1997, following the announcement of the airline's first profit since 1989.

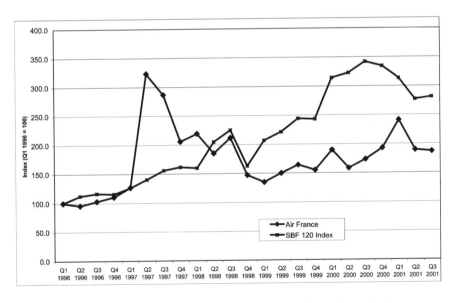

Figure 7.4   **Air France share price trend *vs* the French market**

The exercise of employee allocation, warrants and conversions decreased the State's stake to 56.8 per cent at end March 2000, and to 54.9 per cent at end March 2003. The next stage in the privatisation which reduced the French Government stake from to below 50 per cent was the acquisition of KLM. Air France purchased KLM shares by issuing new Air France shares (11 Air France shares and 10 warrants[14] for 10 KLM shares), which resulted in the dilution of the French Government stake to 44.7 per cent.

Figure 7.5 shows the way the acquisition was structured in order to have time to protect the KLM operations from Air Services Agreement restrictions. Although Air France-KLM only holds 49 per cent of the voting rights in KLM, it owns 100 per cent of the economic rights in the operating airline. It was assumed that by 2007 the KLM operations at Amsterdam would enjoy full traffic rights and the merger could be consummated. At that point, the separate identities would still be maintained under assurances given to KLM and the Dutch State by Air France-KLM, applicable until May 2012. These included the continuation of the hub operation at Schiphol Airport. This specifically guarantees the services from Schiphol to 42 key intercontinental destinations up to 2008 and the balanced development of the Schiphol and Paris hubs for a further three years. This would be monitored by the Dutch Government.[15]

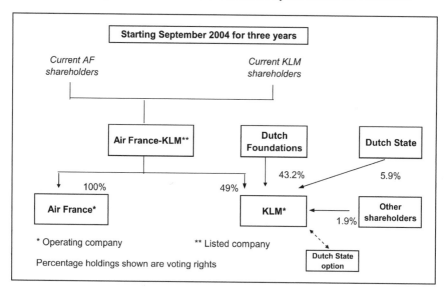

Figure 7.5   Air France-KLM post merger interim structure

In 2004, the French Government placed with institutions 18.4 per cent of the airline for €720 million in January 2005 with an additional 7.6 per cent going to employees (giving them a total of 17.4 per cent), leaving it with 18.7 per cent, a level that it stated it wished to maintain. Since 1999, the Air France share price has ranged from a low of €7.12 to a high of €26.60.

---

14 Each warrant entitled holders to acquire two Air France-KLM shares at a price of €20, with an expiry date in November 2007.

15 De Wit, Jaap and Burghouwt, Guillaume (2005) *Strategies of multi-hub airlines and the implications for national aviation policies*, AirNeth Workshop Report, The Hague.

7.7 The Results so Far

Privatisation has been most marked amongst the largest 25 international airlines although a number of the next tier have either already moved to the private sector (Turkish) or are planned to do so (AeroMexico and LOT Polish Airlines). The major changes so far will be discussed below by region.

North America

There are no airlines in the US either federally owned or state owned. Following 9/11, the Federal government took steps to assist airlines in the form of compensation payments, loans and loan guarantees through the Air Transportation Stabilization Board (see also Chapter 12). In conjunction with the loan guarantees it also received warrants, or options to acquire shares. These were received from Frontier Airlines and World Airways, the former being sold by auction in May 2006.[16]

Air Canada was privatised through an IPO and subsequent share sales over 1988–1989. It filed for bankruptcy in April 2004 and exited later that year under a reorganised holding company, ACE. As part of the reorganisation, Deutsche Bank underwrote a rights issue to unsecured creditors, and it was agreed to repay the US$84 million loan guaranteed by Lufthansa that was outstanding immediately before bankruptcy over the five years years to 2009. This had been provided jointly by Star Alliance partners Lufthansa and United Airlines in support of a buy-back of shares by Air Canada in 1999 to foil a hostile take-over. United's share (US$92 million) was unlikely to have been settled in full.[17]

The Mexican Government had re-nationalised the countries two major airlines – AeroMexico and Mexicana – by transferring their shares in 1995 into a state-owned holding company, Cintra to avoid their bankruptcy. They had originally been privatised back in 1988/1989. Mexicana was sold in 2005 to a privately owned Mexican hotel group (although legal proceedings were initiated the following year over the sale price), and it was planned to sell AeroMexico to the public by auction towards the end of 2006 but this was postponed to 2007.[18]

Caribbean

Air Jamaica was sold to a private Jamaican corporation involved in the hotel and tourism industry in 1994, but it was re-nationalised in 2004 following financial difficulties. A similar fate befell the Trinidad based airline, BWIA. It was sold to US and Caribbean investors in 1995 (with the government retaining 33.5 per cent of the shares), but the government of Trinidad and Tobago increased its stake to 75 per cent

---

16 Air Transportation Stabilization Board, US, Treasury, Press Release (31 May 2006).

17 *Air Canada Management Discussion of Financial Results* 2003.

18 It was originally planned to sell AeroMexico at the same time as Mexicana, but bids did not reach the minimum price required by the government (Kerry Ezard, Air Transport Intelligence News, (22 August 2006).

in 2004, following the failure of a rights issue. BWIA was closed down at the end of 2006, and replaced by a new entity, Caribbean Airlines.

Central and South America

South America initially took the lead in airline privatisations, and while there have been some success stories (notably LAN-Chile), there have also been some major problems. Aerolineas Argentinas was 'privatised' through a sale to the former Iberia holding company (SEPI),[19] although this merely changed its control from one government to another. Later, in June 2000 Aerolineas' majority shareholder, the Spanish state holding company SEPI, announced a 'final' restructuring plan to try and return Aerolineas to profitability by 2003. In June 2001, flights to seven international destinations were suspended and the airline went into administration. SEPI agreed the sale of its 92 per cent stake to the private Spanish company, Marsans Group, in November 2001 who in turn committed to inject $50 million in fresh capital. In December 2002 the airline came out of administration after a Buenos Aires judge accepted its debt restructuring agreement with creditors

Another South American carrier, Viasa, was privatised in the early 1990s, but subsequently went bankrupt in 1998. The largest airline in South America, Varig, was owned by a private foundation, but effectively controlled by the government. Following its bankruptcy in 2006, its cargo division was acquired by private investors (Variglog) who later also took over the operating division of the passenger airline.

The government-owned airline of Chile, LAN-Chile, was privatised in 1989, later becoming LAN Airlines, controlled by Chilean family and industrial interests.

The Panama national airline, COPA, had for many years been partly owned by Continental Airlines of the US. In December 2005, this stake was sold to the public through an IPO and listing on the New York Stock Exchange.[20]

Europe

Significant progress has been made in Europe and by 2006 most of the larger airlines had been privatised, the most recent being Alitalia whose government holding had gradually been eroded by the government not taking up their rights. After a number of attempts at privatising the whole airline, Olympic Airways was split into an operating company (Olympic Airlines) and a ground services company (Olympic Air Services). At the end of 2004, the Greek Government launched another attempt to sell both companies with no success by 2006. Another airline that remains 100 per cent government-owned is Aer Lingus. The unions had opposed previous attempts to privatise it, but in 2006 a sale of up to three-quarters of the government stake was offered through an IPO in September 2006. The other airline that remained in government hands was TAP Air Portugal.

Turkish Airlines had a small holding in private hands (1.83 per cent) since 1990, and tried to sell further shares in 2001 without success. IMF pressure to sell

---

19 American Airlines also took an 8.5 per cent stake via the Spanish holding company.
20 *Aviation Strategy*, March 2006, p. 6.

state-owned assets led to the government selling a 23 per cent stake on the Istanbul exchange in December 2004 at a price of just under seven lira. A further 28.75 per cent was sold in May 2006 leaving the government controlling 46.43 per cent of the airline and a Golden Share.[21] Since 2002 the airline's share price has ranged from a low of five lira to a high of nine lira, and has performed poorly compared to the ISE National 100 index of stocks on the Istanbul exchange. Finnair was still majority government owned at the end of 2005.

In Eastern Europe, LOT Polish Airlines was part-privatised by selling 37.6 per cent to Swissair in 1999. This was later diluted to 25 per cent and, with the bankruptcy of Swissair, remained in the hands of the Swissair administrator until 2005, when it was agreed to offer it for sale in an IPO of the airline. Hungarian national airline, Malev, had also sold a stake to strategic investor, Alitalia, but that was subsequently re-purchased by the Hungarian government. An attempt to sell 99.95 per cent of the airline in 2004 resulted in only one bid that (rumoured to be linked to Aeroflot) was rejected as not meeting the terms of the tender.[22] Bulgaria Air, the national airline of Bulgaria was in 2006 being prepared for privatisation by public tender, with the government retaining a Golden Share.[23]

Africa/Middle East

In Africa, Kenya Airways was an excellent example for others to follow (described above), but this has not yet happened, and South African Airways, a prime candidate, is still 100 per cent state owned. The Nigerian flag carrier, Nigeria Airways, went bankrupt in 2004, and a privately owned Virgin Nigeria Airways was formed to fill the void.[24] The collapse of other state-owned airlines included the multi-nationally owned, Air Afrique, liquidated in 2001, and Ghana Airways in 2004.

Air Madagascar was planned to be privatised in 1999 but the bidders (a consortium that included Air France) suspended their offer when the central bank defaulted on payments to the Ex-Im Bank relating to its B747 aircraft.[25] More recently, in mid-2006 the government of Botswana was considering bids for their national carrier.

Asia/Pacific

Progress in Asia has been mixed. The Thai Airways position in September 2001 was that the government intended to reduce its stake from 93 per cent to 70 per cent later in the year, with the possibility of more than 10 per cent available to a foreign investor. This reversed their previous position, which ruled out foreign investment in the airline. However, the Thai Government gradually reduced their holding to 54 per cent in 2006. Singapore Airlines also remains under majority state control,

---

21 *Ibid.*, (June 2006).

22 Dunn, Graham (2004) *Air Transport Intelligence*, (November), 23.

23 Airline Business, JulyBusiness, A. and July 2006.

24 Fifty-one per cent owned by Nigerian institutional investors and 49 per cent by Virgin Atlantic Airways.

25 McMillan, Ben (2000) *Air Transport Intelligence*, (30 March).

and the Malaysian Government re-purchased its majority in its national flag carrier. The Malaysian private investor received RM8 per share from the government, the same price that he originally paid when he bought his 29 per cent controlling stake. However, RM8 was more than double the market price of the shares (RM3.68) at the time they were bought back.[26] The Asian financial crisis of 1997 and its aftermath clearly upset some plans, and also made it hard for already privatised airlines, Malaysian and Philippine Airlines,[27] to make profits. The Indian Government's progress towards privatising Air India has also been slow, and their plans to allow substantial foreign stakes were later reversed.[28] In Australasia, one of the first airlines to be privatised, Air New Zealand ran into trouble at the end of summer 2001, with the bankruptcy of its subsidiary Ansett. Its bankruptcy in January 2002 resulted in Singapore Airlines' stake being reduced to 6.47 per cent (with a write-down of their investment by S$380.6 million) and the government re-taking control with 80.4 per cent of the airline.

The national carrier of Sri Lanka was privatised in March 1998 by means of a trade sale to Emirates Airlines. The Middle East airline took 40 per cent of Air Lanka, increasing this to 43.63 per cent by 2006, by which time its name had changed to Sri Lankan Airlines. The government retains 51 per cent and employees hold 5.3 per cent of the shares.

All the three largest Chinese airlines have been part-privatised by IPOs and secondary offerings. Air China's IPO took place in December 2004, with the government selling of a 24 per cent stake through a Hong Kong listing. Cathay later acquired 20 per cent though a share swap. The carrier's secondary offer of a further 16 per cent of the total shares issued or 1,639 million shares (reduced from an initial allocation of 2,700 million due to poor demand) to Chinese investors took place in August 2006, with a Shanghai listing.[29] China Southern had previously taken a similar approach, first selling 35 per cent on the Hong Kong stock exchange in February 1997, and a further one billion shares through a Shanghai listing in July 2003. The State retained 50.3 per cent of the shares of the airlines. China Eastern's IPO occurred soon after in July 1997, with their domestic debut following later.

There have been no studies to date which have successfully separated the impact of privatisation *per se* on efficiency, employment or profitability. Some of these gains have clearly been evident in the lead-up to privatisation, and thus one difficulty is the period over which to examine the data. One study suggested that semi-private and privately owned airlines improved their productivity (in revenue per employee) by 5 per cent more than government owned airlines between 1992 and 1997.[30] Another study found that air fares in both the British Airways' and Air Canada's markets

---

26 *Financial Times*, (22 December 2000).

27 Sixty-two per cent of Philippine Airlines was sold to the private PR Holdings in 1992, and by 2006 the government only retained a nominal 4 per cent stake in the airline.

28 Singapore Airlines had planned to join the large industrial conglomerate, the Tata Group, in investing in Air-India, but subsequently withdrew altogether.

29 Philip Tozer in *Aviation Industry News*, 8 August 2006.

30 Baur, U. and Kistner, D. (1999), Airline Privatisation Principles and Lessons Learned, in *Handbook of Airline Finance*, eds Butler and Keller, pp. 71–90.

fell significantly when the control passed from government to private ownership, reflecting expected improvements in economic efficiency and keener competition. At the same time, the stock prices of competitors fell following the announcement.[31]

Privatisation has usually resulted in more liquid market for share trading, but a better working of the marking could only be possible once majority share ownership by foreign nationals is allowed, and restrictive clauses in Air Services Agreements are removed.

---

31 *Privatization and Competition: Industry Effects of the Sale of British Airways and Air Canada*, Social Science Research Network, Working Paper, (31 July 1994).

Chapter 8

Airline Financial Planning and Appraisal

Financial planning is the process whereby an airline's corporate goals, and the strategies designed to meet those goals, are translated into numbers. These numbers cover forecasts of market growth and airline market share, and estimates of resources required to achieve this share. Financial planning ranges from the short-term preparation of budgets to long-term planning, the latter often in conjunction with fleet planning. Its main longer term financial aims are:

- The evaluation of the expected future financial condition of the company.
- The estimation of likely future requirements for finance.

The first requires the estimation of items in an airline's future profit and loss statement. The second focuses on cash flow, which might also include assumptions on long-term finance, as well as working capital or short-term financial needs. Both of these will also need to be tested for the impact of alternative strategic options.

Short to medium-term financial planning is generally described as budget planning and control. It is concerned with the achievement of the firm's objectives, but it is also the principal way in which a company controls costs and improves the utilisation of assets. The control process involves four aspects:

- The development of plans.
- The communication of the information contained in the plans.
- The motivation of employees to achieve the plan goals.
- The evaluation and monitoring of performance.

The difference between longer term financial planning and shorter term budgets lies in the latter's greater detail and ability to provide the basis for the improvement in resource utilisation. The remainder of this chapter will be divided into an examination of airlines' approach first to shorter term budgets, and second to longer term financial planning.

8.1 Budget Preparation and Control

The budget is a formal quantification of management's *short-term* plans. It forces managers to think ahead, and to anticipate and prepare for changing conditions. It is generally prepared for the financial year ahead, by month and often also by quarter. The greater the likely problems of control, the shorter the reporting period should be. More frequent reporting and analysis takes time and resources. For airlines, costs are reported monthly, while the less controllable traffic and revenue side is examined on a daily basis (passenger and cargo reservations, and traffic levels), and as frequently as accounting systems allow for yields.

Continuous budgets are sometimes produced, with an additional month added at the end of the period as soon as one month passes, so as always to give a complete 12-month projection. *Cash budgets* are also useful to avoid situations of idle cash surpluses or worrying cash shortages. A *flexible budget* can be prepared for a range of outputs based, for example, on alternative traffic forecasts and varying levels of aircraft utilisation.

The format of the budget may be broadly similar to that of the longer term corporate or fleet plan. Indeed, the first year of the longer term plan may be the starting point in the preparation of the budget. The integration of the two is clearly important, and longer term goals should not be abandoned for inconsistent short term measures. Budgets are generally coordinated by the finance department, but their preparation involves a high degree of co-operation between departments:

- Passenger and market share forecasts (Marketing).
- Cargo forecasts (Cargo).
- Yield and revenue projections (Marketing/Finance).
- Schedules planning (Marketing, Operations, Engineering).
- Resource and manpower planning (all departments).
- Cost estimates (all departments).
- Budget finalisation (Finance).

Budgets therefore help the coordination between the various parts of the airline. For example, flight operations/scheduling need to liaise closely with engineering on maintenance planning and scheduling.

For an existing firm, budgets are often prepared with reference to the previous year's experience. Zero-based budgets, on the other hand, take nothing as given, and consider the most effective way of achieving output targets. For an airline, capacity plans are converted into a schedule, usually for the coming summer or winter season. This is determined by, and is checked against, passenger and cargo traffic forecasts. Resources are then estimated in order to be able to operate the schedule most effectively, but at a desired level of service. A chart of the daily rotation of each aircraft in the fleet is determined by the requirements of the market, and optimised to take into account airport curfews, maintenance and crew schedules and estimates for turnaround times at airports. Slot constraints are also becoming more important for some airlines. Allowance will be made for contingencies such as flight diversions and delays. Budgets can be built up in various ways and with various levels of detail. They can be for the airline as a whole, by department or by route. A route analysis usually includes the items shown in Table 8.1.

Costs are allocated as far as possible down to the route level to allow a comparison of each route's contribution to overheads. Table 8.1 is one way that this can be done, but airlines might group costs in different ways. This serves as a starting point for an evaluation of the impact of removing, combining or adding routes. It should be stressed, however, that a system-wide or network approach should be adopted. This is because the revenues from one passenger may have to be shared with more than one route. Similarly the ownership costs of one aircraft would need to be spread across a number of routes. The removal of one loss-making route may appear to improve overall profitability, but this may not be the case: once the revenues have been deducted from other routes that were fed from the route that was removed, the profit may actually decline. Similarly, the aircraft fixed costs *saved* by not operating one route may have to be reallocated across the network, resulting in lower profits on these routes.

Budgetary control consists of comparing the estimates of revenues and costs contained in the monthly budgets with the actual revenues earned and costs incurred. Control will also be exercised through the cash and working capital budgets. The variation between forecasts/estimates and actuals will be calculated, and any significant differences highlighted. The likely causes of such differences should be identified, and any necessary action taken.

Table 8.1   Route profitability analysis

	Route A	Route B	Route C
Block hours	1,000	730	950
Return flights	260	365	156
Passengers	43,000	95,000	32,000
Cargo tonnes	480	1,800	1,050
Revenues ($000):			
− Passenger	8,600	11,400	8,000
− Cargo	50	205	100
− Duty-free	140	250	150
− Total	8,790	11,855	8,250
Operating costs ($000):			
Direct operating costs[1]	5,790	4,745	4,750
Contribution	3,000	7,110	3,500
Aircraft related costs	1,480	1,080	1,400
Ground operations	450	630	270
Commercial costs	800	1,780	600
Commissions	350	590	450
Operating result	− 80	3,030	780

1. These usually include fuel, engineering, airport, ATC, crew allowances, catering, security, handling, delay/diversion and sub-chartering costs

Table 8.2 shows a typical airline management accounts' comparison of monthly budget with the actual monthly result. It gives the summary overall position of the airline, although more detail would be available by route, activity, or cost/profit centre. Changes in actual traffic, operating and financial data can easily be seen both in relation to the budget (the variance) and in relation to the same month of the previous year. The financial year-to-date position would normally also be shown for the current and previous years.

Table 8.2   Typical airline management accounts – Budget 2006

	March 2005	March 2006		
	Actual	Actual	Budget	Variance
Passengers carried	28,520	21,547	21,124	423
Passenger-km (000)	4,363	3,306	3,718	− 412
Seat-kms (000)	6,601	5,654	5,767	− 113
Passenger load factor (%)	66.1	58.5	64.5	− 6
Average stage kms	320	345	350	− 5
Aircraft hours/day	7.5	7.3	8	1
Passenger yield (cents)	45	55	50	5
Cost per seat-km (cents)	29.7	33	30	3
Breakeven load factor	66	60	60	0
Operating ratio (%)	100.2	97.5	107.5	− 10.0pts
Expenditure by department ($m)				
Marketing		9.1	9.3	− 0.2
Operations		13.5	12	1.5
Engineering		4	3.5	0.5
Personnel		6.5	6	0.5
Other		3.3	3.7	− 0.4
Total		36.4	34.5	1.9
Expenditure by type ($m)				
Staff costs		23.2	20	3.2
Depreciation		4.7	4.7	0
Aircraft rentals		0.5	0	0.5
Agent commissions		3.9	4.1	− 0.2
Fuel costs		3.5	4.2	− 0.7
Other materials/services		0.6	1.5	0.9
Total		36.4	34.5	1.9

The variance in total expenditure can be broken down into the principal explanatory factors. These might distinguish between capacity (costs would rise if more seat-kms were operated compared to the plan), or price (fuel prices were above those assumed for the budget). They might also include any exchange rate changes that had not been allowed for. A further analysis might reveal:

Staff costs: + $3.2 million, or 16 per cent over budget;

Number of employees up by 5 per cent

Average wage/salary levels up by 10.5 per cent

Fuel costs: − $0.7 million, or down by 17 per cent compared to budget;

Block hours down by 5 per cent; average price down by 12 per cent

Performance indicators should also be shown to give an idea of underlying changes in productivity or service quality. These could include:

- Regularity, or flights operated *vs.* planned.
- Punctuality, or on-time performance.
- ATK capacity per employee.
- Fuel cost per block hour or ATK.
- Landing fees per aircraft departure.
- Average payroll cost per employee.
- Average flying hours per pilot.
- Average flying hours per cabin crew member.
- Reservations cost per passenger.

For example, SAS introduced a productivity target for cockpit and cabin crew in 2004: they planned to increase the number of flying hours per pilot from 550 in 2004 to 700, and flying hours per cabin crew member from 570 in 2004 to 750. More detailed performance data might include fuel burn by aircraft type, or even for each aircraft, number of transactions per payroll clerk, *etc.*

Some of the differences between actual and budget figures will be due to factors beyond the control of management. For example, bad weather at the home base airport or an unexpected increase in fuel price. A distinction should therefore be drawn between controllable and non-controllable costs.

Budgets are the basis for expenditure limits within a particular department or division for a particular period, usually the financial year. Most budgets lapse at the end of the period, so that funds that were allowed, but not spent, cannot be carried forward to the next period. This has obvious advantages in cost control, but can result in the budget holder finding ways to spend the remaining funds before they are withdrawn.

Table 8.3   Example of airline cash budget

US$1,000	January	February	March	April
Total revenues	1,000	1,300	2,100	2,800
Direct costs	1,500	1,450	1,600	1,800
Payroll costs	50	50	50	50
Aircraft rentals	250	—	—	250
Other costs	20	30	30	40
Net cash from operations	− 820	− 230	420	660
Net capital movements	− 200	− 150	—	—
Net cash surplus/(shortfall)	− 1,020	− 380	420	660
Opening balance	1,500	480	100	520
Monthly movement	− 1,020	− 380	420	660
Closing balance	480	100	520	1,180

The budget can be in account or accrual format, or in terms of cash. The latter is vital in determining future working capital needs, which are described in the next section of this chapter. For the cash budget, assumptions will be made on the delay between the date on which the passenger is carried (the accounts) and the date of receipt of the funds. For airlines, this would be around one month for sales through travel agents, and around the same period for expenditure on credit. Cash sales and revenues would be received and incurred in the same month as shown in the accounts.

Table 8.3 highlights the variation of a leisure traffic airline's cash flow by season. For example, a European charter airline would have a cash shortfall in the low winter months and a surplus in the summer season. The table includes the net inflow or outflow of capital which is obtained from the capital budget, the area covered later in this chapter. This budget would also show capital movements, such as debt and equity financing.

8.2   Working Capital Management

The management of an airline's capital can be divided into short-term working capital management (up to one year) and longer term capital budgeting.

The appropriate level of working capital is determined by the levels of current assets (cash, marketable securities, receivables and stocks) and current liabilities (overdrafts, short-term borrowings, accounts payable, and sales in advance of carriage).

The way in which an airline's assets are financed involves a trade-off between risk and profitability. In general, short-term borrowings cost less than long-term borrowings, and short-term investments earn less than long-term ones; thus on the basis of profitability, the aim should be for a low proportion of current to total assets, and a high proportion of current to total liabilities. However, this would result in a very low or negative level of working capital, and a high risk of technical insolvency (an airline unable to meet its cash obligations).

Ideally, each of the airline's assets would be matched with a liability or financing instrument of approximately the same maturity. This would ensure that cyclical and longer term cash needs were met (*i.e.*, zero risk) at minimum cost. In practice, a cushion would be required because of the difficulty in forecasting cash flows with a high degree of accuracy. This would imply a level of current assets somewhat higher than current liabilities. In fact, many airlines operate with the two broadly equal, or with current liabilities less sales in advance of carriage equal to current assets. This is because many advance sales are not reimbursable with a cash payment, and a cushion is provided by an overdraft facility, which can be used at any time.

Each of the elements of working capital will now be examined in more detail. This expands on the definitions given in Chapter 2 (Section 2.3), and the discussion of current and quick ratios in Chapter 3 (Section 3.3).

8.2.1   *Current Assets – Stocks*

Manufacturers tend to hold high levels of stocks or inventories, which include materials, work-in-progress and finished goods. The finished goods tend to be sold on credit. Retailers, on the other hand, carry only finished goods, which are sold for cash. Airlines, and other service industries such as hotels, carry low stocks (mostly materials or consumables), little work-in-progress (repairs on aircraft) and no finished goods. They sell almost entirely on credit.

An airline's product or service is delivered by aircraft and associated equipment, and stocks are required to keep aircraft serviceable. The word *stocks* in the aircraft maintenance context could include spare engines, spare parts, rotables (repairable items) and consumables (short-life items). These are important in maintaining an aircraft in service, and any missing critical items might result in delayed or cancelled flights and substantial costs:

- Overnight and meal costs for delayed passengers.
- Cost of purchasing alternative flights on other airlines.
- Loss of subsequent bookings from dissatisfied customers.

The balance sheet definition of stocks normally covers only consumables or expendables (after an allowance for obsolescence), spare parts and rotables being considered as fixed assets and depreciated in the same way as aircraft. This means that only such items as maintenance consumables, office and catering supplies, fuel and oil are included in the amount shown for stocks.

The normal stock turnover ratio (cost of sales divided by stocks) would be under 10 times for a manufacturer, but is not relevant to services industries such as airlines. The average stock turnover period is another measure that gives an idea of the length of time for which the stocks are held. This is calculated by relating the average stocks held over the period to the cost of stocks of materials consumed during the period:

$$Average\ stock\ turnover\ period\ =\ \frac{Average\ stocks\ held}{Cost\ of\ sales \div 365}$$

For airlines, the cost of sales should only include goods or stockable items consumed, and not services such as airport charges. This figure is not always easily obtainable from published accounts. For BA, the average stocks held can be obtained from current assets in the balance sheet (averaging the beginning and end year positions), and was £72 million in 2000/2001. Cost of sales would include principally fuel and engineering costs, which amounted to just over £1.7 billion in 2000/2001. Assuming, additional relevant costs of in-flight meals, ticket stocks and other items increased this amount to around £2 billion, BA's average stock turnover period for 2000/2001 would have been only 13 days. This stood at 14 days for BA's year ended 31 March 2006.

8.2.2   Current Assets − Debtors or Receivables

Almost all airline sales are on credit, whether through accounts with travel agents or through credit card companies. This involves a cost to the airline of administration, the opportunity cost of the funds not yet received, and the possibility of bad debts (with agents or corporate customers). These will be outweighed by the benefits of increased sales.

Airlines that participate in Bank Settlement Plan arrangements with travel agents do not have to decide the period of credit to extend to their distributors. This is fixed automatically, with funds transferred to net recipients on the 17th day after the month of sale. Agents would also extend credit to their corporate customers, so that reducing the 1 month or so that airlines give to agents would only result in agents having to find extra working capital at high cost.

The average settlement period is calculated by expressing the trade debtors amount on the balance sheet date in terms of the numbers of days' sales.

$$\textit{Average collection period} = \frac{\textit{Trade debtors}}{\textit{Credit sales} \div 365}$$

Ideally, it should be in terms of the number of days' credit sales, but this information is rarely available from the financial statements, and so 'total traffic sales' is used. For British Airways, the average collection period using figures for total sales declined from 36 days in 1999/2000 to 34 days in 2005/2006. The Lufthansa Group recorded 49 days in 2005 and Air France Group 42 days, but both of these include other businesses such as aircraft and engine overhaul and catering. US carriers do not normally separate trade debtors from current debtors or receivables, but using total receivables would result in an American Airlines' period of only 19 days in 2005. Other US carriers have a similar period, with the notable exception of Southwest with only 13 days (because of the low percentage of passengers buying tickets though travel agents). Asian carriers such as Thai and Singapore Airlines had similar periods to BA in 2005/2006, but Cathay Pacific achieved a shorter period of 29 days, well down from its 1997 level of 47 days through different financial arrangements with their travel agents.

8.2.3   *Current Assets – Cash and Marketable Securities*

Cash holdings would usually cover only money that is immediately available, *i.e.*, petty cash and current account balances. However, funds might be placed on short-term deposit with banks for a term of anything between overnight to one year. These funds will earn interest, and the very near term deposits could be considered as *quasi* cash.

There will be an opportunity cost of holding cash in the interest or higher interest income foregone. At times of high inflation, cash holdings will lose their purchasing power. The major reason for holding cash is the unpredictability of cash flows, and the need to have funds available to meet unexpected demands. Many airlines accumulate cash during the peak season, and retain this (or place it on short-term deposit with banks or in government securities) to meet demands in the low season.

An overdraft facility gives airlines the possibility to reduce cash holdings, but this is an expensive form of borrowing, and should be used to cover events such as aircraft grounding or sharp downturns in traffic and revenue which cannot be predicted.

An airline might build up cash and marketable securities, either because it plans major investments in aircraft in the near future, or to fund acquisitions or investments in other companies. British Airways' liquid assets increased to £2.44 billion (US$4.2 billion) at the end of March 2006, from just over £1 billion at the end of March 2002. Removing depreciation, amortisation and currency adjustments from operating expenditure gives a rough figure for cash spend: this was £7,111 million for the 12 months to 31 March 2006, or an average of £19.5 million/day. Thus, BA's end 2006 cash and cash equivalents of £2,440 million would cover 125 days of expenditure. For AMR, their cash and short-term investments of $3,814 million would have covered only 71 days at their average cash spend in 2005 of $53.8 per day, contrasting with Southwest's 147 days.

8.2.4 Current Liabilities

The two key items of working capital in current liabilities are trade creditors and sales in advance of carriage. Overdrafts were discussed in cash above, and there will also be other short term creditors such as the government (taxes due) and shareholders (dividends payable). A new and growing item is accrued frequent flyer programme liabilities.

Trade creditors are a source of short-term finance which depends on suppliers' terms. A free period of credit will generally be extended to customers, after which interest may be charged on late payment. Delaying payments too long might put critical supplies at risk.

That part of current liabilities described as sales in advance of carriage (or advance sales) has the advantage of being short-term borrowing, but of low risk since most of the money will not have to be re-paid (as long as the airline continues trading). While interest does not have to be paid on this money, there is an implicit cost in the difference between the air fare charged and the fare that would otherwise have been offered without the advance payment and non-reimbursable features.

The average settlement period can be calculated in the same way as the average collection period. There is, however, a similar problem in obtaining data from published accounts on credit purchases.

$$Average\ settlement\ period = \frac{Trade\ creditors}{Credit\ purchases \div 365}$$

Assuming that credit purchases approximate to operating expenses less staff costs and depreciation, then British Airways' average settlement period was 58 days in 2005/2006 (well down from 76 days in 2000/2001), and the Lufthansa Group 66 days for its year to end December 2005. The settlement period for financial year 2005 for American Airlines (AMR) was 31 days and South-West 53 days. Cathay Pacific reported 37 days for 2005.

8.3   Financial Planning

8.3.1   *Cash Flow Forecasts*

Financial planning deals with the longer term financial condition of the airline, and in particular the generation of investment proposals, and the process of the analysis and selection of projects from these proposals (capital budgeting). The term *capital* refers to fixed assets, which for the airline is likely to be one or more aircraft, but could also be a major computer or maintenance hangar project. These have a useful life of anything between five and 25 years, and to evaluate whether such investments should be made it is necessary to prepare cash flow forecasts over a similar period.

The starting point for the cash flow forecasts are projections of traffic, yield and revenues. Similarly, operating costs will be estimated from capacity planned to meet the traffic forecasts, as well as input price projections.

Forecasts of cash disbursements should include capital expenditure, progress payments on aircraft acquisitions, future dividend and tax payments, and the proceeds of asset sales. Net cash receipts (receipts less disbursements) are then subtracted from the initial cash balance to give the subsequent cash surplus or cash requirements in each period. If there is a cash shortfall, then the methods of financing should be considered, and the schedule of capital and interest payments incorporated in the cash flow forecasts.

The *pro forma* (projected) profit and loss and balance sheet can be derived from the cash flow forecast. For the profit and loss, the capital expenditures will need to be removed and replaced by a depreciation charge. Profit or loss from asset sales will be substituted for the cash proceeds from such sales.

The *pro forma* balance sheet will be estimated for the end of each forecasting period. The initial balances of fixed assets, current liabilities, *etc.* will be updated using information from the profit and loss and cash flow statements for each period. Thus, the future financial position of the airline will be estimated, and its ability to raise further long-term capital.

In summary, the following financial statements are likely to be prepared in conjunction with any major fleet planning study or other corporate planning exercise:

For investment appraisal
- Investment schedule.
- Cash flow statement.
-

For financial evaluation
- Loan disbursement schedule.
- Summary of finance charges.
- Debt service schedule.
- Debt repayment schedule.
- Cash flow statement.
- Net income statement.
- Balance sheet.

For the investment appraisal, it is not necessary to know likely future sources of finance for the investment being evaluated. For a fuller financial evaluation, however, sources of finance can be evaluated, and their impact on the cash flow, net income or profit and loss statement and balance sheet determined.

The next part of this chapter will deal with the investment appraisal. For this it has been assumed that the investment options have been narrowed down to two alternative aircraft types: the acquisition of a new A330-300 for US$115 million *versus* a new Boeing 777-200 for US$138 million (both including the necessary spares). The aircraft have similar passenger capacity and each will perform the required services between specified or likely future city pairs. Where there is a difference in payload or cargo capacity, this will be reflected in the revenue forecasts. Cost differences will also be reflected in the cost projections. A higher residual value (65 per cent of cost) has been assumed for the B777-200 in the base case, compared to 60 per cent for the A330-300. It should be stressed, however, that this is not necessarily a widely accepted view, and this initial assumption and the figures in Table 8.4 are not based on a real case.

Table 8.4   Aircraft investment appraisal cash flow forecasts (US$ million)

A330-300	2006	2007	2008	2009	2010	2011
Capital cost (incl.spares)	− 115					
Residual value						69
Cash operating revenues		24	28	30	32	35
Cash operating costs		9	9.5	9.9	10.4	10.9
Cash operating result		15	18.6	20.1	21.6	24.1
Net cash flow		15	18.6	20.1	21.6	93.1
PV cash flows @ 8%	124.9					
NPV @ 8%	9.9					
IRR − %	10.4					
B777-200	2001	2002	2003	2004	2005	2006
Capital cost (incl. spares)	− 138					
Residual value						89.7
Cash operating revenues		26	30	35	35	42
Cash operating costs		10	10.5	11	11.6	12.2
Cash operating result		16	19.5	24	23.4	29.8
Net cash flow		16	19.5	24	23.4	119.5
PV cash flows @ 8%	149.1					
NPV @ 8%	11.1					
IRR − %	10.2					

The projections for both aircraft have only been made over five years years, to make it easier to understand the calculations in the absence of a PC spreadsheet. This has necessitated the estimation of a residual value of each aircraft at the end of the five years, and the assumption on this would clearly be critical to the outcome. With forecasts over a longer period, of say 15–20 years, this problem would be less significant. The residual value should ideally be the market value of the aircraft at that time; this is in practice difficult to forecast and the depreciated book value is sometimes used instead.

Taxation should also be incorporated into the financial projections, since they could have a large impact on cash flow. In the UK, unusually high 100 per cent first year capital allowances were allowed against corporation tax for a period ending in 1978. These would have favoured capital intensive fleet replacement decisions.

Expected profitability, or net cash flow, is an essential element in the selection of investment projects, and the following techniques reduce the net revenue streams of different projects (or fleet planning options) to a common measure. This provides a quantitative basis for comparison, although the final selection of aircraft or capital investment may include other non-quantifiable elements. Net cash flows for financial appraisal are normally stated in constant or base year prices. This avoids the problems of forecasting inflation rates for the various cost and revenue items. Above average rates of inflation for particular items will then be reflected in higher real or constant price increases in the item (*e.g.*, fuel costs). Alternatively, all revenues and costs could be forecast in current prices.

8.3.2   Decision Criteria

Various measures are used to combine the project cash flows (or profits) for comparison with the initial investment required. These are used to decide whether to go ahead with a particular project (comparison with the without project case), or to compare a number of different projects.

Accounting rate of return   The average rate of return technique measures the average profit per year and expresses this as a rate of return on the capital invested.

Table 8.5   Example of accounting rate of return

US$ (000)	Project A	Project B	Project C
Investment	10,000	10,000	10,000
Annual profits:			
Year 1	4,000	1,000	2,500
Year 2	3,000	2,000	2,500
Year 3	2,000	3,000	2,500
Year 4	1,000	4,000	2,500
Year 5	0	0	2,500
Total profits	10,000	10,000	12,500
Average annual profit	2,500	2,500	2,500
Return on investment %	25	25	25

The example in Table 8.5 shows three projects of similar initial investment but varying profits and project duration. Apart from difficulties about how to measure profits (pre-tax?) and whether to take the average investment over the life of the project, this technique does not differentiate between profits earned at the end of the first year and profits earned, say, after 20 years. The particular example has been chosen to produce identical rates of return and no preference for any one project; however, even if one project had produced the highest rate of return, selection on this basis might have been misleading due to the different timing of profits.

This ratio cannot be calculated from the data in Table 8.4, since accounting items such as depreciation would have to be deducted from cash profit to get accounting net profit. The ratio is useful in that returns can be compared with the overall return on assets or investments for the firm as a whole, but it is not widely used in investment appraisal.

Pay-back period This technique measures the length of time that a project takes to re-coup the initial investment. Here, cash flows (profits before depreciation) are measured rather than accounting profits. The timing of profits is more important than in the first technique, but no consideration is given to cash flows received after the pay-back period.

Table 8.6   Example of payback period

US$ (1,000)	Project A	Project B
Investment	10,000	10,000
Net cash flows:		
Year 1	4,000	1,000
Year 2	3,000	2,000
Year 3	3,000	1,000
Year 4	0	1,000
Year 5	0	3,000
Year 6	0	3,000
Pay-back period	3.0 years	5.7 years

Project A is selected by this method, although it is possible that the rate of return over its whole life is zero or negative. This illustrates the problem of using this technique, which should only be used as an initial screening device in certain cases. For the airline example shown in Table 8.4, the pay-back period for the used A330-300 is 4.4 years and the Boeing 777-200 is 4.5 years. They are thus very close on this measure, but ideally a longer forecast period would make the results less dependent on the aircraft's residual value which is a large part of the cash return in year five for both aircraft. The assumption on residual value is therefore crucial to the outcome.

Discounted cash flow Discounted cash flow (DCF) techniques take into account the differing timings of cash flows and the variation in project lives. The only mathematical manipulation required is the reciprocal of compound interest.

The essential objective of DCF is to value each year's cash flow on a common time basis. This is usually taken to be the present, although it could equally well be at the end of the period. Profits earned in year 1 could be re-invested in each of the three subsequent years on a compound interest basis; conversely, profits earned in future years can be discounted back to the present, the mathematics of which is given in the following general formula:

$$Net\ Present\ Value = \sum_{t=0}^{n} \frac{CF_t}{(1+i)^t}$$

where CF_t =   Net cash flow in period t

　　i   =   Discount rate or cost of capital

　　n   =   Project life (years)

The Internal Rate of Return (IRR)   The discount rate (i) required to equate the discounted value of future cash flows with the initial investment, or to reduce net present value to zero. This can be calculated by trial and error; for a project requiring an initial investment of $10,000, followed by cash benefits of $6,500, $5,500, $4,500 and $3,500 at the end of the first, second, third and fourth years, this amounts to solving the following equation:

$$0 = -10,000 + \frac{6,500}{(1+i)} + \frac{5,500}{(1+i)^2} + \frac{4,500}{(1+i)^3} + \frac{3,500}{(1+i)^4}$$

The internal rate of return (sometimes referred to as the DCF rate of return of the investment) in this example is 40 per cent. Projects can be ranked according to rate of return, and a project selected if its Internal Rate of Return (IRR) is greater than a specified cut-off value. The major drawback of this technique is the possibility of finding two solutions to the above equation, or two internal rates of return for the same investment. (This occurs when there is a change of sign to negative for future cash flows, as in the case of the need to decommission a nuclear power station at the end of its useful life.) For the airline example shown in the Table 6.4, the IRR for the A330-300 is 10.4 per cent and the Boeing 777-200 is 10.2 per cent.

Net Present Value   Instead of calculating the discount rate required to equate the Net Present Value (NPV) to zero, the rate of return is specified and the NPV is calculated. Projects may be selected with a positive NPV, the discount rate chosen as a minimum target rate of return, ideally based on the weighted average cost of capital to the firm (WACC). Projects may also be ranked according to NPVs. This is the preferred technique in investment appraisal, although it does require the prior selection of the discount rate. One answer to this is to compute NPVs with more than one discount rate to see how sensitive the outcome of project ranking is to changes in this parameter. For the airline example shown in Table 8.4, the Net Present Value for the A330-300 is US$9.9 million and the Boeing 777-200 is US$11.1 million, both using an 8 per cent discount rate.

Profitability Index   This is the ratio of the project's benefits to the project's costs, both discounted to present values at the appropriate discount rate. It is similar to the net present value approach, but has the possible advantage of being independent of the relative size of the projects. For the example in Table 8.4, the A330-300 has an index of 1.064, while the B777-200 has an index of 1.061. This ratio may be useful where there are a number of investments that might be made, but limited capital available for investment (*i.e.*, capital rationing). Here, projects could be ranked by profitability index, and selected from the top of the ranking until the available capital was used up.

8.3.3   Discount Rate Calculation for NPV

The discount rate is selected to represent the cost of capital to the airline, although it should also be appropriate to the particular project that is being evaluated. Since investors do not usually have the opportunity to signal their needs in relation to a particular project, in practice past returns to investors in the airline are taken as a proxy for future returns to the airline and project. This is calculated for both equity and debt finance, or a weighted average based on a past or target future debt/equity ratio.

The cost of debt can be obtained by taking a weighted average rate of interest of existing balance sheet debt. Another approach would be to take the current LIBOR plus the premium suggested by the airline's current credit rating, although that might be affected by shorter-term factors which may not persist over the entire project life.

The cost of equity is computed using the Capital Asset Pricing Model. This assumes that equity markets are 'efficient' in the sense of current stock prices reflecting all relevant available information. Finance theory asserts that shareholders will be compensated for assuming higher risks by receiving higher expected returns. However, the distinction should be made between systematic risk, which is market risk attributable to factors common to all companies (*e.g.*, impact of 11 September 2001 on all airlines), and unsystematic risk, which is unique risk specific to the company or a small group of companies (*e.g.*, US Airways' bankruptcy announcement or the impact of the European Commission's decision on airport charges on Ryanair). CAPM models the expected return related to the systematic risk. According to portfolio theory, unsystematic risk can be diversified away through portfolio selection, and thus no reward is received for assuming this risk.

The covariance between the company's return and the market's return is the company's β value, and is a measure of the systematic risk of the company (see also 3.5). From the β value, CAPM can be used to calculate the equilibrium expected return of a company. The equilibrium expected return of a company, R_e is the sum of the prevailing risk-free rate, R_f, and a 'risk premium' dependent on the β value and the market risk premium $(R_m - R_f)$. This can be expressed as follows:

$$R_e = R_f + \beta(R_m - R_f)$$

In order to estimate β, the following regression equation is used:

$$R_e - R_f = a + b_e(R_m - R_f)$$

Where

R_e	=	the return on equity e,
R_f	=	the risk-free return,
a	=	constant,
R_m	=	the return on the overall stock market,
b_e	=	the equity β.

Although the calculation of β involves a covariance relationship between company return and market return, the exact methodology of estimating β is not explicitly indicated for published values, nor is it apparently unique.[1] The risk-free return is needed for the above formula, and the yield on government bonds is taken as a proxy for this, adjusting for the expected future rate of inflation. Index-linked government bonds can be used for this, or the inflation rate subtracted from the bond yield. Estimates for this have ranged from 2.5 per cent to 3.5 per cent. AMR used 2.93 per cent as the risk-free rate in their 2005 calculation of stock option values using the Black-Scholes model.

An estimate of the equity risk premium is also required. The UK CAA have used a range of 4–5 per cent in past regulation of airport charges, which they later revised down to 3.5 to 4.5 per cent. The UK CAA's discussion paper on the cost of capital also includes US estimates of 3–4 per cent and even lower.[2]

The formula for WACC uses the β values obtained from the above CAPM methodology:

WACC = $g(r_f + \rho).(1\text{-}T) + (1\text{-}g)(r_f + \text{ERP.} \beta)$

Where:

g is the gearing for the airline expressed as ratio of debt to (debt + equity)
r_f is the risk-free rate
ρ is the debt premium
T is the airline's rate of corporate or profits tax
ERP is the equity risk premium
β is the beta value estimated from the CAPM regression

---

1   This is discussed further in Morrell, P. and Turner, S. (2003) 'An evaluation of airline beta values and their application in calculating the cost of equity capital,' in *Journal of Air Transport Management*, 9(4), 201–209.

2   *Heathrow, Gatwick and Stansted Airports' price caps*, 2003–2008: CAA recommendations to the Competition Commission, February 2002, Annex: Cost of capita for Heathrow, Gatwick and Stansted. UK Civil Aviation Authority website.

Gearing (g) can be the airlines existing ratio, or more usually a target future ratio. The first (debt) part of the equation can be replaced by the airline's average existing debt interest rate.

8.3.4   Which Criterion to Choose?

The B777-200 is marginally the preferred alternative using the pay-back period and the NPV criteria, but the Airbus A330-300 comes out better on IRR and profitability index.

The first two criteria do not take into account the time value of money, and can thus be rejected. Both NPV and IRR are valid methods of comparison used in industry, but a different conclusion is drawn depending on which is used. IRR is however widely used, and it is easy to see why this is so, especially in large organisations: the spreadsheet calculations will be done at lower level of management than those making the decision (which for larger projects will be at board level). There might also be a time lag between evaluation and decision. It is thus easier for the board to be given the preferred project IRR and then decide on their target or cut-off rate, taking into account the project's risk, rather than specify the discount rate to be used for each NPV calculation.

Table 8.7   Financial evaluation of alternatives

	A330-300	B777-200
Pay-back period (yrs)	4.4	4.5
Net present value		
(NPV @ 8% in US$ million.)	9.9	11.1
Internal rate of return (%)	10.4	10.2
Profitability index	1.064	1.061

For independent projects, the NPV and IRR criteria always lead to the same accept/ reject decision. This is illustrated in Figure 8.1, where it can be seen if the IRR is greater than the project cost of capital or discount rate, then the NPV using that cost of capital as the discount rate will always be greater than zero.

If the projects are mutually exclusive, as in the case of the A330-300 *vs.* the Boeing 777-200, then if the cost of capital is greater than the rate at which the two lines cross the two methods lead to the selection of the same project. In other words, if the cost of capital is greater than 9.3 per cent then the A330-300's NPV is always greater than the Boeing 777-200's NPV, and the A330-300 also has the higher IRR.

If the cost of capital is less than the cross-over rate, then a conflict exists between NPV and IRR; in such a case, it is preferable to take the project with the higher NPV, since this would add most to shareholder wealth, assuming that the airline can obtain the necessary funds to invest in the project.

It should be noted that projects which have relatively high up-front capital costs will have a curve that is steeper sloping (Figure 1.8) . A sensitivity test that assesses the effect of higher than expected capital costs will result in a rotation of each curve to the right.

Second, a long-term project will have a steeper slope than a short-term one. Changing the profile of the project by moving costs from the near term to the longer term will have the effect of rotating the curve in a clockwise direction.

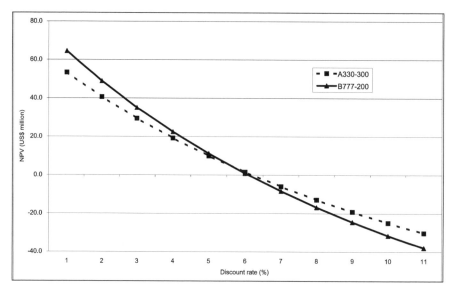

Figure 8.1   NPV *vs* discount rate: A330-300 vs. B777-200

The best decision criterion to use is NPV, assuming that the airline can borrow sufficient funds at the discount rate or cost of capital to finance the investment. In the above example, the B777-200 would be preferred on this basis, but the outcome is very close. In such cases, first a rigorous series of sensitivity tests should be carried out (*see below*). If the B777-200 choice was more sensitive to changes in key assumptions, and might be affected more by, say, external economic shocks, then it may be better to decide on the more robust solution, the A330. Unquantifiable factors, such as the longer term security of spares and other support, may also be taken into account in the final decision.

A survey of airline CFOs in 2005 indicated a strong preference for NPV and pay-back approaches, with accounting rate of return and IRR also widely used.[3]

8.3.5   Risk and uncertainty

Probability (risk) analysis   This relatively complex task involves the estimation of ranges of values and probabilities of the financial inputs to each project. Thus, for each aircraft purchase option, these must be estimated for forecasts of traffic,

---

3   Gibson, W. and Morrell, P. (2005) *Airline finance and aircraft evaluation: evidence from the field.* Paper to ATRS World Conference, Rio de Janeiro, July 2005.

revenues and costs. A series of rate of return calculations is then produced in the form of probability distributions for the rate of return for each aircraft option. The project with the highest probability of exceeding a given rate of return is chosen.

Sensitivity analysis   Sensitivity analysis tests the effects on the financial outcome or ranking of projects of changes in some of the key assumptions used in making the projections, assuming other factors remain unchanged. These tests should be applied in areas of greatest uncertainty such as traffic forecasts, market shares, fuel prices or rates of exchange. Judgement would be required to determine which parameters to change and the range of values to be explored. Sensitivity analysis does not involve the assignment of probabilities to changed assumptions: for example if the central plan assumed fuel prices to be constant in real terms over the forecast period, the alternative might be tested of an increase of 3 per cent *per annum* in real terms. Sensitivity analysis would determine the resultant change in NPV, but would not consider the likelihood of the alternative assumptions. In the example in Table 8.4, the outcome would change if identical assumptions had been taken on residual values (*i.e.*, 60 per cent of first cost in both cases). This would have reduced the B777-200 NPV from $11.1 million to $6.4 million, and its IRR from 10.2 per cent to 9.3 per cent.

Scenario analysis   This technique considers the sensitivity of the NPV or IRR to changes in the key variables and also the range of likely variable values. Thus, a pessimistic set of variables might be chosen to determine the NPV, or an optimistic set, to give a range of outcomes. The optimistic set might include fuel prices declining or remaining constant in real terms, a high GDP forecast, and high market share or low yield dilution. The pessimistic scenario might take a high fuel price increase, low GDP growth, and low market share. It is important that the assumptions for the key variables are consistent with one another for each scenario, *e.g.*, low fuel price escalation is consistent with high GDP growth. The analysis may involve much work on generating alternative assumptions, as well as workshops where these are challenged and honed into a short-list of scenarios to be evaluated.

In conclusion, it needs to emphasised that investment decisions based on the framework and criteria recommended above are only as good as the assumptions used in the evaluation. As many of the relevant factors as possible should be quantified and included in the appraisal, some sort of risk analysis undertaken, and, where appropriate, other unquantifiable factors also addressed.

Monte Carlo simulation is a procedure whereby random numbers are generated using a normal probability distribution of the expected values of the assumptions that were used for the cash flow forecasts. This is similar to Probability analysis described above, but where the probabilities are not known.

The survey of airline CFOs referred to above found that, of the airline managers using the NPV technique, almost two-thirds raised or lowered the discount rate to allow for risk, rather than changing the cash flow forecasts using the techniques

Table 8.8 Start-up airline business plan

	Jul-Sep	Oct	Nov	Dec	Jan	Feb	Mar	Apr	May	Jun	Jul	Aug	Sep
Profit & Loss Account													
Total revenues	0	3,380	3,040	3,440	3,460	3,080	4,340	7,410	12,600	12,660	14,100	13,800	13,650
Total costs	1,500	3,900	3,640	3,540	3,810	3,480	4,510	7,480	11,850	11,460	12,350	11,900	11,950
Operating result	-1,500	-520	-600	-100	-350	-400	-170	-70	750	1,200	1,750	1,900	1,700
Interest paid	0	25	25	25	25	25	25	25	25	25	25	25	25
Interest received	150	61	61	61	43	43	43	23	23	23	39	39	39
Net result	-1,350	-484	-564	-64	-332	-382	-152	-72	748	1,198	1,764	1,914	1,714
Cash Flow Statement													
Cash revenues	0	15	3,380	3,040	3,440	3,460	3,080	4,340	7,410	12,600	12,660	14,100	13,800
Cash expenditure	1,500	2,250	3,400	3,600	3,500	3,500	4,600	7,100	9,000	11,500	10,900	10,800	11,900
Net interest paid	-150	-36	-36	-36	-18	-18	-18	2	2	2	-14	-14	-14
Net cash suplus	-1,350	-2,199	16	-524	-42	-22	-1,502	-2,762	-1,592	1,098	1,774	3,314	1,914
Cumulative cash													
Opening balance	10,000	8,650	6,451	6,467	5,942	5,900	5,878	4,376	1,614	22	1,120	2,894	6,207
Closing balance	8,650	6,451	6,467	5,942	5,900	5,878	4,376	1,614	22	1,120	2,894	6,207	8,121
Balance Sheet	end Sep			end Dec			end Mar			end Jun			end Sep
Fixed assets	1,000			1,895			2,595			7,325			5,715
Current assets													
Trade debtors	0			3,400			4,300			12,600			13,600
Cash/deposits	8,650			5,942			4,376			1,120			8,121
Total Assets	9,650			11,237			11,271			21,045			27,436
Current liabilities													
Trade creditors	500			3,200			4,100			12,000			13,000
Long-term debt	3,000			3,000			3,000			3,000			3,000
Shareholders' funds													
Ordinary shares	7,500			7,500			7,500			7,500			7,500
Retained earnings	-1,350			-2,463			-3,329			-1,455			3,936
Total Liabilities	9,650			11,237			11,271			21,045			27,436
Debt/equity ratio	0.5			0.6			0.7			0.5			0.3

described above.[4] This is clearly easier, but does not provide the discipline of re-visiting the major assumptions upon which the evaluation is based.

8.4   Start-up Airline Business Plan

Many of the essentials of preparing the financial part of a start-up airline business plan have been discussed in the preceding sections of this chapter. The fleet plan will be crucial, in that it brings together decisions on many aspects of marketing, operations and engineering. For a start-up airline, however, the investment appraisal might point to a particular solution, but the realities of the marketplace might dictate something else. There might, for example, be an attractive offer of the right number of aircraft at the right time at a low operating lease rate. ValuJet in the US started with used ex Delta Air Lines DC-9s purchased with cash,[5] and Debonair in the UK with a fleet of used BAe 146s on 16-month operating lease.[6] Other European low cost carriers such as Ryanair, easyJet and Go all started with used B737-200s and -300s, but later ordered new aircraft. JetBlue in the US started with new A320s, but was well financed and presumably had a very attractive offer from Airbus.

Aircraft operating economics in these circumstances take second place to savings, at least in the difficult start-up period, in capital investment. This is because the airline may never take-off at all without the necessary finance; and the last part of this chapter will show that, even when almost all assets are leased rather than owned, the financial requirements to start an airline are still quite substantial.

The three key financial statements in any start-up airline business plan are presented in Table 8.8 for a hypothetical airline. The figures suggest an initial level of traffic of around 500,000 passengers per year, operated perhaps with a fleet of 7–8 short to medium haul aircraft. The investment appraisal has indicated that used, low capital cost, aircraft would produce higher net present values, given the airline's high cost of capital and discount rate. The financial evaluation (see Chapter 10) indicating that an operating lease would be preferable to owning the aircraft, or taking them on finance lease. But considerable working capital will still be needed, and some of the sources of such capital described in Chapter 8 will have been considered.

The scenario described in Table 8.8 is one of an airline starting scheduled operations, say on intra-European routes, at the beginning of October, after spending the previous three months in planning, obtaining licenses, approvals and slots, training, marketing and promotion. In this period no revenues are earned, but considerable expenses would have been incurred. The particular example shows a winter start-up, which might have been dictated by aircraft availability, and gives the airline a chance to become better known before the peak summer season. But it may mean a greater working capital requirement.

The discussion of working capital in 8.2 above suggested that perhaps a short-term capital requirement could be financed on a short-term basis with, say, an overdraft. This would not be appropriate here: first, the airline would not have the security to

4   Gibson and Morrell. Supra.

5   *The Avmark Aviation Economist*, 19 (April/May 1996).

6   *Airfinance Journal*, 13 (July/August 1996).

get past the loss-making earlier months or even years, and would need to spend a considerable amount of time on refinancing their working capital; second, the banks would only offer such finance in conjunction with more permanent finance, and even then only on a self-liquidating basis; and finally the regulatory authorities would be unlikely to license a start-up airline on this basis.

Regulatory authorities in most countries have various financial fitness criteria for licensing start-up airlines. Countries that have more liberal air transport policies and a more competitive environment are likely to have both stricter and less secretive financial requirements. The European Commission published in 1992 common criteria to be used by member states in granting operating licenses for start-up airlines. They required that such airlines should provide a business plan for at least the first two years years of the applicant's operation.[7] In an annex to the regulation, the following information was required from first time applicants:

1. The most recent internal management accounts, and, if available audited accounts for the previous financial year.
2. A projected balance sheet, including (*sic*) profit and loss account, for the following two years.[8]
3. The basis for projected expenditure and income figures on such items as fuel, fares and rates, salaries, maintenance, depreciation, exchange rate fluctuations, airport charges, insurance, *etc.* Traffic/revenue forecasts.
4. Details of the start-up costs incurred in the period from submission of application to commencement of operations and an explanation of how it is (*sic*) proposes to finance these costs.
5. Details of existing and projected sources of finance.
6. Details of shareholders, including nationality and type of shares to be held, and the Articles of Association. If parts of a group of undertakings, information on the relationship between them.
7. Projected cash-flow statements and liquidity plans for the first two years years of operation.
8. Details of the financing of aircraft purchase/leasing including, in the case of leasing, the terms and conditions of contract.[9]

Other provisions were also included for the continuing assessment of existing license holders. It can be seen that Table 8.8 provides some of the information required, but a second year of operation would have to be added, as well as more details on operating revenues and expenses, sources of finance and shareholdings.

---

7   This was increased to three years in Article 5 of a Proposal for a regulation on common rules for the operation of air transport services in the Community, European Commission, COM(2006) 396 final, 18 July 2006.

8   This was increased to three years in Article 5 of a Proposal for a regulation on common rules for the operation of air transport services in the Community, European Commission, COM(2006) 396 final, 18 July 2006.

9   *Official Journal of the European Communities, No* L240, (24 August 1992) p. 7.

Article 5 paragraph 1 of the EU regulation gives two hurdles that need to be overcome before a license can be granted.[10] First, the airline needs to demonstrate that 'it can meet at any time its actual and potential obligations, established under realistic assumptions, for a period of 24 months from the start of operations'. From Table 8.8, it would appear from the projected balance sheet that the airline could at least meet the requirement for the first year. Second, the airline would be able to 'meet its fixed and operational costs incurred from operations according to its business plan and established under realistic assumptions, for a period of three months from the start of operations, without taking into account any income from operations'.[11] This can be tested by looking at the cash flow statement for the imaginary start-up airline in Table 8.8. If all revenues are removed from the first three months, then the cash balance at the end of December would be $6.4 million lower, or a −$493,000. The airline would not therefore pass this hurdle.

However, if some of the future income were already contracted for, it might be possible to include that in the calculations. For example, if the airline had a legal contract to provide charter services for a tour operator in November and December, and that the combined revenues under this contract of $500,000 were included in the planned cash revenues in those months, then this revenue could be included and the airline would pass the test. This modification was not written into the regulation, but it would seem to be a sensible approach to take where significant charter operations are concerned.

In the USA a similar approach is taken by the Department of Transportation before granting an operating certificate. The Air Carrier Fitness Division of DOT states in its guidelines that applicants must provide 'independent third-party verification that it has available to it resources (*e.g.*, cash, lines-of-credit or bank loans) sufficient to cover all of its pre-operating costs ... plus the operating expenses that are reasonably projected to be incurred ... during three months of "normal" operations'.[12] No revenues can be assumed for these first three months, and expenses should be based on projected traffic and revenues, and not reduced because of reduced or no traffic. They prescribe the estimation of the first three months' operating expenses by dividing expenses for the first 12 months by four.

The EU regulations could, in certain cases, be somewhat less strict than those of the US DOT. The interpretation of the EU Regulation by the UK CAA states that 'in considering the extent to which all of the operational costs should be included the CAA may take into account the proportion of flying which could be cancelled without impact on the core business...'.[13] This is in the context of licensing charter carriers that operate *ad hoc* flights outside their core business of series charters for tour operators. Such airlines are less common in the US.

---

10 *Official Journal of the European Communities*, supra, p. 4.

11 This is considerably less strict that the rule applied by Microsoft, where enough cash must be available to operate the company for at least one year, even if no one paid them; see Gates, W. (1996), *The Road Ahead*, revised edn, p. 45.

12 Air Carrier Fitness Division (2002) *How to Become a Certificated Air Carrier*, Office of the Secretary, US Department of Transportation, 202-366-9721.

13 Financial framework for the grant of a Type A operating license, UK CAA, www.caa.co.uk, Section 4.2.

Chapter 9

Risk Management:
Foreign Currency and Fuel Price

9.1 Exchange Rate Volatility

International airlines sell tickets in many different countries and currencies, even in places where they do not have their own operations. They also incur operating expenses in the currencies of the countries they serve, and buy capital equipment from the major aerospace exporting countries such as the US, Canada, UK, France, Brazil and Germany.

It would be impossible for there to be a perfect match in both amounts and timing of foreign currency receipts and expenses. An airline may achieve some sort of balance over the year as a whole in receipts and expenses in a certain currency, but there will be weeks and months of surpluses followed by periods of shortfall. This can be managed by borrowing and lending in this one currency, and thus not involving conversion into another currency or any exchange risk. But net surpluses in a foreign currency would have to be exchanged into the local currency, which is the currency in which most costs are incurred and ultimately any profits would be retained or distributed. Here, there will be a time lag between income and expenditure which involves a risk of a movement in the exchange rate, and therefore a foreign exchange loss or gain. An airline's treasury has the task of managing revenues, expenditures, assets and liabilities in both local and foreign currencies, and thus minimising the risks of exposure to large currency movements.

Since the late 1960s, exchange rates of currencies have floated with respect to other major currencies, subject to central bank intervention, in pursuit of economic and monetary goals. Some currencies are pegged to major currencies, such as the US dollar, or a basket of the currencies of their major trading partners. Some countries do not manage their exchange rates as a policy objective, leaving them to float freely.

The Bank for International Settlements (BIS) estimates the importance of the various currencies in global foreign exchange market trading: the US dollar accounted for 45 per cent of daily turnover in April 1989, falling only slightly to 44.5 per cent in April 2004. The second most important currency is the Euro with just under 19 per cent, followed by the Japanese Yen with around 10 per cent and the UK pound with 8.5 per cent. The UK pound has increased somewhat in importance (up from 7.5 per cent in 1989) while the Yen has fallen from 14.5 per cent.

The European exchange rate mechanism attempted to limit the fluctuations between European currencies, but market pressures and a lack of coordination of

EU monetary policies had placed the future of this system in doubt. However, 12 EU countries introduced a common currency (the 'euro' or €) in 2000, with the complete phasing out of national currencies by March 2002. Only the UK, Denmark and Sweden remained outside the euro area, such that their monetary policy was not applied by the European Central Bank, as was the case with the others. This change made life easier for Europe's major airlines (not only the ones whose countries have signed up), in terms of reduced currency risks and transaction costs, but there are also costs involved in the change-over.

Fluctuations occur because of changes in the supply of and demand for the currency. For example, if the UK was running a balance of trade deficit, then more traders would be selling pounds to pay for imports than exporters are buying pounds with the foreign currency proceeds from their foreign sales. This would weaken the pound, or the pound would depreciate against the currencies it traded with. Exporters might delay invoicing in a currency that they expect to depreciate, in the hope of gain, while importers might do the opposite. These 'leads and lags' would further increase downward pressure on the currency.

Here exporters and importers are taking a position on future currency movements which is no different from money traders, often called speculators.[1] The latter execute orders for others, as well as trying to profit on their own account from movements in currencies and interest rates. This can also add considerable buying or selling pressures to a currency that cannot be counteracted by buying or selling by that country's central bank, even if it wished to. However, the argument that governments and central bankers are now increasingly powerless in the face of global market dealers has been rebutted by the strength of the dollar, following statements and actions by central bankers from the G7 countries in April 1995.

In the past few years, exporters of capital have also become more important in exchange rate determination. Foreign direct investment has been high from countries like Japan which have a high domestic savings rate and visible trade surplus. This has taken the form of Japanese investors buying foreign assets (see Chapter 10, Japanese leveraged leases) or foreign stocks and shares, or of Japanese companies establishing offshore manufacturing plant in countries such as China and Federation of Malaysia. This has the effect of weakening the yen against other currencies.

Market economics suggests that currency depreciation resulting from a trade deficit would automatically make exports more competitive and lead to a reduction in the trade deficit and thus an appreciation of the currency. One of the problems of this equilibrium theory is that depreciation leads to higher import prices and increases domestic inflation, which in turn reduces the move towards greater international competitiveness. Thus, a country is trapped in a downwards spiral of inflation and depreciation. Extreme examples of this have occurred at various times in the past, notable in Brazil and other Latin American countries, many African countries, and more recently Russia and some CIS countries.

---

1   The now well-known fund manager and investor, George Soros, was reported to have made a considerable sum from speculating on sterling's depreciation in 1992; see Kaletsky, A. *The Times*, 26 October 1992.

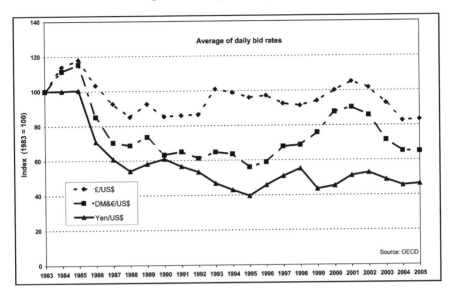

Figure 9.1   Key currency exchange rates *vs* US dollar, 1983–2005

It can be seen from Figure 9.1 that even the world's major currencies are subject to quite sharp fluctuations in the space of only one or two years years. A fall of the US dollar against the yen and Deutschemark (DM) between 1985 and 1988 of above 40 per cent, and the pound by just under 30 per cent, illustrates this point. The Euro (€) joined the list of major world currencies in 1999, and completely replaced the Deutschemark and other EU currencies in 2002. Since, its introduction, however, it has weakened against the US dollar, falling 15 per cent between 1999 and 2000.

Purchasing power parity (PPP) theory states that under liberalised international trade a basket of goods in one country should cost the same as a basket of goods in another country. If domestic prices rise in one country, then the exchange rate between that country and another should change to restore the price equality between the two baskets of goods. Exchange rates should, according to this theory, be determined purely by relative price movements. It is doubtful if this would happen even in the long term because of the increasing element of goods and services that are not traded internationally in the basket of typical domestic purchases; in the short or even medium-term many exchange rates persist in being significantly out of line with the rates that equate the price levels in each country. For this reason, the use of market exchange rates causes distortions in international comparisons, for example of airline costs or yields. These can be removed by the use of PPP rates of exchange which are published on a regular basis by the Organisation for Economic Co-operation and Development (OECD) for most major currencies.[2]

Currency changes can have a significant effect on the pattern, and in some cases the size, of air travel demand. An improvement in the pound against the US dollar

2   These are based on the consumer prices of a basket of goods, and are published in the OECD's Main Economic Indicators.

between 1986 and 1989 encouraged some UK sun-seekers to switch from European destinations such as Spain to Florida. On the other hand, the greater depreciation of the pound against the French franc compared to the Spanish peseta and Italian lira between 1992 and 1994/1995 led to the latter countries becoming relatively more attractive to UK tourists. In 1997, Thailand, Federation of Malaysia, Indonesia and other Asian countries also became much more attractive to foreign tourists, following their currency depreciation, but it also seriously inhibited foreign travel by residents.

Few tourists buy the foreign currency needed for a foreign holiday in advance, although there was some evidence that Germans did this when the US dollar was particularly weak against the mark in spring 1995.[3] However, many still plan and book their holidays well in advance of travel, even though some leave booking until the last minute to try to take advantage of special offers. This means that currency depreciation would result in less spending on discretionary items while on holiday, rather than cancellation, and perhaps only affect demand in the following season.

9.2 Airline Trading Exposure to Currency Movements

Currency changes can also have a serious impact on an airline's reported profitability. This might stem from its trading activities, which are examined here, or it may come from the restatement of foreign currency denominated assets or liabilities, which are discussed in the next section. For example, Singapore Airlines announced in October 1996 that its results for the first half of the financial year had been hit by both higher fuel prices and the strong Singapore dollar.[4] The depreciation of key revenue earning currencies such as the yen and DM contributed to a decline in yields expressed in Singapore dollars of 6.7 per cent.

Airlines often report the adverse effect of foreign exchange movements on profits, but rarely the converse. In order to explore the possible trading impact of marked exchange rate movements, a simplified example has been constructed. This assumes trading only in the local currency (£ sterling) and one foreign currency (US$), and treats airlines either as exporters or importers, depending on the currencies in which its operating revenues and expenses are incurred.

For an international airline to be an exporter, the following is likely to hold true:

- Its costs will be primarily in the local currency.
- The majority of its revenues will be in foreign currency.

The example in Table 9.1 assumes 60 per cent of revenues will be in foreign currencies and 60 per cent of expenses will be in the local currency, which is a fairly good approximation of many major international scheduled airlines (*e.g.*, KLM in 1995/1996).

---

3 *Financial Times* Foreign Exchange Supplement, (6 June 1995), p. vi.

4 *Financial Times*, (29 October 1996), p. 27.

Table 9.1   Effect of exchange rate depreciation on profits of exporter airline

	Revenues	Expenses	Difference
Local Currency (£)	40	60	− 20
Foreign Currency in $	*120*	*80*	*40*
Foreign Currency in £			
(At exchange rate of $2.00 per £)	60	40	20
TOTAL (£)	100	100	0
Profit in £			0
Foreign Currency in £			
(At exchange rate of $1.50 per £)	80	53	27
Local Currency (£)	40	60	− 20
TOTAL (£)	120	113	7
Change in Profit (£)			+7

The initial position is one of zero local currency trading profit at the rate of exchange of $2 to the £. The impact on profits of a depreciation of sterling of 25 per cent to $1.50 to the £ (which actually occurred between 1990 and 1993) is then evaluated, assuming other factors remaining constant.

This example has shown how the depreciation of a currency helps exporter airlines by increasing the local value of their foreign earnings by a greater amount (£20) than the increase in the local value of foreign expenses (£13), resulting in a profit improvement (£7). However, it would also allow them to reduce foreign selling prices or fares and stimulate traffic without risk of reducing their sterling revenues.

International charter airlines whose revenues are almost entirely from their own country's residents will be net importers (they will need to import aircraft and fuel, both incurred in foreign currency). Foreign currency revenues for these carriers are unlikely to exceed 20 per cent. Finnair, a scheduled airline with a large charter operation, also provides an example of an airline which has relatively low foreign exchange revenues (35 per cent in 1995/1996) and high local currency costs (65 per cent). The impact of a similar sterling depreciation is shown in Table 9.2.

For the importer airline, the depreciation of a currency increases the local value of their foreign earnings by a smaller amount (£7) than the increase in the local value of foreign expenses (£13), resulting in a profit deterioration (£6). There would also be very little scope for them to increase revenues or stimulate traffic by reducing foreign selling prices or fares.

Thus, the depreciation of the UK pound sterling will have a beneficial impact on British Airways, but will hurt a charter carrier such as Britannia Airways (and contributed to the bankruptcy of Laker Airways). But it should be noted that a currency depreciation also has an initially adverse effect on the net exporter by making its costs incurred in foreign currency immediately more expensive. The effect on revenues will generally take longer because of the advance nature of ticket sales. It will also depend on whether the airline uses the depreciation as an opportunity to lower local currency fares, or offer more attractive discount fares, and the price elasticity of its potential markets. This last effect is clearly very difficult to quantify, but often neglected in airline profit announcements and related commentaries.

Table 9.2   Effect of exchange rate depreciation on profits of importer airline

	Revenues	Expenses	Difference
Local Currency (£)	80	60	20
Foreign Currency in $	*40*	*80*	*– 40*
Foreign Currency in £			
(At exchange rate of $2.00 per £)	20	40	20
TOTAL (£)	100	100	0
Profit in £			0
Foreign Currency in £			
(At exchange rate of $1.50 per £)	27	53	– 26
Local Currency (£)	80	60	20
TOTAL (£)	107	113	– 6
Change in Profit (£)			– 6

Furthermore, in the longer term the rate of inflation of prices in general in the local currency will increase, increasing the exporter's local currency costs and eroding the profit increase. There might also be an effect on the exporter airline's local market, which will find foreign holidays more expensive as a result of the depreciation of their currency. But in reality airlines operate to many different countries, some of whose currencies are bound to fare worse than the local one, and switching between countries is the more likely response.

It is the major currencies in which an airline trades that will provide the greatest exposure to large foreign exchange movements. One example of an international airline that has regularly published details of the importance of this is SAS, which does not fit easily into the above example, since it has three *domestic* currencies. With quite large domestic markets, it tends to be long in two of its home currencies. However, its long-haul hub is in Denmark resulting in quite high costs there, but revenues are smaller partly due to the smaller domestic market. It is short in US dollars, a common position for many airlines stemming from the fact that capital costs,[5] fuel, some airport charges and US station and sales costs are all in dollars.

Table 9.3   SAS revenue and cost currency breakdown in 2005 (per cent)

Currency	Revenues	Costs	± % Pts
Swedish krona	21	18	+ 3
Norwegian krona	28	19	+ 9
Danish krona	11	14	– 3
Euro (€)	24	18	+ 6
US$	7	26	– 19
Pound sterling (£)	5	3	+ 2
Other	4	2	+ 2
Total	100	100	+ 0

Source: SAS Group Annual Report, 2005

---

5   Airbus now prices its aircraft in both US dollars and Euros (€), although € deals are rare.

The data in Table 9.3 meant that, of SAS's 2005 EBITDA of SEK3,000 million, the airline had surpluses of SEK5,900 million of Norwegian Krona, SEK3,900 million of euros, SEK2,200 million of Swedish Krona and SEK1,300 million of UK sterling. It had a deficit of SEK11,000 million in US dollars, and SEK1,600 million of Danish Krona. In contrast to SAS which earns a large part of revenues in its home currency, Turkish Airlines derived only 16 per cent of operating revenues from Turkish New Lira in 2004, 45 per cent coming from euros and as much as 16 per cent from US dollars. This is because of its strong sales to incoming European tourists and those of Turkish origin living in Germany. The airline's expenditure was split between its home currency (48 per cent), US dollars (32 per cent), euros (13 per cent) and other currencies (7 per cent).

British Airways earns just under 60 per cent of its revenues in around 140 different foreign currencies (30 per cent in US$), and incurs about 50 per cent of its costs abroad (30 per cent in US$). US carriers like Delta Air Lines have 75–80 per cent of their revenues and an even higher percentage of expenses in US dollars, and are thus affected little by changes in exchange rates. A 1992 study of American Airlines did, however, find that a weaker US dollar boosted short-run cash flows, but that this might also in the longer run weaken the US economy and reduce American travel.[6]

Qantas estimated the sensitivity of their profit forecasts with respect to the key currencies in which it trades, namely the US dollar, the Japanese yen and the UK pound.[7] They examined the effect of a 5 per cent movement in the exchange rates of these currencies, and estimated the following impacts:

Table 9.4   Impact of currency changes on Qantas after-tax profit for 1995/1996

	Depreciation	Appreciation
Uniform movement of 5 per cent in A$ against all currencies	11%	−10%
Movement of 5 per cent in A$ against US$	−22%	20%
Movement of 5 per cent in A$ against Japanese Yen	3%	−3%
Movement of 5 per cent in A$ against UK pound	3%	−3%

The after-tax profit forecast for Qantas stated in the prospectus of A$237 million for the financial year 1995/1996 assumed an A$/US$ exchange rate to average 0.76 over the year, A$/Yen to average 72.2, and A$/UK£ to average 0.47. Profits actually turned out to be higher than expected at A$247 million, not helped by an appreciation of the Australian dollar, which averaged 76.6, or 6 per cent higher then predicted. The A$/£ rate was 0.49, or a 4 per cent appreciation of Australian dollar, which again

---

6   Bilson, J. (1992), Managing Economic Exposure to Foreign Exchange Risk: A Case Study of American Airlines, *The Economist*, 6 June.

7   Qantas Airways Limited, Offering Memorandum, (22 June 1995).

would have tended to reduce profits. (The forecast of A\$ 0.76 to the US dollar turned out to be right.)

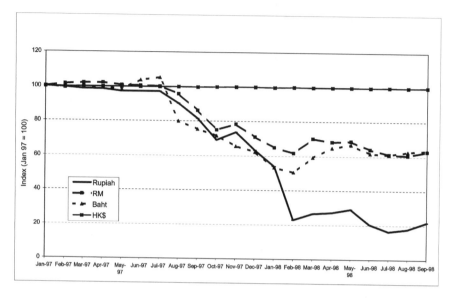

Figure 9.2   Selected Asian exchange rates *vs* US dollar, 1997/1998

The Asian financial crisis of 1997 and 1998 resulted in the very rapid depreciation of many Asian currencies. Those airlines that were short of US dollars found themselves having to buy them at significantly higher prices post-1997 compared to before.

Table 9.5   Asian airline US dollar mismatch

Airline	US\$ revenues % total	US\$ costs as % total	Net impact* (%)
Air New Zealand	15	23	– 0.4
Cathay Pacific	20	20	0
Japan Airlines	10	15	– 0.2
Korean Air	20	25	– 0.3
Asiana	18	52	– 1.6
Malaysian Airlines	10	28	– 0.8
Singapore Airlines	25	23	0.1
Qantas Airways	5	15	– 0.5
Philippine Airlines	15	33	– 0.9
Thai Airways	15	24	– 0.4

* Net impact on operating margin of a 5 per cent average local currency depreciation against the US\$

Source: US-Asean Business Council (1999)

Table 9.5 gives an idea of how sensitive various Asian airlines were to the depreciation of their local currencies.[8] Unfortunately, the source did not give data for Garuda, but it is likely that its situation was not dissimilar to Malaysian, both having large domestic markets generating negligible foreign currency revenues. The net impact on operating ratios is shown for a 5 per cent depreciation. In the case of Thai Airways the local currency fell by around 50 per cent, which would have shaved 4 per cent points off their operating ratio. This is without considering any net economic effects of a reduction in travel by nationals, offset by the boost to tourism from the more attractive rates. The most extreme example, Asiana was faced with a 30 per cent drop in its local currency between 1997 and 1998, which would have reduced its operating ratio by almost 10 per cent points.

The analysis in Table 9.5 ignores the possible benefits from revenues generated in relative strong currencies other than the US dollar. Philippine Airlines carries a large number of nationals living and working abroad who buy their tickets in foreign currency. The table also misses the important impact of foreign debt repayments, which are addressed in the next section.

9.3   Airline Balance Sheet Exposure to Currency Movements

Airlines can also experience large reported foreign exchange profits or losses as a result of borrowing money or acquiring aircraft in foreign currencies. SAS provides an example of this, with large exchange losses being charged against 1992 profits as a result of a revaluation of long-term debt, following the November 1992 float of the Swedish krona, and its subsequent decline of 20 per cent against the DM and 15 per cent against the ECU.[9] This was somewhat offset by exchange gains from liquid funds placed in foreign currencies.

An example of two transactions involving foreign currencies and an airline's balance sheet is given below.

Example 1

An airline sells tickets to the value of US$100,000 on 1 December, but has not received the funds by the end of the financial year at end December. The sale is translated into £ at the rate ruling at the date of the transaction (or the rate for the month through the IATA clearing house), say US$2.00/£. The passengers travelled before the end of the year, so that revenue amounting to £50,000 will be included in the Profit and Loss statement for the year. However, since the invoice had not been paid by year end, debtors (accounts receivable) will have to include the $100,000 outstanding, but this will be converted into sterling at the year end rate of exchange, which is perhaps only US$1.5/£. Thus, debtors will include £66,667, the difference between this and the revenue amount of £50,000 being credited to the profit and loss

---

8   US-ASEAN Business Council Inc. (1999), *ASEA and Asia Pacific: Civil aviation and airport development*.

9   SAS Annual Report (1992), p. 27.

statement as an exchange gain, such that retained earnings will ultimately offset the change in debtors or current assets.

Once the money is received in the following January, the dollars are converted to pounds at the new spot rate (US$1.60/£), and the £62,500 is added to cash balances in current assets. The exchange gain is thus £12,500, rather less than the £16,667 allowed for in the previous financial year, so an adjustment is made in the current financial year for the difference of £4,167.

Example 2

An airline buys an aircraft for US$1 million on 1 March, and this is entered in the balance sheet under fixed assets at the rate of exchange ruling at the date of the transaction. It will then be depreciated in the normal way based on this sterling amount, say £500,000 (US$2.00/£). At the end of the financial year, this amount is not adjusted to reflect any change in the $/£ rate since the date of acquisition. The aircraft is, however, a foreign asset and any foreign exchange gain or loss will eventually be realised, but only once the asset is sold. Alternatively, the aircraft value can be adjusted at the end of each reporting period, using the new rate of exchange. Long-term debt associated with the acquisition of such aircraft, however, is usually adjusted periodically for exchange rate changes.

British Airways (and many other airlines) generally translate foreign currency balances into sterling (or their reporting currencies) at the rates of exchange ruling at the balance sheet date. Changes in the sterling value of outstanding foreign currency loans and finance leases used for the acquisition of aircraft and investments are reflected in the cost of those assets. Profits and losses arising on translation are normally dealt with through the profit and loss account, although some airlines make adjustments solely on the balance sheet.

9.4   Airline Foreign Exchange Risk Management

Airlines will try to reduce foreign exchange exposure, or the risk of loss, by matching revenues and payments, as well as assets and liabilities, in each currency. This is called a natural hedge. It may be possible to achieve this is some currencies, and, where there is an imbalance, increase expenditure in the countries where excess revenues are earned.

For example, British Airways earns a surplus in French francs, and reduces this by buying wine and food in France for its in-flight catering. In some countries, revenues cannot be remitted to the home currency and are effectively blocked in a rapidly depreciating local currency. The advantages of adopting a similar strategy here are clearly much more sizeable, but there is generally less scope for making such purchases in these countries. The possibility of running sales conferences there might not achieve the desired result if the local hotels insist on charging in US dollars or another hard currency (as the airline would probably now be doing for its own local sales). Sometimes, however, state owned airlines come to some arrangement for funding the local embassy in return for payments to the airline in the home country.

Where surpluses are earned, and natural hedges impossible, they can either be sold on the spot market (for immediate delivery into the local currency), or they can be sold on the forward market (and *vice versa*). The forward market is a realistic alternative for delivery of the local (or foreign) currency equivalent in up to 12 months into the future, but beyond that period would tend to be too expensive, or there would be no market available. Forward market prices are quoted for major currencies for three, six, nine and 12 months ahead. A forward market contract will commit the airline to buy a fixed amount of a given currency at a future date at a given exchange rate.

An alternative to dealing on the forward market is to buy or sell an option which gives the holder the right, but not obligation to exchange a given amount of currency at a certain rate, at a future date. A premium will have to be paid for buying the option to purchase currency (a put option), or sell currency (a call option). This money is lost, but the holder can then either exercise the option if the subsequent trend in the spot rate is unfavourable, or throw away the option if the spot market is favourable. A European option remains with the buyer until the exercise date, but an American option can be traded in the intervening period, and there will be a market price for buying and selling options.

A major investment paid for in a foreign currency is a good example of whether to hedge, and which method an airline should choose. Once a firm order has been signed for an aircraft, an airline will be committed to delivering the cost of the aircraft in one or two years years' time. The example below is based on a UK based airline contracting to buy a B747-400 for delivery in one years' time at a cost of US$140 million. It is assumed that down-payments and natural hedges result in US$100 being required at delivery date. There are three possible strategies:

a) Do nothing; wait until delivery date and then buy the US$100 million in the *spot market*, at the then rate of exchange;
b) Hedge the risk of an adverse movement in the $/£ exchange rate by buying the $100 million *forward*;
c) Hedge the risk of an adverse movement in the $/£ exchange rate by buying a *call option* to buy the US$100 million in one year's time at the current forward rate;

or a combination of the above.

Do nothing (Strategy A)

The spot rate is the exchange rate at which dollars can be purchased with pounds for immediate delivery. It changes continuously as a result of supply and demand. Assume that it was $1.5205 to the £ at the time the contract was signed. In 12 months' time, however, it could be lower, hence the exchange risk. On the other hand, if it rose, then the aircraft's price would effectively be reduced.

Hedge with forward Purchase (Strategy B)

The forward exchange rate is the rate at which pounds can be purchased with dollars at a future date. Assume the 12 months' forward rate was $1.4905 at the time the contract was signed. The airline could therefore purchase US dollars forward with the local currency it would have available in 12 months' time. It would then do nothing until the forward contract due date (*i.e.*, in 12 months) when it would buy the $100 million with £67 million of local currency (*i.e.*, the pounds converted at the contract rate of $1.4905).

Hedge with Call Option (Strategy C)

A call option is the right to buy a currency at some future date at an agreed rate of exchange. This right must be purchased at a price which varies according to supply and demand. Assume that a call option to buy US dollars in one year's time at the current forward rate of £1 = $1.4905 costs 5.1 per cent of the US$ amount. This option can either be exercised in one year's time, with the dollars purchased at the forward rate ($1.4905) costing £67 million, plus the 5.1 per cent cost of the option. Depending on how the spot rate actually moves over the year ahead, the option might not be exercised, with the dollars instead bought at the spot rate ruling at the time, plus 5.1 per cent, which is the cost of the option.

Figure 9.3 shows how the local currency cost of the remaining payment for the aircraft will vary with the eventual spot rate in one year's time. It can be seen that if the spot rate had turned out to be below 1.4905 (the original forward rate), then alternative (b) of assuring in the cost of £67 million with a forward contract would have been best. If the spot rate had turned out to be above 1.4905, then the 'do nothing' strategy (a) would have been best (*i.e.*, dealing on the spot market at the time of delivery). In retrospect, the option strategy is never the best strategy, regardless of how the spot market actually moves over the year. The option is the worst strategy if the spot rate moves very little, and better than the worst strategy if rates move significantly up or down. The forward purchase is the least risky strategy, locking in the cost of the aircraft in £ sterling at £67 million, but the aircraft might have cost less if the rate had hardened.

An actual example of a hedging strategy which involved a combination of (a) and (b) above was provided by Lufthansa. In early 1985, the airline bought 20 Boeing 737–300 aircraft at a cost of $500 million to be paid in on delivery in a year's time. The spot $/DM rate at the time was around DM3.20. The airline decided that a decline in the dollar was imminent, but that they should hedge 50 per cent of the cost with a forward contract, just in case the markets once again confounded the forecasters. The forward exchange rate was DM3.20, thus locking in half the cost of $250 million at DM800 million.

The dollar in fact rallied to about DM 3.45 before falling to DM 2.30 over the next 12 months. The total cost of the aircraft in local currency was then the DM 800 million from the forward deal plus a further DM 575 million at the spot price of DM 2.30, giving a total of DM 1.375 billion. In retrospect, the 'do nothing' strategy on the full $500 million would have cost only DM1.15 billion, or DM 225 million less than they ended up paying. Alternatively, a forward hedge for the full $500 million would have resulted in a total cost of DM1.6 billion, or DM225 million more. It is, of course, easy to be wise after the event, and the subsequent summoning of Lufthansa's chief executive to the Transport Minister[10] was probably more of a gesture to calm the political storm that had arisen than a reprimand.

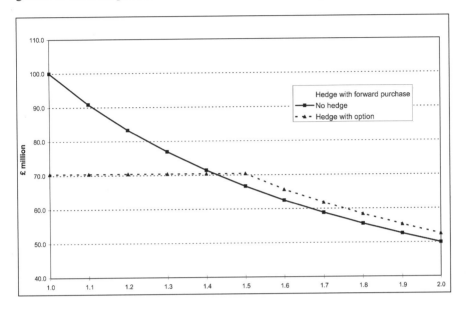

Figure 9.3   Cost of hedging *vs* eventual spot rate

Perhaps a better way of looking at Lufthansa's dilemma would be to go back to the fleet planning and NPV analysis that the airline would have undertaken before confirming the order for the aircraft (see Section 8.3). This would have included assumptions on the DM/$ exchange rate, and ought to have been tested against various possible exchange rate outcomes. Because of the impact of any subsequent exchange rate movements on both costs and revenues, it may not have been necessary to hedge the purchase cost at all. However, the effect on the project NPV of alternative foreign exchange strategies could have been tested against actual spot rate outcomes. These strategies should also have included options, particularly in view of the volatility of the exchange rate in question.

It should be concluded that dealing in the forward or options markets (also called 'derivatives') is a way of managing risk, but it does not remove it altogether. It is rather the exchange of an unacceptable risk (*i.e.*, that the aircraft end up costing significantly more than planned for) for an acceptable risk (*e.g.*, that other airlines might acquire aircraft more cheaply). It could also be seen as the payment of a premium to insure against the risk of a serious financial loss in the future.

---

10 *Financial Times*, 24 February 1986.

In a 1992 survey of 23 major international airlines,[11] it was found that 21 used natural foreign currency hedges (matching foreign currency revenues with expenses), while 17 airlines hedged with forward contracts. Eight airlines used options for hedging, with only two of those trading in options. Only seven airlines borrowed in currencies with operating revenue surpluses, the majority either borrowing in local currencies or borrowing in US$ to finance US$ assets.

9.5   Fuel Price Exposure

9.5.1   *The Need and Means to Hedge Fuel*

Airlines use three approaches in dealing with fuel prices. First, they try to increase the fuel efficiency of their operations. Second, they try to pass cost increase on to their customers as price increases or surcharges. And third, they hedge fuel costs using physical or derivative markets.

Increasing fuel efficiency in the short-term relies on changing operating procedures (*e.g.*, cruise speed) or tankering policies.[12] Most of these are already exhausted, and there are limits to how much can be achieved, given safety requirements. Replacing existing aircraft with more fuel efficient ones can take place gradually. This has the same effect as a permanent policy of hedging fuel, as it reduces profit volatility from fuel price changes.

Airlines have passed fuel increases on to customers on the cargo side of the business for many years. Lufthansa and others published an index of fuel prices, the trigger points, and the resulting surcharge amounts. FedEx does not hedge fuel at all since it can rely largely on these surcharges.

On the passenger side, surcharges were rarer, but recently most of the major EU and Asian airlines have done this with some success. On the other hand, US airlines operating within the US seldom make such increases stick (ATA, 2004).[13] Low cost airlines there now account for near one-third of capacity, and the competitive situation is more intense than in other parts of the world.

It is also the norm in many other industries to pass on increases in input prices in the short term, while investing in more fuel-efficient systems in the longer term. Table 9.6 shows that many European airlines differentiated their surcharges between short and long-haul trips. Interestingly, KLM's approach was very different from that of their new owner, Air France. In Asia, there was a larger variation in surcharge

---

11 KPMG/IATA (1992), *Accounting Policies, Disclosure and Financial Trends in the International Airline Industry*, KPMG, August. p. 24

12 Modern jet aircraft minimum cost speeds can be slightly higher than minimum fuel burn speeds, because labour, maintenance, and ownership costs accrue with time. However, the differences are small. Tankering fuel from low-cost to higher-cost airports costs fuel burn, and can be reduced when costs are high everywhere. Again, tankering involves a small fraction of most airline operations.

13 Air Transport Association of America (2004), *ATA's Response in Unisys*, R2A Scorecard, 2, No. 11, September p. 5.

amounts, while only one US airline had introduced surcharges on international flights by August 2004.

Airlines are exposed to unexpected movements in fuel prices in the same way as they are for the price of foreign currencies. This is not strictly a financial risk, since fuel is a commodity, similar to others used by airlines such food or maintenance materials. The difference is the amount of fuel they require, and the fact that they use the same type of refined crude oil product, jet A1 kerosene, throughout the world for their jet and turbo-prop operations. The fact that it is a commodity means that airlines can avail themselves of similar derivative contracts that they do in the foreign exchange markets, and it is for this reason that it has been included here.

Table 9.6   Fuel surcharges announced by major airlines in 2004

Airline	Date	US$ or equivalent*	
		Short/medium haul	Long haul
Europe:			
Air France	August 2004	3.66	14.64
British Airways	August 2004	4.55	10.92
BMI	August 2004	4.55	10.92
KLM	August 2004	4.88	4.88
Lufthansa	August 2004	2.44	8.54
North America:			
United Airlines	June 2004	*n/a*	5%
Asia/Pacific:			
Air China	2004	7.00	7.00
Air New Zealand	May 2004	3.93–9.83	13.11
All Nippon	May 2004	5%	5%
Cathay Pacific	August 2004	*n/a*	13.85–18.97
China Eastern	2004	7.00	7.00
China Southern	2004	7.00	7.00
Dragonair	August 2004	5.38–6.92	*n/a*
Qantas	August 2004	7.11	15.64
Singapore	August 2004	4–7	12
Virgin Blue	August 2004	7.11	*n/a*

* converted at average exchange rates in August 2004

Airlines buy fuel at the major airports around the world from the major multinational fuel companies or their subsidiaries.[14] These companies are responsible for fuel storage and its delivery to the aircraft on the apron at the airport.

---

14 Very occasionally, airlines have jointly purchased and stored their own fuel at certain airports to assure supply at a reasonable price.

For short/medium haul flights, airlines do not always need to pick up fuel at the destination airport, and at smaller airports it is sometimes not available. However, if the fuel is cheaper at the destination, they may top up their tanks, and engage in tankering fuel to reduce fuel costs.

The contracts with the major oil companies all include a clause which allows them to adjust price in line with world market price movements. They also add a handling charge to recover their costs of storage, tankering or hydrant installations, and sometimes an airport concession fee. Thus, if world markets increase sharply, as they did in 1999/2000 and again in 2005/2006, then airlines experience marked upward pressures on costs, with little time lag after significant crude oil price increases.

To hedge the risk of these strong upward pressures on fuel costs, which can easily result in an operating profit becoming a loss, airlines have a number of derivatives which they can buy, involving one of the following. Fuel price risk can be managed in a three ways: forward contracts, futures contracts, and derivatives such as options, collars, and swaps

Forward contracts are 'over the counter' agreements between two parties whereby one purchases a fixed amount of fuel from the other at a fixed price at some future date. Airline fuel suppliers such as Air BP enter into such agreements, but their tailor-made nature is not a convenient instrument for third parties or speculators. Parties also have full counter-party risk – that is risk that the airline or the supplier goes bankrupt before the deal is closed.

Futures contracts are better suited to both hedging and trading, since they are usually set up through exchanges that set standard contracts and protect against counter-party risk. One party to the contract agrees to deliver to another a standardised quantity of oil at an agreed price (the 'strike' price) on an agreed date in the future. These are conventionally reversed on the due date, so no physical delivery takes place. In fact, according to NYMEX, less than 1 per cent of trades result in the delivery of the underlying commodity, in this case crude oil and related products.

The main exchanges offering oil futures contracts are the International Petroleum Exchange (IPE) in London and NYMEX in New York. The former's futures are in Brent crude oil, one contract being for 1,000 barrels. The quality of the oil is assured, and contracts can be fixed for each month up to two years ahead, and then half-yearly to three years out. The liquidity for contracts beyond one year forward declines significantly and there is a Clearing House that guarantees the financial performance of contracts with the help of margin requirements.

Derivatives consist of an option or a right to buy (or sell) a given amount of fuel at a specific date at a stated 'strike' price. Strike prices are available spaced both above and below current futures prices. The cost of an option is based on the underlying futures, and if exercised (there no obligation to do so) will result in a corresponding futures position. A call option (right to purchase) offers flexibility over a future, because it gives the holder the possibility to protect against a price rise, while at the same time giving the opportunity to participate in a decline. Options (and swaps) can also be taken out with other parties (*e.g.*, approved counter-parties such as banks) in aviation fuel, in addition to crude oil. Jet fuel is rarely traded on any exchanges and thus must be 'over the counter'. These involve counter-party risk for both sides, and thus financially weak airlines find it hard to find others willing to take this risk.[15] Options are available in both Brent gas oil and crude at IPE.

More recently, airlines have moved toward using combinations of a call and a put option called a 'collar'. The call protects the holder from price increases above a strike price above the current future, at a cost of the option premium that must be paid at the outset. The holder of this call also sells a put option that limits the advantage it can take of price reductions below another strike price, below the current future. The total cost of taking the two options is the call option premium paid less the put option premium received. This is popular with airlines since it locks in the price that will be paid for fuel between two known values. A collar limits the speculative risk to a small range of price moves.

Swaps are tailor-made futures contracts whereby an airline locks in payments at future dates based on current fuel or oil price. These could be arranged with a supplier such as Air BP. The airline would buy a swap for a period of, say, one year at a certain strike price for a specified amount of jet fuel per month. The actual prices for each month is then compared with the swap price, and if the price is higher the counter-party would pay the airline the price difference times the amount of fuel. However, if the prices were lower, then the airline would pay the difference. They lock in a given price, as with forward contracts.

In summary, aviation fuel itself can only be hedged through over-the-counter arrangements with the additional counter-party risk. Hedging oil on exchanges such as NYMEX or SIMEX (that regulate standardised contracts) eliminates counter-party risk. These markets also are more liquid, and allow an airline to sell before due date. For longer periods into the future only crude oil instruments have good liquidity. Jet fuel contracts only have liquidity for shorter periods.

Hedging using jet kerosene clearly fully reflects price movements in the commodity that the airline actually needs to operate its aircraft.[16] Apart from a little-traded Japanese market, there are no exchange-traded futures available in aviation fuel, although over-the-counter contracts can be arranged.

The most liquid market available for the most closely related product is crude oil, with contracts available in both Brent and US WTI crude. No markets exist for OPEC produced oil products, although the market prices for these track very closely the above two supplies.

Aviation fuel prices have in the past tracked crude prices fairly closely, apart from period of very steep increases in crude prices, for example at the beginning of the 1970s, 1980s and 2000s.[17] Thus, crude oil derivatives are seen by some as a good proxy for fuel price movements. On the other hand, it is at times of instability when crude is a less good hedge that airlines need hedging most.

---

15 Jet Fuel Intelligence (2005), New Asian Carriers View Hedging as two-Edged Sword, *Energy Intelligence*, XV, No. 6, February.

16 Leaving aside the aviation gasoline that airlines operating small piston-engined aircraft require.

17 At these times, a sharp increase in the demand for jet aviation fuel by the military tends to increase its price relative to crude.

9.5.2   *Airline Fuel Hedging Practice*

Most major passenger airlines in the US, Europe, and Asia now hedge at least part of their future fuel needs. State-owned airlines hedge when they are allowed to, and they have a uniquely valid reason for doing so. Most newer carriers do not hedge at first, because they are using their credit to finance high growth rates. The oldest low-cost carrier, Southwest, has excellent credit and does hedge, although Southwest also has ties to the Texas oil industry and local relationships may have influenced this decision. A survey of treasurers from 25 of the world's largest airlines in 1991 revealed that 13 engaged in fuel futures transactions, managing exposures six months to two years years into the future (KPMG/IATA, 1992).[18]

Three of the eight largest US majors were not hedged for 2004, and one (American Airlines) was only hedged for six months of that year.

**Table 9.7   Percentage of 2004 fuel needs hedged at 31 December 2003:
US majors**

	% hedged	Av. US cents/gallon	Value $ million	Product	Instruments
Southwest	82	*n/a*	251	Crude and heating oil	Options, collars and swaps
Delta	32	76.46	97	Crude and heating oil	
US Airways	30	*n/a*	38	Crude and heating oil	Swaps and collars
American*	12	*n/a*	54	Jet fuel and crude	Swaps and options
America West	11	*n/a*	21	*n/a*	Collars
Continental	0				
Northwest	0				
United	0				

* Approximate average for whole year; 21 per cent hedged for first quarter

Source: Airline 10K reports for 2003

All the major European network airlines had hedged a significant part of their 2005/2006 fuel needs at the date of publication of their 2004 annual report. British Airways were somewhat under-covered, but subsequently increased their hedging activity (Table 9.8).

Less information was available from the annual reports of Asian airlines. However, in general, less hedging seems to have been undertaken by the still predominately state owned airlines. Both Thai Airways and Malaysian reported an upper limit of 50

---

18 KPMG/IATA (1992) *Accounting Policies, Disclosure and Financial Trends in the International Airline Industry*, KPMG, August.

per cent on the volume of expected fuel uplift that could be hedged, with All Nippon also reporting an unspecified limit.

State-owned Air India gained permission to hedge in 2003. Since the state is not a portfolio investor, reducing profit swings may be more justified for such owners.

Table 9.8   FY2004/2005 fuel needs hedged at YE2003/2004: Largest non-US carriers

	% hedged*	Av. cents/ gallon*	Value** $m	Products	Instruments
British Airways (2003/2004)	41	68.1	53	*n/a*	Collars and swaps
KLM (2003/2004)	80	*n/a*	*n/a*		*n/a*
Air France (2003/2004)	78	*n/a*	*n/a*		*n/a*
Iberia (2003)	54	55–62	*n/a*	Jet NWE	Swaps and options
Lufthansa (2003)	72	72.6*	72	Crude/ heating oil	*n/a*
Air New Zealand (2003/2004)	47	bands	84	WTI crude and jet	Options and collars
Cathay Pacific (2003)	25	*n/a*	*n/a*	*n/a*	Various
Singapore Airlines (2003/2004)	*n/a*	*n/a*	59		Options and swaps
Thai Airways (2003/2004)	12				Various
Emirates (2003/2004)	19	*n/a*	*n/a*	*n/a*	Options and futures

* average price locked into to hedge contracts (for Lufthansa on only 35 per cent of annual needs); ** market value of fuel hedge derivatives at financial year end

Source: Airline annual reports and websites.

Korean Airlines reported a gain of Won 282 million from a forward fuel contract in FY2003, reducing their average fuel price paid by 34 per cent. Qantas offset 73 per cent of their 2003/2004 increased fuel price paid through various unspecified hedging activities. Singapore Airlines were able to offset almost all the price element of their 2002/2003 increase in fuel costs by hedging, and in the following financial year a S$135 million fuel cost increase from higher prices was made S$1 million worse by hedging losses.

The major Chinese airlines (*e.g.*, China Southern, China Eastern and Air China) were (as of end 2004) obliged to purchase their domestic fuel needs from the state oil company at Chinese (PRC) spot prices. They were not permitted to hedge fuel (or foreign exchange) price risks.

As discussed above, futures are used by some airlines, but the growing forms of fuel price hedging are options, swaps and collars, with collars seen as being less speculative. Crude and heating oil contracts are more widely used than jet kerosene, since they can be traded on an exchange. Airlines rarely cover more than 18 months to two years into the future, with most treasurers looking to cover a part of their requirements over the next budget or financial year.

Many airlines are finding it increasingly difficult and expensive to access credit for fuel hedging purposes. To alleviate this problem and to reduce the costs associated with risk premiums, IATA is working with leading banks worldwide to use the IATA Clearing House for the settlement of hedging transactions.

Chapter 10

Aircraft Leasing

A lease is a contract whereby the owner of an asset (the lessor) grants to another party (the lessee) the exclusive right to the use of the asset for an agreed period, in return for the periodic payment of rent. Leases may be for houses, offices, telephones, cars trucks or computers. In this chapter, the focus will be on aircraft, although there is no difference in principle with the arrangements for aircraft and any other asset.

Leasing should not be confused with hire purchase, which also features periodic payments from the user to the owner of the asset. The key difference between the two is that hire purchase agreements are essentially a deferred payment mechanism for the user eventually to own the asset. This could be over a five-year period for a fax or photocopy machine. Since the intention is to own the asset after a few years, the tax benefits of ownership can be used by the asset operator from the outset. It is this ownership feature that distinguishes hire purchase from leasing.

An aircraft lease is a contract between a lessor and a lessee such that the lessee:

- Selects the aircraft specifications.
- Makes specified payments to the lessor for an obligatory period.
- Is granted exclusive use of the aircraft for that period.
- Does not own the aircraft at any time during the lease term.

The lessor could be a bank or specialist leasing company, or it could be a company set up by high tax-paying investors seeking capital allowances to offset against their income, thereby reducing their tax payments. The lessee will normally be an airline.

The airline may or may not have an option to acquire the leased aircraft, or share in the proceeds from the sale of the aircraft at the end of the lease term. Certain characteristics of a lease follow from these broad definitions:

- The lessor cannot terminate the lease provided the lessee meets the conditions specified.
- The lessor is not responsible for the suitability of the aircraft to the lessee's business.
- The lease may be extended at the end of the obligatory period for a further period.

The advantages of leasing to the airline are:

- Volume discounts for aircraft purchase can be passed on to airline (particularly attractive to smaller airlines).
- The conservation of an airline's working capital and credit capacity.
- The provision of up to 100 per cent of finance, with no deposits or pre-payments (up to 33 per cent of the cost of the aircraft paid in advance to

manufacturers, or 15 per cent of the cost required by banks to be paid by the airline as a condition of loan finance).
- Shifting the obsolescence risk of aircraft to lessor (shorter term leases).
- No aircraft trading experience needed.
- The possibility of excluding lease finance from the balance sheet (see Appendix 2.2 at the end of Chapter 2 for more on this).

Possible disadvantages could be:

- A higher cost than, say, debt finance for purchase.
- The profit from eventual sale of the aircraft going to the lessor (as title holder).
- Higher gearing than, say, purchase with equity finance.
- Aircraft specification not tailor-made for lessee airline (short-term leases).

Leasing is clearly advantageous to manufacturers and lessors, since it increases opportunities for business. The documentation for leasing is usually simpler than debt or equity financing. The greatest disadvantage is the risk that insufficient care will be taken of the equipment.

The fastest growth in leasing was during the 1980s, especially the second half. In 1980, the share of commercial jets owned or managed by operating lessors was around 4 per cent, climbing to almost 18 per cent in 1990, and to 28 per cent by 2004.[1] The number of airlines either leasing all or some of their fleet rose from 59 per cent in 1986 to 85 per cent in 1999, and those with an all leased fleet from 46 airlines (15 per cent) in 1986 to 278 airlines (40 per cent) in 1999 (Figure 10.1).

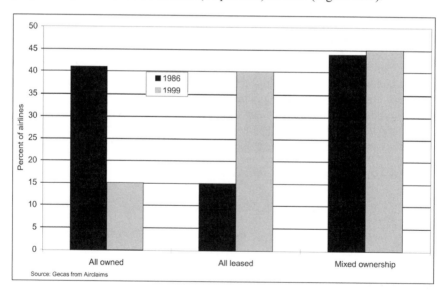

Figure 10.1   Number of airlines owning and leasing aircraft

Source: GECAS, from Airclaims

---

1   Ashcroft, Robert (2005) *A Powerful Force in Commercial Aviation*, UBS Investment Research Q-Series.

Table 10.1 gives the share of the total fleet acquired through finance or operating leases for some of the largest world airlines. Data were not available for some of the larger Asian airlines, and others did not break down finance leased aircraft. Operating leases accounted for 35.3 per cent of the fleet for all regions combined, with a slightly higher share for the North American airlines. Finance leases have been popular in the US, but the European airlines find this an attractive form of finance, especially BA (mainly through Japanese Leveraged Leases) and Iberia.

Of the LCCs included in Table 10.1, easyJet and Air Asia both make considerable use of operating leases, and to a lesser extent JetBlue in the US. Of the network carriers, Iberia also has a high share of its fleet on operating lease, as does Continental in the US and Air New Zealand in the Asia/Pacific region.

Table 10.1   Leased aircraft shares by region for selected airlines

	Total	% finance lease	% operating lease
AMR (end 12/2005)	1,001	9.4	24.0
Delta (end 12/2005)	649	6.6	31.3
Continental (end 12/2005)	630	0.5	76.5
Northwest (end 12/2005)	580	1.0	43.3
United (end 12/2005)	460	12.4	37.6
Southwest (end 12/2005)	445	2.0	18.9
JetBlue (end 12/2005)	92	0.0	33.7
Total/average US	3,857	5.5	38.0
Lufthansa (end 12/2005)	432	5.1	16.4
Air France-KLM (end 3/2006)	397	16.9	36.8
British Airways (end 3/2006)	284	0.0	27.1
Alitalia (end 12/2005)	175	6.9	24.0
Iberia (end 12/2005)	149	9.4	59.7
EasyJet (end 9/2005)	109	0.0	83.5
Ryanair (end 3/2005)	87	0.0	14.9
Total/average Europe	1,633	12.2	32.4
Qantas (end 6/2005)	200	*n/a*	26.0
Air China (end 6/2004)	136	36.8	16.9
SIA Group (end 3/2006)	118	4.2	21.2
Cathay Pacific (end 12/2005)	96	56.3	13.5
Air New Zealand (end 6/2005)	89	*n/a*	49.4
Air Asia (end 2005)	26	0.0	84.6
Total/average Asia/Pacific	665	*n/a*	26.9

Source: Airline annual reports

10.1   Finance Lease

Finance leases accounted for around 30 per cent of newer jet aircraft financing in 1997 for the world, and around one-half of financing for North American airlines, but has declined significantly since then due to the withdrawal of Japanese Leveraged

Leases and the decline of US tax leases. A finance lease can be for between 10 and 26 years but more likely for a period of at least 10–12 years. It is non-cancellable, or cancellable only with a major penalty. The lessor expects to gain a normal profit on the asset from one airline through a combination of rentals, tax benefits and conservative residual value assumptions, without being involved in, or necessarily having an understanding of, the lessee's business. The lessee is likely to have a purchase option at the end of the lease term, at fair market value, for a percentage of the cost, or for a nominal (very low) price.

The normal risks and benefits of ownership are the responsibility of the lessee, although they are not the legal owner of the aircraft at any time during the lease period (title may or may not be eventually transferred to the lessee). Because the lease period is for the major part of the aircraft's life, finance leases are often called *full pay-out* leases. It follows that the lessee is responsible for repairs, maintenance and insurance of the aircraft, and that the risk of obsolescence lies with the lessee. The lessor does not consider the residual value of the aircraft at the end of the lease period important, and does not need to be technically knowledgeable about the aircraft or airline business.

The lessor may demand that the lessee pay a specified number of rentals on the first day of the lease payment, with a corresponding rental holiday at the end of the lease term.

10.1.1   Japanese Leveraged Leases

A leveraged lease is one where the aircraft is acquired using a large amount of debt finance and a small amount of equity finance. Equity is normally between 20 and 40 per cent of the total value of the aircraft, resulting in high gearing and thus high risk and potential reward for the equity investors. Equity investors are prepared to accept this risk, often because they are able to capture significant tax benefits from having title to the asset.

One form of leveraged lease is the Japanese Leveraged Lease (JLL). This involves the establishment of a special purpose company to acquire the aircraft, with between 20 per cent and 30 per cent of the finance coming from equity provided by Japanese investors, and the remainder from a bank or group of banks. The equity share must exceed 20 per cent to satisfy the Japanese tax authorities.[2] The aircraft is acquired by an airline, immediately sold to the special purpose company, and leased back under normal finance lease terms for 10 years (narrow bodied aircraft) or 12 years (wide bodies). This approach permits the airline to claim tax allowances from the tax authorities in its own country, and the Japanese investors also to claim full tax allowances on the same asset. This is known as 'double dipping'. It clearly gives substantial benefits to both lessee and lessor, and results in the airline having a very attractive cost of finance. The discounted present value of the allowances could amount to between 6–11 per cent of the cost of the aircraft.

---

2   One group of Japanese investors, who have in the past supplied such equity, has been Petinko (Pinball) game operators, having few capital investments which can be used to reduce their taxable profits.

Four other conditions must be fulfilled: the aircraft must be new, the rental payments must not vary over the lease term, the lease must not exceed 120 per cent of the depreciation life, and the final payment from the lessee must not be greater than 45 per cent of the original value of the aircraft.

In 1990, approximately US$9 billion, or about 20 per cent of the value of all aircraft deliveries, was financed by JLLs. By 1992, this had halved to around $4.5 billion.[3] In 1994, $4.9 billion was arranged, followed by $3.7 billion in 1995. The largest equity providers and arrangers in 1995/1996 were Orix Aviation (15.7 per cent of the total), NBB (10.8 per cent) and Fuji (10.3 per cent).[4] The leading JLL borrowers in 1995/1996 were All Nippon Airways ($652 million), BA ($411 million) and United ($403 million).

The attractiveness of this form of financing can be seen in the cost of borrowing: the margin over LIBOR has ranged from a low of just under 30 basis points (0.3 per cent) for British Airways in 1995 to 120 basis points for China Southern in 1993.[5] To put this in perspective, the inter-bank rates for lending between major international banks are around 22–23 basis points over LIBOR.

However, JLLs were not available to any airline. Japanese equity investors prefer well-known airlines, preferably those with government guarantees or high credit ratings such as British Airways, KLM or Lufthansa.

Unfortunately, at the end of the 1990s, JLLs were withdrawn, and an attractive source of finance that was made considerable use of by airlines such as BA disappeared. Japanese Operating Leases were then offered with similar, albeit not so large, advantages, but these did not fill the gap left by JLLs. JLLs were originally encouraged as a way of exporting the foreign currency generated by Japan's large trade surpluses; these surpluses have recently disappeared, and so there was less need to encourage these and other ways of capital exports.

10.1.2 US Leveraged Leases

Financial leases at favourable rates have also been available in other countries, such as the US and in recent years Germany. US based leveraged leases provide the maximum benefits for deals relating to aircraft based and registered in that country. However, foreign airlines had been able to make use of the US Foreign Sales Corporation (FSC) provisions, which were designed to foster exports of US manufactured aircraft. Tax exemptions were available on foreign generated lease income for FSCs, as long as the aircraft has at least a 50 per cent US content, and at least 50 per cent of the flight miles operated by the aircraft are outside the USA. FSCs were, however, quite costly in terms of documentation and administration, and only high value aircraft, such as JAL's B747-400s, could support these costs. Lease terms ranged between 10 and 20 years, with typical terms for aircraft leased to non-US airlines of between 12 and 15 years. FSC's were subsequently outlawed, following EU country claims to the World Trade Organization that they provided

---

3 *Airfinance Journal* (1994), No. 160, p. 22.

4 *Airfinance Journal* (1996), *Where on Earth Is the Slump?*, May.

5 *Airfinance Journal* (1994), No. 160, pp. 26–27.

unfair subsidies. However, they were soon replaced by a similar cross-border lease structure, the Extra Territorial Income (ETI).

Before the development of FSCs, US leases required a lessee to be placed between the US lessor and the non-US lessee. This was necessary to avoid the provisions of the 1984 Pickle Bill (named after its sponsor, a Texas congressman named Pickle), which disallowed investment tax credits for property leased to non-US taxpayers. These leases were called 'Pickle leases', but were not economically very attractive.

10.1.3   European Leveraged Leases

The German aircraft lease market increased rapidly over the three years to 1996 to reach more than $1.5 billion. These leases have been similar in structure to JLLs, and their growth has been dependent on the high marginal tax rates that also apply in Japan. Air France, Cathay Pacific and Lufthansa were the three leading lessees in 1995/1996, and a high percentage of leases involved Airbus aircraft (65 per cent).[6] Of the other European aircraft finance lease markets, the next largest was the UK with only around $0.5 million of aircraft financed a year.

10.1.4   Extendible Operating Leases

Finance leases, with walk-away options at various break-points, appear to be more like operating leases (*see below*), but the intention of both lessor and lessee is generally to pay off the full cost of the aircraft. An example of this was British Airways' extendible operating leases on their Boeing 767s, where the airline could walk away at no cost after 5, 7, 9, 11, and 13-year breakpoints. Manufacturer's guarantees were used to underwrite the aircraft values at each breakpoint.

A slightly different example was United Airlines' lease of 29 A320-200 aircraft from Airbus. These are on 22- to 24-year operating leases, which are cancellable on 11 months' notice during the initial 10 years of the lease period. As operating leases, these are not placed on United's balance sheet. United also benefits from the early termination option in the assessment of the airline by the ratings agencies (*e.g.*, S&P and Moody).

10.2   Operating Lease

Although the dividing line between finance and operating leases has recently become more blurred, but the key features of an operating lease are:

*   It allows airlines to respond rapidly to changes in market conditions.
*   It is of shorter term, usually between one and seven years, or an average of five years, and can be returned to the lessor at relatively short notice and without major penalty.
*   The lessee cannot choose the aircraft specification (except for good customer first user of aircraft).

---

6   *Airfinance Journal*, (May 1996), pp. 31–32.

- An airline gains the use of an aircraft without the obligation to pay off its full cost.
- The lessor expects to profit from either selling or re-leasing the aircraft.
- The lessee is usually responsible for the maintenance of the aircraft but often has to pay to the lessor a maintenance reserve.

The aircraft's residual value is important to the lessor, and is a key factor in determining the lease rentals that can be offered. The cost of re-marketing or placing the aircraft with another lessor also needs to be considered in rate negotiations, given that aircraft may be placed with at least three different operators over their lifetime. Operating lease rentals vary quite significantly over the economic cycle, with lessors often accepting a short-term drop in monthly rentals to avoid re-marketing or even parking aircraft.

Operating leases may have a purchase option for the lessee to buy the aircraft at the end of the lease term, sometimes at a fair market value and sometimes at a stated price. There will almost definitely be an option for the lessee to extend the lease for a further two to four period.

The lessor assumes the risks of aircraft obsolescence and needs to know the aircraft and airline business (and ensure that maintenance and overhaul is carried out to high standards). There are specialist asset management firms that take care of the technical management of operating leases for the aircraft owners. They can also deal with the commercial side of the business (rent collection, contracts, *etc.*) as well as re-marketing, repossession, placing and sales. Examples of such firms are Airstream International, ALM, Fortis, Babcock and Brown and Pembroke Capital. The last two jointly manage the ALPs securitisation portfolio of aircraft described in the next chapter.[7] With the increasing trend towards the separation of ownership and operation of aircraft, firms like these have an assured future. The lease rental in the example in Table 10.2 was largely fixed. An alternative might assume an initial monthly rental of $300,000 based on the six-month US dollar LIBOR of, say, 6 per cent. This rental would be adjusted up or down every six months, depending on LIBOR on the revision date.

The return condition of the aircraft is very important to an operating lessor, since they will wish to place it with another operator with the minimum of delay. For example, if an aircraft had been delivered to an airline fresh from its 'C' check (an intermediate maintenance check on an airframe that is required every 3,500–4,500 hours of operation), the lessee would be expected to return it in a similar condition at the end of the lease term. A fund, or maintenance reserve, is usually established for the major overhauls (or 'D' checks), which the lessee will contribute to, and out of which any such work that needs to be performed will be paid. For better risk airlines, this would be dealt with at the end of the lease term.

---

7   *Aircraft Economics*, No. 28, November/December 1996.

Table 10.2   Typical operating lease terms

Aircraft type:	2 used Airbus A320-200 aircraft, each with IAE V2500-A1 engines
Delivery date:	April 1996
Lease term:	Three years from delivery date
Lease rental:	Payable monthly in advance to a bank account nominated by the Lessor, in accordance with the following schedule:

Months 1–9	US$300,000; fixed
Months 10–12	US$1,000 per block hour
Months 13–24	US$350,000; fixed
Months 25–36	US$400,000; fixed

Security deposit:	US$900,000 per aircraft
Maintenance reserves:	On the 10th day of each month, the Lessee shall pay a Maintenance reserve in respect of the hours operated during the previous month.

Airframe:	US$125.00 per block hour
Engines:	US$150.00 per engine, per block hour
APU:	US$30.00 per block hour
Landing gear:	US$10.00 per block hour

Delivery condition:	On delivery, the aircraft shall conform to the following conditions:

Configuration:	180Y Galleys: G1 and G5
Toilets:	LA, LE and LD
Engines:	Approx. 6,500 hours and 3,250 cycles
Airframe:	Approx. 6,500 hours and 3,250 cycles
IFE:	Lessor shall install at its own expense a Sony Transcom IFE system. Lessee shall pay lessor additional monthly rental equivalent to 1.5 per cent of the total installed cost of such system.

The lessee will have to comply with any airworthiness directives and service bulletins that are issued by the regulatory authorities or manufacturers. These will usually require a hangar inspection and sometimes modification of airframe or components. Since such work adds value to the aircraft, the cost is often shared between the two parties, sometimes once a certain threshold has been reached.

Other contract conditions required by the lessor will be a security deposit, which will depend on the creditworthiness of the lessee, and could amount to 1–2 months' worth of rentals. If the lease terms are complied with, then this money will be returned in full. Interest on the deposit (and the maintenance reserve) is subject to negotiation, and may be applied as part of the rental payment. Approval would be required for sub-leasing the aircraft, and the use and installation of other equipment on the aircraft.[8] The terms of the aircraft hull insurance would also be reviewed by the lessor

Operating lessors have usually signed contracts for most of the aircraft that they will take delivery of over the next two years, but after that the orders are more speculative. For example, in March 2000, ILFC had contracts for the lease of all of its 67 aircraft to be delivered in 2001, 62 out of the 66 aircraft arriving in 2002, 25 out of the 68 aircraft expected in 2003, 5 out of 67 in 2004, and four out of the remaining 220 deliveries.[9]

Many airlines in Russia and the CIS countries have had to rely on operating leases to obtain western aircraft, due to the problems with export credits and debt finance. Few of these countries have the aircraft registers, legal and accounting systems which satisfy western lenders. Even operating leases run into problems: ILFC leased a B757-200 to Baikal Airlines in June 1994 for a five-year term, but the aircraft was returned to the lessor in summer 1996 because of the government's insistence that $16 million were paid in backdated import tax.[10]

Start-up airlines in both the US and Europe also tend to take aircraft on operating lease: the Colorado based airline, Western Pacific Airlines, obtained its first 12 B737-300s on five- to ten-year operating lease, while the UK start-up Debonair leased their seven BAe 146s from US Air Leasing for a short initial 16-month period, with power by the hour maintenance on airframe and engines.[11] More recently, both easyJet and Air Asia both expanded rapidly using operating leases.

10.3   Japanese Operating Lease (JOL)

Japanese Operating Leases (JOL) effective took over from the Japanese Leveraged Leases (JLL) that were discontinued at the end of the 1990s (see 10.1 above). The starting point for both is the demand from Japanese investors for tax benefits from capital investments, the aircraft providing a convenient vehicle. The first crucial difference between the two is that the aircraft is placed with the airline on an operating and not a finance lease, with a maximum term of 10 years for narrow bodied and 12 years for wide bodied aircraft. The second that stems from the first is that tax benefits are only available in Japan and not to the aircraft operator (apart from the rentals). However, the Japanese investors obtain generous tax write-offs such that an attractive lease rental is possible (although not as attractive as for the JLL). JOLs took off in 2001, and were running at around US$2–3 billion a year for the next five years, with a range of operators benefiting from them (both network carriers and smaller LCCs).

As with the JLLs, it seemed possible by the end of 2005 that the Japanese permissive treatment of JOLs might be terminated, as occurred with JLLs in 1999.

---

8   Margo, R. (1996) Aircraft leasing: the airline's objectives, *Air and Space Law*, Vol. XXI, No. 4/5.

9   International Lease Finance Corporation, SEC, *Form 10-K filing for fiscal year ended December 31, 2000.*

10   *Airfinance Journal*, November (1996).

11   *Airfinance Journal*, November (1996).

10.4   Wet Lease

A wet lease is the leasing of an aircraft complete with cockpit and cabin crew, and other technical support. The lessor is usually responsible for maintenance and hull insurance. This type of lease is generally for a very short period, say for operations over a number of months or summer season. Haj pilgrimage flights are often operated on this basis. The aircraft retains the paint scheme and logo of the lessor, although a temporary sticker can be used to show the lessee's name on the fuselage. A wet lease is often described as an ACMI lease (*i.e.*, an aircraft, crew, maintenance and insurance lease), although in this case the aircraft is generally considered to be an integral part of the lessee's fleet.

Quite often the lessor will provide only the aircraft and some of the operational support services. For example, the lessee may wish to use their own cabin crew because of language requirements. This can be described as a 'damp lease,' the name given to a lease that falls between a dry lease and a wet lease.

A wet lease has many similarities with the chartering of an aircraft, the key difference being the fact that the lessee would have the necessary operating licenses and permits, and operate flights with the wet leased aircraft under its own flight designator.[12] A chartered aircraft would operate under the designator of the owner/operator or the aircraft.

Since 1990 a number of wet leasing specialists have established themselves, notably Atlas Air (which spent six months in Chapter 11 in 2004 following the post 9/11 downturn) and Gemini in the US and Air Atlanta Icelandic. These generally operate freighter aircraft and try to negotiate two- to three-year contracts, although two to 12 months is the norm, possibly because of opposition from regulatory authorities to longer wet lease contracts with foreign registered aircraft.[13] The longer term contract is likely to include painting the aircraft in the lessee's livery (*e.g.*, Atlas Air's lease to British Airways World Cargo), and the agreement is based on a price per block hour operated with a minimum number of hours charged.[14]

10.5   Sale and Leaseback

Sales and leaseback occurs when airlines which own aircraft often decide to realise the capital value of the aircraft, but at the same time continue to operate them. This may be because they have cash flow problems, but it may also be for the following reasons:

- To meet capital requirements for new aircraft or investments.
- To realise the current value of an aircraft that is likely to be retired in a few years' time, especially when the market price of the aircraft will probably decline significantly over that period.

---

12 This is important for the lessor, since the owner of the flight code (lessee) is invoiced for charges such as airport and en-route.

13 The UK CAA required Atlas Air to lease their B747 freighter aircraft to BA through a majority UK owned company, Global Supply Systems.

14 Endres, G. (2006) Surrogate supply, *Airline Business*, July.

The typical duration for such deals is three to five years. The other party involved (the lessor) is likely to be a bank, which will structure the lease to gain tax benefits. The risk to the bank is relatively low, first because the term is short and second because the lessee will probably be a good credit risk airline, perhaps one that is already well known to the bank.

In 1990, British Airways sold 20 B737-200s at what in retrospect was a very advantageous price ($6–7 million more per aircraft than the market value six years later) and leased them back. Ten of the same aircraft type were sold and leased back for six years by Varig, and 11 by Canadian International for five and a half years.

Appendix 10.1   Lease Rental Calculations

The formula for calculating lease rentals varies according to whether the payment is in advance or arrears, although the structure is similar to the one for term loans:

$$\text{Periodic rental payment} = PV \div a$$

where: PV   =   the present value, or equipment cost

a   =   the rental factor, which for payments in *arrears* is:

$$\frac{1-(1+i)^{-n}}{i}$$

And for *payments in advance*:

$$a = \frac{1-(1+i)^{-(n-x)}}{i} + x$$

where: x   =   number of rentals payable in advance

n   =   number of payments in lease term

i =   interest rate per period

Assuming the Equipment Cost (PV) is $10 million

Lease term = 10 years, or n = 120

Lease or interest rate = 12.5 per cent, or i = 12.5 ÷ (12 × 100)

The rental factor (a) for payment in arrears is:

$$\frac{1-(1+0.010417)^{-120}}{0.010417} = 68.317$$

Thus, the Monthly Rental Amount = $10,000,000 ÷ $68.317 = $146,376

Using the formula for payments in advance (x = 1) gives a monthly rental of $144,867.

Appendix 10.2   Lease *vs* Buy Decision

Major considerations in the choice of financing for the acquisition of an aircraft are the cost, taxation issues, and flexibility. If the purchase option is selected, then a term loan is generally the instrument used by the majority of airlines outside the US. The Eurobond market can be cheaper than a term loan, but is only available to household names of high credit rating. US public bond markets are accessed by US carriers, with high risk, low credit rating airlines issuing high interest bonds to investors (also called *junk* bonds).

For term loans, in addition to the interest charges, the airline must also pay the bank for the preparation of the loan documents and commitment fees. Underwriting fees are also payable for bond issues.

Equity finance may be considered, either to expand the capital base of an airline in line with increased turnover, or when other avenues are not available, for example when the level of gearing is already too high to obtain loan finance at reasonable cost. Equity finance may be raised through a private transaction, *i.e.*, when a 100 per cent government owner subscribes more capital. This may be less expensive than a public offer of shares which may subsequently be quoted on a stock market.

Leasing, whether for short or longer periods is becoming increasingly popular, not always where an airline has no other sources of finance available.

Whether an airline leases or purchases outright an aircraft an evaluation will be made of the expected return from the investment, from projections of revenues and costs. If the results are positive, then alternative methods of finance will be considered by calculating the net present value of the financing costs for each option:

- Calculate the NPV of the lease alternative.
- Calculate the NPV of the buy alternative.
- Choose the alternative with the lowest NPV cost.

Simplified example:

Aircraft cost:	US$10,000,000
Acquisition date:	31 December 2000
Remaining asset life:	5 years
Lease terms:	US$ 2.8 million *per annum* in arrears
Airline bank borrowing rate:	13 per cent *per annum*
Airline financial year end:	31 December
Airline Pays no Corporation Tax	
'Buy alternative' financing:	100 per cent from retained earnings

From the table below it can be seen that the airline would be marginally better off by leasing than buying. The actual calculation would be much more complex, and would include taxation issues, purchase progress payments, commitment fees, residual values, *etc*.

Date	Rentals (US$)	Discount factor	PV (US$)
31/12/2001	2,800,000	0.885	2,478,000
31/12/2002	2,800,000	0.783	2,192,400
31/12/2003	2,800,000	0.693	1,940,400
31/13/2004	2,800,000	0.613	1,716,400
31/12/2005	2,800,000	0.543	1,520,400
Aggregate present value of rentals			9,847,600
Aircraft purchase price			− 10,000,000
Difference			152,400

Tax paying lessee

An evaluation for a tax paying lessee must take into account the delay between the payment of interest or rental and the cash benefit of tax relief. The following formula derives an acceptable approximation (for small values of n) for the after tax discount rate from the pre-tax rate:

$$R_2 = R_1 - \frac{R_1 * T}{(1 + R_1 * T)^n}$$

where: R_1 = Lessee's pre-tax borrowing rate (13 per cent)

R_2 = Lessee's after tax rate

T = Rate of corporation tax (35 per cent)

n = Delay of tax payment in years

Assuming the average tax delay is 18 months from the mid-point of the year, R_2 is calculated from the above formula to be 8.74 per cent. The tax credit has been determined by assuming that the asset could be written off over four years, with the airline paying corporation tax at 35 per cent. The discount factor in the NPV calculation is shown on the opposite page.

Thus, the difference in the present values of the buy and lease alternative in the table below show the former to be more costly by $289,265. With accelerated tax allowances, purchasing the aircraft would become the cheaper option.

These examples have shown how increasing complexity can be introduced into the evaluation. On the purchase side, advance payments to manufacturers would also need to be introduced, as well as alternative financing options (see Appendix 5.1 for term loan calculations). This would require a breakdown of the annual periods into quarters or even months, and the use of computerised spreadsheets.

Date	Rental or cost ($)	Tax credit (@ 35 per cent)	Total net benefits ($)	Discount factor	Present value of net benefits ($)
Purchase:					
31/12/2000	− 10,000,000	—	− 10,000,000	1	− 10,000,000
31/12/2001	—	875,000	875,000	0.92	805,000
31/12/2002	—	875,000	875,000	0.846	740,250
31/12/2003	—	875,000	875,000	0.778	680,750
31/12/2004	—	875,000	875,000	0.715	625,625
				NPV =	− 7,148,375
Lease:					
31/12/2000	—		—		—
31/12/2001	− 2,800,000	—	− 2,800,000	0.92	− 2,576,000
31/12/2002	− 2,800,000	980,000	− 1,820,000	0.846	− 1,539,720
31/12/2003	− 2,800,000	980,000	− 1,820,000	0.778	− 1,415,960
31/12/2004	− 2,800,000	980,000	− 1,820,000	0.715	− 1,301,300
31/12/2005	− 2,800,000	980,000	− 1,820,000	0.658	− 1,197,560
31/12/2006	—	980,000	980,000	0.605	592,900
				NPV =	− 7,437,640

Chapter 11

Aircraft Securitisation

Securitisation, which started in the US in the mid-1970s, is the conversion of identifiable and predictable cash flows into securities. The advantages of this to lenders are:

- Risk is spread over a number of lenders.
- Risk may be spread over a number of world regions.
- Greater size reduces costs of administration.
- The loan or asset is removed from the balance sheet.

For the borrower, the cost of finance would be significantly lower than would otherwise be the case.

Securitisation involves the re-packaging of cash flows or receivables into securities which are then sold to investors. This is often done in different tranches, each tranche having different rights and risks attached. Higher credit ratings, and thus lower borrowing costs, can be achieved than would be possible for the separate parties involved in each lease or mortgage. Ratings are given to each of the securities by agencies such as Standard & Poor's or Moody, thereby making them more saleable to institutions. The cash flows could be short-term, for example with the sale of accounts receivables from travel agents, or on credit cards. They could be medium-term, with the sale of five- to ten-year aircraft operating lease or vehicle loan receivables. Or they could be long-term, with the sale of home mortgage receivables of loan principal and interest.

In the case of house mortgages, the loan portfolio is sold to a third party company by the bank that originally provided the finance. This bank would continue to earn fees from the management of the portfolio, and the loans would be removed from the balance sheet to allow it to expand its business.

There has, however, been some debate about whether securitised assets should be removed from the balance sheet, even though substantially all of the risks and rewards of owning the assets has been transferred (sold) to another company. A London law firm, Freshfields, described securitisation as:

> The packaging of assets, backed by appropriate credit enhancement and liquidity support, into a tradable form through an issue of highly rated securities, which are secured on the assets and serviced from the cash flows which they yield.[1]

---

1   Verchère, I. (1994) *The Air Transport Industry in Crisis*, EIU, p. 119.

Aircraft finance ranges from the traditional structures which rely on airline credit to those which rely on aircraft value. As one goes from left to right along the spectrum shown in Figure 11.1, the financing is less related to the airline's corporate credit rating and more to the aircraft asset risk. On the far right, the securitisations are not linked at all to an airline's credit rating.[2]

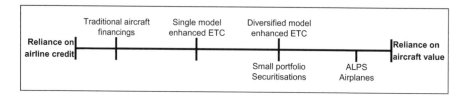

Figure 11.1   Aircraft financing spectrum

Source: Standard and Poor's

The remainder of this chapter will describe the securitisation of aircraft and similar financing structures, which has important implications for the long-term financing of the industry. They also provided one of the means for Guinness Peat Aviation (GPA) to recover from near bankruptcy (see 5.3.3).

11.1   Equipment Trust Certificates

The Equipment Trust Certificate (ETC) is often described as a securitisation. However, the ETC is created more for tax reasons than for the spreading of risk and lowering borrowing costs. It would typically include only one or two aircraft.

A trustee issues equipment trust certificates to investors, and uses the funds raised to buy the aircraft, which is then leased to the airline which ordered it. It is, however, a form of secured debt financing, and not a true lease since the aircraft is ultimately owned by the airline. It would provide protection from airline bankruptcy in the same way as securitisation, but so would secured debt finance.

The certificates can generally be sold to institutions at a slightly higher rating than that of the airline. They often have the added attraction of being tradable.

A modified version of the, ETC is the Enhanced Equipment Trust Certificate (EETC), which looks more like the aircraft securitisations described below, and is further to the right in terms of relying more on asset risk in Figure 11.1. Rather than selling one type of certificate or bond, the EETC divides these into different categories, each of which has a different risk/reward profile in terms of security and access to lease rental cash flows. A structure of this type will give the senior (lower risk) certificates a much higher credit rating than under the, ETC. But the essential difference of aircraft ownership between EETC and securitisation still remains, the latter spreading the risk over more than one airline.

---

2   Standard & Poor's, (2001), *Aircraft Securitization Criteria*, www.standardandpoors. com/ratings, pp. 3–4.

The EETC was developed in the US in the 1990s as a means for non-investment grade airlines to source funds using investment grade ratings, with the added advantage of giving more protection to the owner of the aircraft in the event of Chapter 11 bankruptcy.

An example of an EETC was the refinancing of 13 A320s operated by Northwest Airlines, and originally financed by Airbus. This involved the sale by a trustee of $352m of notes of four classes, with the highest class rated A by Standard & Poor's. The notes are secured by the 13 aircraft, which are leased back from the trust/partnership by Northwest.[3]

More recently, American Airlines refinanced its acquisition of TWA with a $1.3 billion EETC. This offered five classes of securities or notes, with the A class rated AAA and A2 by S&P and Moody respectively. The initial loan to value ratio for the top class was 41 per cent, giving a large cushion in case the underlying aircraft needed to be sold in a weak market. The lowest class, the D notes, were rated BBB/Baa2, and had a loan to value ratio of 66.5 per cent. Maturities of the notes ranged from seven to 20 years, and the coupons (interest rates) ranged from 142 basis points (1.42 per cent) over prime rate to 270 basis points. The collateral was 32 MD-11s, 10 B737-800s and four B777s, all belonging to TWA.[4]

Outside the US, EETCs are still rare, with only Qantas and Iberia using them by the middle of 2001, the latter denominated in euros. Iberia later issued Iberbond, 2004, a complex deal that combined an EETC structure with Japanese Operating Leases. It was secured against 20 A319/A320/A321 aircraft valued at US$933 million, and the debt was denominated in a mixture of US dollars and Euros.

11.2   ALPS 92-1 Securitisation

The first international securitisation of aircraft was offered by Guinness Peat Aviation (GPA) in mid-1992, with the help of Citicorp Investment Bank and Lehman Brothers International. A total of 14 aircraft valued at US$380 million were leased to the the various airlines at the time of launch of ALPS 92-1, with their share of aircraft appraisal value indicated in brackets as seen in Table 11.1.[5]

The North and Central America regional share of aircraft value was 28.5 per cent, the European share 42.2 per cent and the Asian share 29.4 per cent. All except Malev and China Southern are now majority owned by private interests, although BWIA, Air Jamaica and Philippine Airlines were government controlled at the time of the issue.

The portfolio of aircraft consisted of six B737s (various series), one B757, one B767ER, one B747, 2 MD-82/83, one A300, one A320 and one Fokker 100. This gave a spread of manufacturers and sizes, but not of range capability (only two long-haul aircraft).

---

3   *Transport Finance* (13 January 1995).

4   *Airfinance Journal* (June 2001), 18.

5   Radley, A.B. (1994), *Future Strategies in Aircraft Leasing*, MSc Thesis, Cranfield University, September.

The assets were sold to a Jersey-based special purpose company, which was financed by equity and $380 million worth of bonds (the senior debt portion of which was rated AA by Standard and Poor) to be repaid from the cash flows generated from the lease payments, plus the proceeds of any subsequent sales of aircraft in the portfolio. Equity investors would get 10–12 per cent semi-annual dividends, plus a share in any residual value of the aircraft at maturity. Investors in the company were various European financial institutions, principally banks (39 per cent), fund managers (32 per cent) and insurance companies (16 per cent).

Table 11.1   ALPS 92-1 aircraft portfolio

North America:	Canadian (7.4%)
Caribbean:	Air Jamaica (6.0%), BWIA (5.4%)
Latin America:	TAESA (9.7%)
Europe:	Sun Express (5.5%), Malev (5.6%), Istanbul Airlines (5.%), British Midland (5.7%), Spanair (15.0%, Portugalia (4.6%)
Asia:	Asiana (5.6%), China Southern (5.0%), Philippine Airlines (13.4%), Korean Air (5.4%)

Table 11.2   ALPS 92-1 bond amounts and interest rates

	Amount $ million	Interest Rate
Subclass *A*-1 Certificates	208.4	7.75% fixed
Subclass *A*-2 Certificates	104.2	6 million LIBOR + 0.8%
Subclass *A*-3 Certificates	70.4	3 million LIBOR + 0.7%
Class M Certificates	34.0	6 million LIBOR + 6.1%
Class B Certificates	104.0	12.00%
Total	521.0	

Source: ALPS 92-1 Offering Circular

GPA was appointed to provide administrative and management services to the company for a fee of 0.15 per cent of the initial purchase price of the aircraft. They would also provide support in the form of re-marketing and re-leasing the aircraft.

11.3   ALPS 94-1 Securitisation

GPA's second aircraft securitisation in 1994 packaged 18 aircraft valued at US$980 million. Aircraft included in the portfolio had a low average age, and the success of the sale was helped by the upturn in aircraft values and lease rates, although some concern was expressed by potential investors that any forced sale of a number of aircraft at the next downturn might result in low values and losses.

The special purpose company was given more flexibility than under the terms of ALPS 92-1 in selling aircraft to pay down the debt. Aircraft were also required to be sold, once their lease term had expired. If any lessee defaulted, then a new lease and aircraft should be substituted in the portfolio from a designated back-up pool of aircraft.

11.4   Airplanes 96 Securitisation

The main purpose of the Airplanes securitisation in early 1996 was to further downsize GPA and remove just over $4 billion in debt off its balance sheet. The number of aircraft remaining under GPA ownership was reduced by 229 aircraft to 129 (down from its high of 380 in 1993). This left GPA with around $1 billion in debt, secured on individual aircraft in their fleet.

This securitisation dwarfed previous ones in sheer size. The portfolio of 229 aircraft were placed with 83 lessees. The $4 billion in bonds were successfully placed on the market by emphasising the growing attraction of operating leases to both large and small airlines, the spread of risk across regions (see Table 11.3), and the involvement of GE in the management of the leases. Investors would also be totally insulated from any further problems that might be faced by GPA. Morgan Stanley was the bank responsible for selling the bonds, in return for which they earned $20 million in fees (or 0.5 per cent of the total value).

Table 11.3   Airplanes securitisation – Aircraft numbers and values

Lessee region	Number of aircraft	% of total value
Africa	3	0.7
Asia	24	15.0
Australia	4	0.3
Europe	66	34.4
North America	44	17.3
Latin America	75	28.4
Other	4	1.1
Off-lease	9	2.8
Total	229	100.0

Source: Airfinance Journal, July/August 1996

One concern of potential investors in the bonds was the numbers of aircraft involved and the possible affect on aircraft prices, at for example the bottom of the next recession, if even 10 per cent of the total portfolio were offered for sale as a result of a lessee bankruptcy. This was addressed by a greater emphasis of the cash flows from the lease rentals as opposed to the security from aircraft residual values.

As with previous securitisations, efforts were made to give a spread of both regions of operation and of aircraft types. As with ALPS 92-1, the senior bonds were rated AA by Standard & Poor's, ensuring their acceptance by institutional investors.

Table 11.4   Airplanes securitisation – Bond amounts and interest rates

	Initial amount (US $ million)	Interest Rate
Subclass *A*-1 Certificates	850	LIBOR +0.25%
Subclass *A*-2 Certificates	750	LIBOR +0.32%
Subclass *A*-3 Certificates	500	LIBOR +0.47%
Subclass *A*-4 Certificates	200	LIBOR +0.62%
Subclass *A*-5 Certificates	598	LIBOR +0.35%
Class B Certificates	375	LIBOR +1.1%
Class C Certificates	375	8.15%
Class D Certificates	400	10.88%
Total	4,048	

Source: *Airfinance Journal*, July/August 1996

11.5   ALPS 96-1 Securitisation

ALPS 96-1 was the refinancing of the original ALPS 92-1 securitisation which resulted in the withdrawal of GPA and GECAS. GPA was repaid its share of the class M bonds. Babcock and Brown took over as the managers of the portfolio from GPA.[6]

Only one of the original 14 aircraft was replaced:[7] the B737-300 originally leased to the Turkish carrier, Sun Express, was sold for US$25 million at a book loss of $1.6 million. This aircraft was replaced by a B767-300ER belonging to Whirlpool Financial Corporation, which had recently come off lease. Otherwise all the original lessees were unchanged with the exception of an MD 82 which was now leased to TWA (replacing Korean Air) and a B757-200 now with Transwede (replacing TAESA).

---

6   *Airfinance Journal*, (July/August 1996), pp. 20–21.

7   GPA did have problems with a number of other leases, for example in connection with eight DC9s to a Mexican carrier and a number of leases with the Brazilian airline, VASP, but these were not in the portfolio.

The new appraised value of the 14 aircraft was $455 million, compared to the $522 million value under ALPS 92-1. Aircraft like the Airbus A300B4 had seen their value fall from $31 million in 1992 to only $13 million in 1996. The B767-300ER leased to Spanair, however, only declined from $78 million in 1992 to $68 million in 1996.

11.6   More Recent Securitisations (2005/2006)

The first securitisation since 2003 was offered by AerCap (previously debisdebís Airfinance) in September 2005 for US$942 million. This was followed at the end of 2006 by Aviation Capital Group which securitised leases on 74 aircraft to finance its purchase of operating lessor, Boullioun. The ACG Trust III deal raised US$1.86 billion, by issuing a triple A rated *G*-1 tranche ($1.62 billion), an A-rated *B*-1 tranche ($117.5 million) and a tranche ($122.5 million) rated at BBB − (non investment grade). Most of the aircraft portfolio consisted of newer narrow bodied aircraft, with over 50 per cent B737-800s and A320-200s, and an overall average age of only 4.8 years.[8]

Aircastle, a fast growing operating lessor, securitised leases valued at US$560 million in June 2006, in addition to their IPO which raised $194 million to repay debt.

11.7   Conclusions

Securitisation has not been widely used since its establishment at the beginning of the 1990s. If were solely a device for GPA to avoid bankruptcy, then the next major economic downturn may see another impetus to its use. Its future will also clearly depend on future trends in operating leases: will they continue to increase in importance, particularly in areas like Asia, where they have not to date been so popular? This is part of the larger question of the separation of ownership and operation of assets. Next is the question of accounting practice, and whether securitised assets will be removed from balance sheets.

The advantages are persuasive, and centre on the reduced cost of borrowing for airlines: before the ALPS 92-192−1 securitisation, banks had lent GPA 75 per cent of the value of its leases at LIBOR plus 2 per cent. When the leases were securitised, the special purpose company could borrow 87 per cent of their value at LIBOR plus 1.4 per cent.[9]

Possible disadvantages of securitisation are a weakening of the relationship between the lessee and the lessor, as well as the additional workload imposed on the airline as a result of the increased number of parties involved. Second, it might be argued that the contracting out of the monitoring and technical administration tasks to specialist firms might prove to be less thorough than when they were performed by the operating lessors themselves.

---

8   *Airfinance Journal*, February (2006).
9   *Financial Times*, Supplement on International Capital Markets, (10 June 1996).

EETCs, as an alternative form of securitisation not involving operating lessors, look likely to become popular outside the US, and if they took off in other parts of the world they could provide a replacement to JLLs and other taxed based financing.

Chapter 12

Airline Bankruptcy

The term 'bankruptcy' is often limited to personal insolvency, but has become widely used in relation to business failures. Insolvency is the inability of a company to meet its debts as they become due. Creditors may give the company more time to pay, but eventually they may force the company to liquidate what assets it can to meet its debts. This process of liquidation is normally also referred to as bankruptcy. It may be forced by outside creditors, or it may be a voluntary liquidation suggested by directors and agreed by shareholders. The company may cease trading or operating at this point, or it may continue trading while it is re-structured and measures introduced to return at least part of the company to profitability.

Airline bankruptcy, or the risk of bankruptcy, has become more likely with increasing airline privatisation. While government-owned airlines do not generally go bankrupt, even larger privately owned ones do, as was the case with Sabena once it had moved to the private sector. Terrorist and health scares add further instability to an industry that is in any case very cyclical. The airline industry is also characterised by high operational and financial gearing (see Chapter 3). This leads to severe cash shortfalls during periods of unanticipated, sometimes prolonged downturns.

Bankruptcy or the liquidation of an airline clearly involves laying off staff and the stranding of passengers who have completed only one leg of a multi-sector trip. Thus, many countries have legislation to try to re-organise the company, and to continue its operation while this process is undertaken.

It is important to note that most of an airline's assets will probably already be mortgaged or used for security for loans at the time it is close to bankruptcy. This will reduce the possibility of selling assets to raise cash to keep going. Pan American managed to defer bankruptcy by selling off assets such as its New York City tower block offices and route rights, but this was an exception.

The second point is that most of an airline's assets are aircraft, and the owners of these aircraft (lessors) or secured creditors probably prefer to keep those aircraft flying and earning some revenue, rather than to have to re-possess them and try to sell them in a very weak market (a 'fire' or 'distress sale').

The number of privately owned airlines that are susceptible to bankruptcy varies widely throughout the world, with the majority experienced in North America. Bankruptcy laws also differ by country. The next sections examine these by major world region, taking the most prominent airline failures as examples.

12.1 North America

The US Bankruptcy code is designed to avoid the adverse effects of liquidation by giving a company time to reorganise and some protection from creditors during this period. Liquidation ('Chapter 7' of the code) would mean the grounding of aircraft, stranding passengers, cutting off air service to some cities and unemployment.

The code gives a company the chance to file for this protection, known as 'Chapter 11'. In doing so, it is often referred to as Debtor-in-Possession (DIP). When a firm gets to this point, it has generally (but not always) almost depleted its cash reserves, so that finance is needed to continue operations in Chapter 11. Loans are thus sought that are described as DIP financing, and which are accorded higher security than would be available outside Chapter 11. The arguments as to whether the availability of this finance prolongs the reorganisation period and leads to over-investment are summarised in Dahiya *et al.* (2003). They concluded that there was no evidence that this was the case.

The debtors are given more time to come up with a credible business plan than in many other countries. However, creditors need to approve this before the airline can emerge from Chapter 11. Such agreement to the plan discharges the debtor from all debts arising up to the effective date of the plan.

The US bankruptcy code gives companies in Chapter 11 relief from creditors, which includes the deferment of principal and interest payments on lending. This would normally cover payments to operating lessors and those extending certain types of lending secured on aircraft. However, the code's Section 1,110 forces the airline to put right any arrears in rental or related payments and continue paying them, or return the aircraft to the owners (after a grace period). The law was amended in 1994 to strengthen further the rights of these creditors and broaden the scope of transactions that qualify.

The Air Transport Association of America (ATA) has listed all US airlines that went bankrupt since deregulation in 1978. Before that time, bankruptcies were very rare, since the Civil Aeronautics Board tended to prevent this happening by arranging marriages between weak and stronger airlines.

Table 12.1   Key US airline Chapter 11 entry and exit

	Entered	Emerged	Months
Braniff (1)	May-82	Apr 84	23
Continental (1)	Sep-83	Sep-86	36
Eastern	Mar-89	Jan-91	22
Braniff (2)	Sep-89	Nov-89	2
Continental (2)	Dec-90	Apr-93	28
Pan American	Jan-91	Dec-91	11
Midway	Mar-91	Nov-91	8
America West	Jun-91	Aug-94	38
TWA	Feb-92	Nov-93	21
US Airways (1)	Aug 02	Mar 03	7
United	Dec 02	Feb 06	37
US Airways (2)	Sep 04	Sep 05	12

Source: *The evolution of the airline industry*, Morrison and Winston, Brookings, 1995 and Author

Up to the end of 2004, ATA listed 144 airlines that had filed for Chapter 11 (many of which later emerged), and only 14 for Chapter 7 liquidation. The only two sizeable airlines that filed for Chapter 7 (Eastern Airlines and Midway Airlines) had previous already filed for Chapter 11 but emerged. Pan Am had filed for Chapter 11 and not emerged. Most recently, US Airways went into Chapter 11 in August 2002, emerged in March 2003 only to return in September 2004.

The most popular month for declaring bankruptcy was January, followed by March, September and December. These were all winter months when airline cash flow is traditionally weaker. As expected, May, June and July had the fewest declarations since both creditors and airline managements tended to persuade each other that positive summer cash flows might prevent the eventual need for such a drastic step.

The first major US airline to file for Chapter 11 bankruptcy following deregulation was Braniff Airlines. They remained under Chapter 11 protection from May 1982 until acquired by the Hyatt Corporation in April 1984. The name was retained and the airline slimmed down and re-focused on the business market.

Continental Airlines was the next to go in September 1983, and did not emerge until three years later.

A number of studies have investigated the role of Chapter 11 in allowing those airlines with temporary relief from incurring some costs to unfairly lower their prices. Barla and Koo (1999) concluded that Chapter 11 airlines did lower their prices after declaring bankruptcy (by an average of 2.3 per cent). This was possible because of cost reductions of around 4 per cent. However, their rivals that had not yet filed for bankruptcy tended to lower prices by an average of 4.4 per cent. Much larger air fare reductions were clearly evident in markets where they competed with the failing carriers, with the intention of driving them permanently out of business.

Borenstein and Rose (1995) concluded in an earlier study that airlines approaching bankruptcy tend to reduce fares, but rivals' fares are largely unaffected and the price discount disappears after filing for Chapter 11.

Another study (Morrison and Winston, 1995) examined all the examples of Chapter 11 airlines (see table above) that entered bankruptcy between 1983 and 1994. They concluded that the effect of bankrupt carriers on the revenues of other carriers was small. They also found that seriously weakened airlines lose market through loss of image, fear of loss of frequent flyer miles and difficulties in negotiating deals with corporations and large travel agents. This allows the other carriers to raise prices. Whether the subsequent price response fitted the first or second model depended on how healthy the airline was when filing for Chapter 11.

Continental first filed in 1983 when it was not in too bad shape,[1] and the industry lost from having to respond to fare discounting by Continental. The converse was true when Eastern filed in March 1989 and Continental for the second time in 1990.

The same study showed that, of the three largest airlines, Delta had tended to gain revenue as a result of the bankruptcies, United lost the most and American lost less.

---

1   It had apparently not defaulted on any loans and still had $60 million in cash (Gudmundsson, 1998).

What previous studies have not addressed is the extent to which a bankrupt airline's costs are lower that others, as a result of Chapter 11 protection. Any concessions obtained from labour stem either from a voluntary agreement (from fear of shut-down) or by invoking Section 1113c of the code to force cuts from entirely new contracts.[2] Section 1110 limits protection from interest and rental payments on many secured financings, leaving only some financing and capital charges. However, pension contributions are sometimes suspended, giving some cost advantage.

Other criticisms of Chapter 11 have focused on the large professional fees that are incurred.[3] For example, United Airlines' parent company has hired legal, aircraft, lease and management consultants to help with its reorganisation. A fee committee was established just to examine the detailed submissions for reimbursement of fees from advisers representing the various interests (*e.g.*, McKinsey, Babcock and Brown, Deloittes, PriceWaterhouse and KPMG). Its report to the court was over 500 pages long.

A report to the US President and Congress in 1993 proposed that the time limit on Chapter 11 carriers filing reorganisation plans be strictly enforced, and that time limits should also be placed on such airlines accepting or rejecting scarce airport gate leases. By 2004, nothing had changed in this respect, but another proposal on lessor rights has been addressed.[4] This might have gone some way towards meeting the criticism of Weiss and Wruck (1998), whose analysis of the Eastern Airlines bankruptcy concluded that the Chapter 11 process allowed Eastern's value to drop by over 50 per cent because of 'an over-protective court insulated Eastern from market forces and allowed value-destroying operations to continue long after it was clear that Eastern should have been shut down'.

US Airline Stabilization Board

The Air Transportation Safety and System Stabilization Act was introduced on 22 September 2001 to bring some stability to and restore confidence in the US airline industry following the terrorist attacks of 9/11. The Act established the Board to implement its programmes of compensation and loan guarantees. Its membership comprised representatives from the Department of Transportation, the Treasury and the General Accounting Office, as well as the non-partisan Alan Greenspan, the Federal Reserve Board chairman (later replaced by his nominee, Edward Gramlich).

Compensation was paid to air carriers that suffered losses as a direct result of 9/11, including increased insurance premiums. A total of just above US$4.6 billion was paid to 427 carriers. For example, United Airlines received $774 million, American Airlines $694 million and Southwest $283 million.

---

2 The bankruptcy code now makes it more difficult for airlines to terminate labour contracts, following the experience of Continental Airlines in the 1980s.

3 *Change, Challenge and Competition, a Report to the President and Congress by the National Commission to Ensure a Strong Competitive Airline Industry*, (August 1993).

4 *Ibid.*

The Act also gave the Board power to offer guarantees on loans of up to $10 billion. By the middle of 2004, applications had been received for $2.9 billion, with approvals for only $1.6 billion. Approvals were granted to US Airways ($900 million), America West ($379.6 million), ATA Airlines ($148.5 million), Frontier ($63 million), Aloha ($40.5 million) and World Airways ($27 million). Nine airlines had their requests turned down, by far the largest being the $1.1 billion from United Airlines.

The loan guarantees usually came with onerous covenants, including security on all unencumbered assets, satisfactory debt ratio, fixed charge coverage ratio and adequate liquidity. The Board also receives warrants entitling it to purchase common stock in the airline.

The US Airways loan guarantees allowed the carrier to obtain loans with a term of six years, and at a much lower rate of interest than it would otherwise have paid (close to that paid by large banks). There was an annual charge set initially at 4 per cent of the guaranteed amount ($900 million). The Board received 7.635 million warrants that gave it the option to purchase common stock at $7.42 per share (which would give it around 14 per cent of the voting shares).

As at the beginning of 2005, no warrants had been exercised, and so the US airlines were still free of government ownership.

Canada has a close equivalent to the US's Chapter 11: The Companies' Creditors Arrangement Act (CCAA). Air Canada filed for and received protection under CCAA on 1 April 2003. The court appointed Ernst and Young as 'Monitors' whose role was manage the process for the court. Air Canada had been struggling for some time, and had been faced with many of the pressures that US carriers faced, post 9/11, with the added constraints that it had agreed to upon the acquisition of CP Air in 2000.

Air Canada published a reorganisation plan in July 2004, and emerged from bankruptcy protection at the end of September 2004. The airline became a subsidiary of ACE Aviation Holdings. Deutsche Bank and other creditors had 88 per cent of the shares in this holding company, Cerberus Capital Management 9.2 per cent, and the balance for management. To comply with foreign ownership restrictions, some owners received a higher percentage of voting shares.

12.2 Latin America

At the end of 2004, there were six Latin American airlines close to bankruptcy: Aerolineas Argentinas, VASP and Varig in Brazil, Avianca and Intercontinental in Colombia, and Nuevo Continente in Peru. Avianca had been in US Chapter 11 since March 2003, but emerged after the court approved a restructuring plan that involved a Brazilian company investing US$63 million for a 75 per cent controlling interest. The Brazilian Government is unlikely to let Varig go under, but the fate of the other three is less assured.[5]

---

5 *Airline Business*, December (2004).

The Argentinian national carrier had filed for bankruptcy protection in mid-2001, and was later acquired by a Spanish consortium that included a Spanish tour company and Spanair. Its restructuring plan was approved in December 2002. By the end of 2004, it was expected to emerge from bankruptcy protection, with the Spanish owners planning to sell 45 per cent of the equity to the public through an IPO.

12.3   Europe

In Europe, a Chapter 11 equivalent does not exist. The closest to this is the UK's 'administration' where a court appoints an administrator to run the business, usually a firm of accountants. It thus differs significantly from Chapter 11 in the US where the existing management may stay in place. Assets may be sold, but the aim is to save at least part as a going concern.

An example of a UK airline going into administration was Air Europe, or its parent tour operator, International Leisure Group (ILG). This occurred in March 1991, after considerable effort had been expended in trying to get new investors. ILG's bankruptcy was precipitated by the bankruptcy in Switzerland of one of ILG's major shareholders (Omni Group), and Citigroup's (one of the major creditors') desire to repossess and sell the aircraft on which it had secured its lending. Once in 'administration' ILG's tour operator bond of £63 million was called in to repatriate holidaymakers stranded abroad, and at that stage continued operations were not possible. Because of this, it was suggested that there was an overwhelming case for Chapter 11 type of protection to enable a more rational outcome to be obtained.[6]

In Germany, many equity shareholders are the major commercial banks. These try to avoid bankruptcies of their associates or subsidiaries by appointing new management. This gives it a chance to survive, by rationalisation or selling poorly performing assets, with bankruptcy as the last resort.

An example of this was the demise of German charter carrier, Aero Lloyd in October 2003. Bayerischer Landesbank owned 66 per cent of the airline, and had been trying sell it to a strategic investor. Once it decided to stop funding the ailing carrier, an insolvency administrator was appointed by a German court. At that point the re-emergence of a much slimmed-down airline, operating only 12 aircraft with half the number of employees, was possible. However, in spite of some additional funding from the Bavarian bank, nothing came of this plan, and the airline was broken up.

In France, a company that stops paying creditors must declare bankruptcy, and a court appoints officials to help management (usually the existing team) draw up a rationalisation plan. This procedure is similar to Chapter 11, but has a time limit of 18 months for the process to be completed. If not, liquidation takes place.

One of the larger French airline bankruptcies was Air Liberté, which finally stopped operations for good in January 2003. It had filed for bankruptcy in June 2001, about a year after British Airways had sold the airline to Taitbout Antibes, and it had been combined with SAir Group owned Air Littoral and Air Outre-Mer

---

6   *Avmark Aviation Economist*, (March/April 1991), p. 9.

(AOM), to try to give it a better chance of survival. The then still solvent SAir had a 49.5 per cent stake in the new airline group, and had agreed to inject a further $175 million. easyJet had been interested in buying the airline and its slots at Paris Orly Airport, but was deterred by the level of the company's debts. It was finally kept going by a French Government loan.

SAir Group filed for protection from creditors in October 2001 after two of its largest lenders, UBS and Swiss Bank decided not to extend further loans to the group. By the beginning of December, all main airline leasing and operating companies were granted further protection to allow Crossair to take over a substantial part of Swissair's airline operations. This deal was made possible by financial support from the Swiss Government, which in turn had persuaded some of the largest Swiss corporations to lend to the new national carrier.

The collapse of SAir Group also caused the bankruptcy of the Belgian national carrier, Sabena, in which the Swiss airline had a 49 per cent, and effective control. This occurred at the beginning of November 2001, and resulted in the saving of only a small part of Sabena's operations. These were limited to regional and some intra-EU trunk routes that were sold to a new airline, SN Brussels that acquired Sabena's regional subsidiary, DAT.

Alitalia, a major state-owned EU carrier, has been close to bankruptcy on a number of occasions between 1997 and 2004. The Italian Government has continued to inject new capital into the airline to keep it going, while at the same time trying to prevent the EU competition authorities in Brussels from imposing restrictions on it.

In this respect, the European Commission decided to approve in 1995 the major capital injection of Lira 2,750 billion subject to 10 conditions. One of those was:

> Until 31 December 2000 Alitalia shall refrain from offering fares lower than those offered by its competitors for equivalent services supplied on the routes which it operates.
> *(OJ L322/44, Article 1, paragraph 7, European Commission, 25 November 1997)*

In approving a further tranche of state aid to Alitalia (Lira 500 billion), the Commission noted in June 1998 that two conditions imposed in the 1997 decision had not been met. One was the requirement that Alitalia did not engage in price leadership. The Commission did not see this as an obstacle to the further subsidy being paid, given the Italian Government promise that 'Alitalia had discontinued its promotional campaigns (involving low-price tickets) within the European Economic Area and reverted to the basic fare structure.'

However, the Italian authorities presented yet another restructuring plan for Alitalia to the Commission in October 2004. This was soon followed by a complaint from eight European airlines to the Commission on Alitalia's current plan to cut fares while expanding capacity.

The privately owned Italian airline, Volare, went bankrupt in December 2004, after the Italian Government had appointed an administrator to try to rescue the airline. A plan was submitted to the aviation authority, but lack of financing resulted in the withdrawal of their license.[7]

---

7   *Aviation Strategy*, (November 2004).

12.4 Australasia

Most of the flag carriers in Asia are still majority owned by their national governments, and thus not likely to be allowed to go bankrupt. Some smaller, privately owned airlines have over the years gone into liquidation: a number of Thai airlines, notably Air Siam, and many small carriers in Indonesia have gone out of business over the years.

In Japan, equity holders and employees tend to have priority, and informal rescues rather than court-administered bankruptcies tend to be most common. All of the three new entrants have been bankrupt or close to it, but all have continued operating as a result of various rescue packages: Skymark received a large capital injection, Air Do was supported by All Nippon Airways and Skynet Asia went into a type of 'Chapter 11'.

Few Asian countries have the procedures for restructuring ailing airlines that North America and Europe do, and creditors tend to have limited rights. Creditors with liens over aircraft have a better chance of re-possession if their aircraft are operated internationally, rather than solely on domestic flights. Steps can more easily be taken to seize aircraft when parked at foreign airports, where legal enforcement of rights is easier.

The most prominent airline bankruptcy in Asia was that of Philippine Airlines (PAL), whose finances deteriorated fast after the 1997 Asian financial crisis. By mid-1998, PAL had debts of over US$2 billion, around half involving US and EU export credit agencies. The airline went into receivership following a pilots' strike in June 1998. A rehabilitation plan was only approved by the country's Securities Exchange Commission in May 1999. This involved a two-year management contract with Lufthansa Consulting, and the dilution of majority owner Lucio Tan's stake from 70 per cent to 54 per cent. Before this approval, the US Exim bank had threatened to re-possess the four B747-400s that were the security for its loans, because the plan did not have the required approval of more than two-thirds of creditors.

In Australia, the long-established airline, Ansett was placed in voluntary administration by its owners (Air New Zealand) on 12 September 2001 (one day after 9/11), and finally ceased operating in March 2002. Some regional subsidiary airlines continued to operate for a while, but assets were gradually sold off over that year (including their Sydney Airport terminal to the airport owners). The proceeds of the sale of assets went to the secured creditors. Creditors had previously voted against liquidation, give the state of the industry at that time. Any such 'fire-sales' would have been at very low prices.

Australia deregulated its domestic market in 1990, which was followed by the entry of Compass Airlines. After about one year's operation they failed to find new equity and a receiver was called in. Regional airline, Impulse, started trunk operations in 2000, but also went out of business in May 2001 after institutional investors withdrew support. Qantas then took over the airline.

The background to Ansett is interesting in that it explains one of the factors behind the bankruptcy of the New Zealand national carrier, which owned 100 per cent of Ansett at the time of its demise. Air New Zealand had purchased 50 per cent of Ansett from TNT Corporation which jointly owned the Australian domestic carrier alongside News Ltd. Singapore Airlines later tried to buy the 50 per cent stake held by News Ltd, but Air New Zealand exercised its pre-emption right and took 100 per cent control. Singapore Airlines subsequently bought 25 per cent of Air New Zealand.

Following the bankruptcy of Ansett, Air New Zealand came under financial pressure, and trading in its shares was suspended on a number of occasions over the following two months. Its future was assured, however, when the New Zealand government injected NZ$885 million (about US$370 million) into the airline in new equity and convertible stock. This was carried out on 18 January 2002, giving the government 74 per cent of the ordinary stock and 82 per cent of the voting rights. Singapore Airlines' stake was reduced from 24.99 per cent on 31 August 2001 to 6.47 per cent in August 2003. The OECD's report on the New Zealand economy in 2002[8] urged the government to sell its shares in the national airline to focus funds on 'higher social priorities'. The government has announced its commitment to do this, but had not done so by August 2004.

12.5 Summary

Airlines that are close to liquidation do not often lack suitors to acquire part or all of its assets, or take control to implement a survival plan. This often occurs without the necessity to file for Chapter 11 or receivership. In the US, a Chapter 11 filing, or even a threat of this often acts as a catalyst to new agreements by employees and suppliers. Chapter 11 in North America favours existing management, and has been criticised for allowing airlines that have no hope of longer term survival to compete, possibly unfairly, with existing carriers, although there is scant evidence of this.

In Europe, 'administration' hands over the day-to-day management to an independent individual or firm that is appointed by the court. Their remit is to get the best deal for creditors and shareholders: this may be achieved by continued operation of the airline, but this is probably more difficult than in Chapter 11. The administrator is often faced by loss of confidence by one or more major secured creditor, in addition to loss of potential customers and continued cash flow crises. In some cases, the aviation authority withdraws the airline's operating license to prevent further market disruption.

All bankruptcies lead to the significant dilution of the interests of the existing equity holders. Usually, a sizeable part of the outside creditors will be banks and lessors with security over one or more aircraft. This may suggest a lower likelihood of reorganisation and continued operations. In fact, airline financial problems also tend to coincide with a very depressed market for used aircraft sales. This means that secured debtors would prefer that the aircraft is kept in service with the ailing airline and generating some revenue, rather than them incurring the risks and costs of re-possession and sale or re-lease.

8   *Economic Survey of New Zealand 2002*, OECD, May 2002.

Unsecured creditors will be suppliers of airport, ATC and fuel services, passengers and shippers with paid-for tickets and others. Airports often force settlement of outstanding debts by blocking an aircraft of the airline in question if it has landed at its airport. ATC authorities also have similar powers to prevent an aircraft from taking off until its debts have been paid. Other unsecured creditors are not so lucky, although they may be able to vote on a proposed re-organisation plan. With the growing popularity of frequent flyer membership, there may be millions of unsecured creditors who have earned miles but not yet redeemed them. It would be impossible to include all of these in any re-organisation process.

Chapter 13

Industry Financial Prospects

Just as the industry experiences cycles in past financial performance, so does the optimism of forecasters and commentators oscillate even more widely. This depends on where in the cycle the predictions are made. In the midst of the early 1980s downturn dire predictions were being made on the ability of the industry to finance expected growth. A similar prognosis was being offered in the early 1990s, but before the forecasters have decided to make downward adjustments in their demand forecasts, traffic had picked up and profitability had returned to the industry. IATA were then in a better position to issue dire warnings of impending constraints from the lack of airport and ATC capacity.[1] As Chapter 1 has shown signs started to appear in 2000 and 2001 that another industry downturn was beginning, although opinions varied as to the depth and length of the impending recession. The terrorist attacks of 9/11 converted the downturn into a major slump, the consequences of which were obviously very severe in the US, but also spread to other world regions. The recovery took place over the period 2002–2006, against a background of buoyant demand. By 2006, some regions had only just regained traffic levels experienced in the 1999/2000 peak, but by then airlines had to contend with an era of persistently high fuel prices.

This chapter will take as a starting point the latest forecasts of air traffic, revenues and costs, as well as investment (principally aircraft) needs. A forecasting horizon of 10 years is considered as long enough into the future to include any future downturn, even though some industry forecasts extend to 20 years or more.

13.1   World Airline Traffic and Financial Forecasts

Most of the recent longer term forecasts of world air traffic are assuming average growth rates of around 5 per cent a year, with significant regional variations. These tend to be based on simple econometric models which relate traffic growth to growth in world GDP. In this respect, they can only be as good as the GDP forecasts which are produced by firms such as Global Insight, Standard & Poor's, or international organisations like The World Bank. Some forecasting models also try to incorporate a fare or yield variable, given the price elastic nature of a large part of the market.

Short-term forecasts of up to five years years ahead are provided by IATA. These are generally built up from individual airline forecasts. Care needs to be taken in identifying whether the forecasts are measured in passenger-kms or in passengers (or include air cargo). The Avitas forecasts referred to in Table 13.1 are for air traffic, without specifying units of measurement. Generally, passenger-kms would

---

1   *Janes's Airport Review,* (1996), p. 9.

be expected to grow faster than passengers. There has been a gradual shift for both business and leisure travellers going further afield, and trip length has been increasing at between 0.5 and 1.0 per cent a year. This is evident in the differences between ICAO's two forecasts in Table 13.1.

Table 13.1   World air traffic and GDP forecasts

	Average annual growth rates (%)	
	Total passenger-kms	Real GDP
Airbus (2004–24)	5.3	*n/a*
Boeing (2005–25)	4.8	2.9
Rolls Royce (2004–24)	5.0	*n/a*
ICAO (2002–15)	4.4	2.5
ICAO (2002–15)*	3.5	2.5
Avitas (2004–24)	4.7	3.1

* in terms of passengers

Table 13.2 looks at the projections from the two major aircraft manufacturers in more detail. These are from forecasts published in 2005, and both are in passenger-kms for the more heavily travelled groups of routes. It can be seen that they are largely in agreement on the trans-Pacific, Europe-Asia and domestic China and USA, but Airbus are more bullish overall and especially for intra-European routes. Boeing is somewhat more optimistic on domestic USA, which has a high weight in the total world forecast. Some researchers examine domestic USA markets for signs of maturity. US traffic bounced back with 8 per cent growth domestically in 2004, slowing to 3 per cent growth the following year, and the two major manufacturers expect it to continue to grow at this rate, not much above the GDP forecast growth. Based on past trends, a rough and ready guide to air traffic growth is to assume twice the growth in GDP, with this multiplier declining to one as maturity is approached.

Table 13.2   Air traffic forecasts by region: Airbus *vs* Boeing

	Average annual growth rates (%), 2004/2005 to 2024/2025	
	Airbus	Boeing
Intra-Europe	5.0	3.4
Europe-North America	4.9	4.6
Asia-North America	6.3	6.0
Europe-Asia	5.9	5.4
Domestic USA	3.2	3.5*
Domestic China	8.7	8.8
World	5.3	4.8

* includes domestic Canada, and Canada–US

Both airports and Air Traffic Control organisations also produce long-term forecasts, some of which are published. For example, EUROCONTROL forecast IFR flights 20 years into the future, their December 2004 release giving a range of between 2.3 per cent and 3.4 per cent a year between 2004 and 2025.

Table 13.3   IATA short/medium-term forecasts

	Estimate 2005 *vs* 2004	% pa 2005 to 2009
North Atlantic	5.0	5.3
Trans-Pacific	7.4	5.8
Europe-Asia/Pacific	6.8	5.9
Europe-Middle East	8.4	6.6
Within Asia/Pacific	8.7	6.8
Within Europe	5.7	5.1
Total international	6.7	5.6Sec

The IATA forecasts in Table 13.3 were published in late 2005, and indicate strong traffic growth for all regions in 2005, especially within Asia/Pacific and between Europe and the Middle East. These two regions are also forecast to grow fastest over 2005–2009, the former due to the high growth in China and India and the latter fuelled by a number of start-up airlines based in the region.

13.2   World Airline Capital Expenditure Projections

An average of almost 90 per cent of capital expenditure by the world's airlines has historically gone towards aircraft. Future aircraft needs are derived from the above traffic forecasts by making further key assumptions on load factors, flight frequencies, aircraft utilisation, and aircraft retirements. The latter are hard to predict, given uncertainties in future fuel and maintenance costs, and whether aircraft will be modified to meet new noise and emission rules. For example, most or all aircraft such as B727-200s and B737-200s were phased out by 2002, the year in which these aircraft did not meet the noise standards without expensive hushkitting or re-engining. Assumptions on the future degree of hubbing and passenger transfers are also required, with point-to-point services recently boosting traffic in many world regions. Boeing see a relative decline in hubbing with more hub by-pass flights, while Airbus are more optimistic on hubs. The Boeing argument rests on passenger preference for non-stop flights and increasing hub congestion; the Airbus view is supported by the economics of hubs and concentration of population in Asia with few secondary airports.

Table 13.4 focuses on aircraft deliveries and retirements and reflects the differing philosophies of the major manufacturers. The retirement figures may vary insofar as they include or exclude aircraft that are in storage and never expected to return to airline service. Boeing's view is of a higher rate of deliveries and also a greater number of retirements a year, the lower average price per delivery indicating higher turnover and demand of smaller capacity aircraft. Rolls-Royce is closer to the Boeing forecast and is probably more optimistic at the regional jet end of the spectrum.

Table 13.4   Commercial jet aircraft delivery/retirement forecasts

	Deliveries per year	Retirements per year	Investment per aircraft/year (million)
Rolls-Royce (2004–2024)	1,395	637	$69.1
Boeing (2005–2024)	1,285	467	$81.7
Airbus (2004–2024)	866	215	$109.6

Embraer forecasts jet deliveries for aircraft of seating capacity between 30 and 120 seats: they expect deliveries of these aircraft to average just under 400 a year between 2005 and 2025, at an average value of US$45 million per aircraft.

The volume of retirements started to increase again at the end of the 1990s, reaching over 300 aircraft in 1998, although some of these were to be converted into freighters. Both Rolls-Royce and Boeing expect retirements to increase in the future.

Deliveries of jet aircraft hit a low of 486 in 1995 and climbed back to 1,200 in 2001, with investment banks forecasting a continuation of this trend to 1,400 in 2003, before turning down again. The delivery forecasts in Table 13.4 obviously include two complete cycles, but there is still a marked difference in manufacturer predictions.

One of the key differences in the last downturn is the increased dependence of the manufacturers on the operating lessors. Thus, for the firm orders outstanding in the first quarter 2001, 38.8 per cent of Airbus's 1,016 aircraft backlog was accounted for by operating lessors (and 31 per cent at that time unplaced with airlines). For Boeing the position was slightly better with 30.6 per cent of its 1,084 aircraft backlog, with 22 per cent unplaced.[2]

13.3   World Airline Financial Requirement Forecasts

If the major aircraft manufacturer forecasts discussed above turn out to be accurate, there will be a need for between US$1.9 trillion (Airbus) and US$2.1 trillion (Boeing) to finance the cost of the aircraft over the next 20 years, both at 2004 prices. This amounts to around $100 billion a year, and looks large in comparison with 2004 cash generated by the world's airlines from internal sources of only $16 billion (see the beginning of Chapter 5). However, 2004 was not a good year for the airlines, with many North American airlines struggling to be cash positive.

---

2   *European Aviation Review* 3, J P Morgan Securities Ltd, Equity Research (12 June 2001).

Boeing give a detailed breakdown of forecast aircraft demand by region over the 20 years to 2024 (Table 13.5). This shows the continued dominance of North America, Europe and Asia, but with demand in Asia for larger more expensive aircraft.

Table 13.5   Boeing airplane demand by region (2004–2023)

Region of airline	Aircraft	Value US$ billion	Average value per aircraft ($m)
North America	8,799	585	66
Europe	6,695	527	79
Asia Pacific	7,163	769	107
Latin America	1,743	98	56
Middle East	869	115	132
Africa	425	34	80
Total/average	25,694	2,128	83

Source: Boeing Current Market Outlook, 2005

Included in Boeing's projection of 7,163 aircraft for the Asia/Pacific region is a demand for 2,612 aircraft from China, valued at $213 billion in 2,004 dollars. This gives an average of $82 million per aircraft, lower than the Asia/Pacific average due to the need to build up regional and feeder routes with smaller aircraft.

Airbus gives the top 10 end-user nations in their overall forecast of $1.9 trillion passenger and cargo aircraft demand over 2004–2023. The US is top with $412.7 billion worth of passenger aircraft, followed by China with $241.7 billion and the UK with $119.2 billion. Single aisle and small jets account for 40 per cent of total delivered value, 25 per cent for intermediate and long-range twins, large aircraft 22 per cent and small twin aisle and regional aircraft 13 per cent.[3]

Boeing's prediction in 1993 of a large decline in Japanese involvement in future aircraft financing now seems to have been somewhat of an overreaction to the early 1990s Japanese withdrawal. However, the withdrawal of the JLL in the late 1990s left a gap the Japanese Operating Lease (JOL) has not completely filled. JLL had financed up to $12 billion of aircraft a year, whereas the JOL so far only accounts for $2-3 billion a year (see Section 10.3). Equity issues have probably played a more important role than anticipated, as airlines have been privatised and free to raise this type of capital which their owners had been unable to provide in the past. New entrants have also raised equity, both in North America and in Europe, with an increasing number of venture capital firms looking for business. This might be an even greater source of funds in the future, following the collapse of the dot.com bubble, although continued regulatory and ownership restrictions limit the number of such possibilities.

---

3   Airbus (2005), *Global Market Forecast* 2004–2023.

Public debt has certainly been more important in aircraft financing in the US, principally through the EETCs. For the rest of the world, public debt has been channelled into aircraft finance via the operating lessors. The Boeing forecast was probably wrong on the negligible role of US banks, and certainly on the Japanese Banks.

Export credits still play a large part, in conjunction with bank lending, providing at least $10-15 billion in finance a year. In the longer term, there could well be the *exit* from the industry of some of the household name airlines, as financiers and investors become more selective, and variations in the cost of capital between good and bad risk airlines becomes greater. It will also be interesting to see whether foreign ownership restrictions will be removed, and international mergers and acquisitions allowed. The further growth of the operating lessor sector is also expected by some observers, although aircraft manufacturers view such a trend with some concern.

In the longer term, aircraft orders will adjust to a level that can attract the necessary finance at a price that allows a reasonable return to be made to aircraft owners. Such adjustment may be painful both to existing airlines and lessors that have over-ordered aircraft, but it will also mean many start-up airlines will not attract the necessary finance to satisfy licensing authorities.

Bibliography

AAE (1990), Pan Am: What Will it Sell Next?, *The Avmark Aviation Economist*, 7(3), April, Avmark International, London, pp. 2–4.

Allegis Corporation (1988), *Addressing Airline Issues, 1987 Annual Report*, Chicago.

Airbus (2005), *Global Market Forecast 2004–2023*, Airbus S.A.S., Toulouse.

Air Carrier Fitness Division (2002), *How to Become a Certificated Air Carrier*, Office of the Secretary, US Department of Transportation, 202-366-9721.

Air Transport Association of America (2004), *ATA's Response in Unisys*, R2A Scorecard, 2(11), September, p. 5.

Ashcroft, Robert (2005) *A Powerful Force in Commercial Aviation*, UBS Investment Research Q-Series, UBS, New York.

Ashworth, M. and Forsythe, P. (1984), *Civil Aviation Policy and the Privatisation of British Airways*, Institute for Fiscal Studies, London.

Atrill, P. and McLaney, E. (1995), *Accounting and Finance for Non-Specialists*, Prentice-Hall, London.

Barker, A., Ross, T. and Wood, S. (1996), *Airline Valuation Guide*, September, SBC Warburg, London.

Barla, P. and Koo, B. (1999), Bankruptcy Protection and Pricing Strategies in the US Airline Industry, *Transportation Research*, E 35, pp. 101–120.

Baur, U. and Kistner, D. (1999), Airline Privatisation Principles and Lessons Learned, in *Handbook of Airline Finance*, eds Butler and Keller, pp. 71–90.

Bilson, J. (1992), Managing Economic Exposure to Foreign Exchange Risk: A Case Study of American Airlines, in *Stocks and currencies, The Economist*, 6 June, p. 113.

Boeing Commercial Airplane, Co., (1996), *Current Market Outlook*, Boeing, Seattle.

Borenstein, A. and Rose, N. (1995), Bankruptcy and Pricing in US Airline Markets, *American Economic Review*, 85, No. 3, pp. 415–435.

British Airways (1987), *Offer for Sale on Behalf of the Secretary of State for Transport*, Hill Samuel & Co. Ltd, January.

British Airways (2003), *Memorandum and Articles of Association*, website as at 15 July, www.bashares.com.

Butler, G.F. and Keller, M.R., eds, (1999), *Handbook of Airline Finance*, Aviation Week (McGraw-Hill), New York.

CAA (1984), *Airline Competition Policy*, CAP500, Civil Aviation Authority, London.

Chang, Y-C *et al.* (2004), The evolution of airline ownership and control provisions, *Journal of Air Transport Management* 10, pp. 161–172.

Clark, P. (2001), *Buying the Big Jets: Fleet Planning for Airlines*, Aldershot: Ashgate Publishing.

Commission of the European Communities (2001), *Proposal for a Regulation of the European Parliament and of the Council amending. Council Regulation (EEC) No. 95/93 of 18 January 1993 on common rules for the allocation of slots at Community airports. COM(2001)335*, Brussels, 20 June.

Cranfield University (1996), *Single Market, Review 1996 – Air Transport*, Department of Air Transport, European Commission.

Creaton, S. (2004), *Ryanair: How a Small Irish Airline Conquered Europe*, Aurum Press, London.

Cunningham, L.F., Slovin, M.B., Wood, W.R. and Zaima, J.K. (1988), Systematic Risk in the Deregulated Airline Industry, *Journal of Transport Economics and Policy*, 22(3), pp. 345–353.

Dahiya, S., John, K., Puri, M. and Ramirez, G. (2003), Debtor-in-possession Financing and Bankruptcy Resolution: Empirical Evidence, *Journal of Financial Economics*, 69, pp. 259–280.

Darryl, A., ed. (2002), *Handbook of Airline Economics*, 2nd edn, Aviation Week, McGraw-Hill, New York.

de Wit, J. and Burghouwt, G. (2005), *Strategies of Multi-Hub Airlines and the Implications for National Aviation Policies*, AirNeth Workshop Report, The Hague.

Dixon, R. (1994), *Investment Appraisal: A Guide for Managers*, revised edn, The Chartered Institute of Management Accountants, Kogan Page, London.

Doganis, R. (2001), *The Airline Business in the 21st Century*, Routledge, London.

Doganis, R. (2002), *Flying off Course: The Economics of International Airlines*, 3rd edn, Routledge, London.

Endres, G. (2006), Surrogate supply, *Airline Business*, 22(7), July, pp. 56–58.

Expanding Horizons, A Report by the Comité des Sages for Air Transport to the European Commission, (1994), pp. 29–31.

European Investment Bank (2004), *Evaluation of EIB Financing of Airlines: A Synthesis Report*, European Investment Bank, Luxembourg.

Feldman, J. (1993), The Eagle Has Landed, *Air Transport World*, December, p. 44.

Fisher, F.M. (1987), Pan-American to United: the Pacific Division Transfer Case, *Rand Journal of Economics*, 18(4), pp. 492–508.

Foley, M.A. (1989), *Impact of Operating Lessors on Aircraft Demand*, Paper delivered at 1989 Geneva Forum, 17 February 1989.

Gates, W. (1996), *The Road Ahead*, revised edn, Penguin, London.

Gibson, W. and Morrell, P. (2005), *Airline Finance and Aircraft Evaluation: Evidence from the Field*, Paper to ATRS World Conference, Rio de Janeiro, July 2005.

Haanappel, P.P.C. (1994), Airport Slots and Market Access: Some Basic Notions and Solutions, *Air and Space Law*, XIX, No. 4/5, pp. 198–199.

Hai, N. (1994), *An Evaluation of Scheduled Airline Traffic Rights*, MSc thesis: Cranfield University, England.

Hall, S., ed. (1989), *Aircraft Financing*, Euromoney Publications, London.

Holloway, S. (1992), *Aircraft Acquisition Finance*, Pitman, London.

Holmes, G. and Sugden, A. (2004), *Interpreting Company Reports and Accounts, Woodhead-Faulkner*, Hemel Hempstead, UK, ninth edn.

Howard, B. (1982), The Iron Lady at DOT, *Forbes*, 7 June.

HSBC James Capel (1996), *British Airways: Selling Slot(s),* November, pp. 31–33.

IATA (1982), *Airline Needs and Sources of Capital,* IATA Financial and Economic Studies Sub-Committee, Geneva.

IATA (1994), *Airline Accounting Guideline No. 1: Explanatory foreword and translation of long-term foreign currency borrowings*, Exposure Draft, in association with KPMG Peat Marwick, August.

IATA (2006), *World Air Transport Statistics*, International Air Transport Association, Geneva.

ICAO (1996), *The World of Civil Aviation, 1995–1998*, Circular 265, Montreal.

ICAO (2004), *Outlook for Air Transport to the Year 2015*, Circular 304 AT/127, Montreal.

ICAO (2005), *The World of Civil Aviation, 2003–2006*, Circular307-AT/129, Montreal.

ILO (1991), *How to Read a Balance Sheet*, Geneva: International Labour Office, 2nd (Revised Edition).

International Lease Finance Corporation, SEC, Form 10-K Filing for Fiscal Year Ended December 31, 2000.

Jet Finance S.A. (1995), *Analysis of the comparative ability of the European airline industry to finance investments*, a report prepared for the Commission of the European Communities, June.

Jet Fuel Intelligence (2005), New Asian Carriers View Hedging as two-Edged Sword, *Energy Intelligence*, XV, No. 6, February, 1–3.

Key, S.L., ed. (1989), *The Ernst and Young Guide to Mergers and Acquisitions*, John Wiley & Sons, New York.

KPMG/IAAIA (1994), *Airline Internal Audit*, KPMG in association with the International Association of Airline Internal Auditors, November, London.

KPMG/IATA (1992), *Accounting Policies, Disclosure and Financial Trends in the International Airline Industry*, International Air Transport Association, August, Geneva.

KPMG/IATA (1995), *Strategic Issues and Current Trends in the International Airline Industry*, KPMG, London.

Littlejohns, A. and McGairl, S. (1998), *Aircraft Financing*, third edn, Euromoney Publications, London.

Mandall, R. (1979), *Financing Capital Requirements of the US Airline Industry in the 1980s*, Lexington Books, D.C. Heath & Co, Lexington, Massachusetts, USA.

Margo, R. (1996) Aircraft Leasing: The Airline's Objectives, *Air and Space Law*, XXI, No. 4/5, pp. 166–174.

McKenzie, W. (1998), *The Financial Times Guide to Using and Interpreting Company Accounts*, Second Edition, FT Prentice Hall, London.

McMillan, B. (2000), *Air Madagascar Sale Back on Track after Bank Default*, Air Transport Intelligence, accessed 30 March, www.rati.com.

Meldrun, A. (2001), *Financing Start-up Airlines: Private Equity*, presentation to Airline Finance course at Cranfield University, 1 March, England.

Miller, K. (1993), *Air Finance for Eastern Europe*, MSc thesis: Cranfield University, England.

Milne, I.R. (2005), *Debt burden*, from Bridging the GAAP, *Airline Business*, February, pp. 54–56.

Morrell, P. and Turner, S. (2003), 'An Evaluation of Airline Beta Values and their

Application in Calculating the Cost of Equity Capital', in *Journal of Air Transport Management*, **9**(4), pp. 201–209.

Morrison, S. and Winston, C. (1995), *The Evolution of the Airline Industry*, The Brookings Institution, Washington, DC, USA.

NatWest Securities (1996), *Strategic Assessment of British Airways*, January, NatWest Securities Ltd, London.

Official Journal of the European Communities, No. L.240, 24 August 1992.

Peters, T.J. and Waterman, R.H., Jr (1982), *In Search of Excellence: Lessons from America's Best-run Companies*, Harper & Row, New York.

Qantas Airways Ltd (1995), *Offering Memorandum for 750 million Ordinary Shares*, 22 June.

Radley, A.B. (1994), *Future Strategies in Aircraft Leasing*, MSc thesis: Cranfield University, September, England.

Reed, Arthur, (1990), *Airline: The Inside Story of British Airways*, BBC Books, London, pp. 47–48.

Reid, W. and Myddelton, D.R. (2005), *The Meaning of Company Accounts*, 8th edn, Aldershot: Gower Publishing.

Rosenberg, B. and Guy, J. (1976), *Prediction of βs from Investment Fundamentals*, *Financial Analysts Journal*, 32(4), pp. 62–70.

Symonds, J.P. (1991), *Aircraft Finance: A Study of Future Supply and Demand*, MSc thesis: Cranfield University, England.

Taneja, N.K. (1982), *Airline Planning: Corporate, Financial and Marketing*, Lexington Books, D.C. Heath & Co, Lexington, Massachusetts, USA.

Transportation Research Board (1991), *Winds of Change: Domestic Air Transport Since Deregulation*, National Research Council, Washington, DC, USA.

TravelTechnics Ltd (1992), *A Failed Partnership: Factors Contributing to Failures in the US Airline Industry*, for International Institute for Tourism Studies, October.

Verchère, I. (1994), *The Air Transport Industry in Crisis*, Chapter 8, pp. 105–121, EIU Publishing, London.

Walsh, C. (1997), *Key Management Ratios: How to Analyze, Compare and Control the Figures that Drive Company Value*, FT Prentice Hall, London.

Weiss, L.A. and Wruck, K.H. (1998), Information Problems, Conflicts of Interest, and Asset Stripping, Chapter 11's Failure in the Case of Eastern Airlines, *Journal of Financial Economics*, 45, pp. 55–97.

Wells, A.T. (2003), *Air Transportation: A Management Perspective*, Brooks/Cole, Belmont, fifth edn, California, USA.

Glossary of Terms

Accelerated depreciation	A rate of depreciation higher than the normal rate, generally for tax purposes.
Accounting concepts	The basic assumptions underlying the preparation of accounts, including 'going concern', 'accruals', 'consistency' and 'prudence'.
Accounting policies	The specific accounting bases judged by the business to be most appropriate to its circumstances and therefore adopted in the preparation of its accounts, *e.g.*, of the various methods of accounting for depreciation, the policy adopted may be to depreciate plant over a five-year period.
Accounting records	The 'books' in which a business records the transactions it has entered into. For companies, minimum standards of accounting records are required by law.
Accrual	An expense or a proportion thereof not invoiced before the balance sheet date but included in the accounts − sometimes on an estimated basis.
Accruals concept	Income and expenses are recognised in the period in which they are earned or incurred, rather than the period in which they happen to be received or paid.
Advance corporation tax	The tax a company is required to pay (at the basic income tax) rate when it makes a distribution. The amount paid can be subsequently set off against the company's corporation tax liability for that year.
American Depositary Receipt (ADR) or Share (ADS)	Certificates issued by a US depository bank, representing foreign shares held by the bank, usually by a branch or correspondent in the country of issue. One ADS may represent a portion of a foreign share, one share or a bundle of shares of a foreign corporation. ADS are subject to the same currency, political, and economic risks as the underlying foreign share.

Amortisation	An estimate of the proportion of the cost of an intangible fixed asset which has been consumed. Also the reduction in loan outstandings in accordance with an agreed repayment schedule.
Asset	Any property or rights owned by the company that have a monetary value.
Asset-based financing	A form of financing in which the risk is related to the value of the equipment, rather than the company.
Associated company	*See* Related company.
Balance sheet	A statement describing the financial position of a business at a particular date.
Balloon payment	A payment which follows a series of lower periodic rentals paid over the term of the lease. Although normally paid at the end of the lease period, balloon payments may also occur during the lease term.
Bank settlement plan (BSP)	Agreement between airlines and travel agents, whereby all air ticket issue and settlements within a particular country are handled by a 'clearing bank'. Although BSPs are established through the IATA mechanism, they are not to be confused with the IATA clearing house for settling inter-airline accounts in different currencies.
Basis point	One basis point is one-hundredth of 1 per cent.
Bond	Documentary promise to repay long-term borrowed money with interest at a definite or determinable future date (usually issued by larger firms with a public listing).
Call option	An option to purchase an asset at a set price at a particular future date.
Cape Town Treaty	The Cape Town Convention on international interests in mobile equipment; signed in Cape Town in November 2001. This is an international registry for security rights in aircraft, aircraft engines and helicopters that will reduce the risks of lending for aircraft financiers, and thus reduce the cost of credit.

Capital allowance	An allowance against profits given for tax purposes in respect of expenditure on fixed assets during the period.
Capital assets	Assets acquired with the expectation that they will remain in service for a number of accounting periods.
Capital costs	Depreciation and interest on capital investment.
Capital employed	The aggregate amount of long-term funds invested in or lent to the business and used by it in carrying out its operations.
Capital lease	A lease which transfers substantially all the risks and benefits of ownership of the leased equipment to the lessee.
Capitalisation	The treatment of costs as assets to be included in the balance sheet rather than as expenses to be written off in the profit and loss account.
Cash flow	In company accounts, a statement of cash balances based on estimated cash inflows and outflows over a given period. In cost-benefit analysis or investment appraisal, the anticipated net benefit or cash stream for a project.
Cash Value Added (CVA)	An economic measure of profit which takes into account the economic cost of capital; provides a better measure of shareholder value than accounting profits.
Consistency concept	The requirements that once an accounting policy for a particular item in the accounts has been adopted the same policy should be used from one period to the next. Any change in policy must be fully disclosed.
Consolidation	Method of combining the accounts of a group of companies into one balance sheet and profit and loss account for the group as a whole.
Contingent liability	A liability dependent upon the outcome of a future event.
Costs of goods sold	Those costs (usually raw materials, labour and production overheads) directly attributed to goods that have been sold. The difference between sales and cost of goods sold gives a measure of gross profit.

Creditors	Amounts due to those who have supplied goods or services to the business.
Cross-border lease	A lease in which the lessor and lessee are in different countries or different legal systems.
Current asset	An asset which, if not already in cash form, is expected to be converted into cash within 12 months of the balance sheet date.
Current cost convention	A basis of accounting under which revenue is compared with the current (rather than the historic) cost of resources used up in earning it in and assets are stated in the balance sheet at their current value to the business (usually equivalent to net current replacement cost).
Current liability	An amount owed which will have to be paid within 12 months of the balance sheet date or money received in advance of carriage.
Current ratio	The comparison between current assets and current liabilities in a balance sheet, providing a measure of business liquidity.
Debentures	Long-term loans, usually secured on the company's assets.
Debt	A form of financing where the borrower pays interest at an agreed rate and is liable to repay the principal by an agreed date.
Debt/equity ratio	A measure of the financial structure of a firm which is used in assessment of financial risk.
Debtors	Amounts due from customers to whom goods or services have been sold but for which they have not yet paid.
Default	An event defined in a lease agreement, such as failure to pay rent or perform some obligation required under the terms of a lease.
Defeasance	A situation where the lessee borrows at one rate and deposits at a higher rate, with the deposit used to fulfil the rental obligations in the lease. Since the deposit is at a higher rate, the sum deposited is less than the total borrowed-financed amount and the lessee obtains an up-front cash benefit which can be used to increase the net present value benefit of the transaction.
Deferred asset/liability	An amount receivable or payable more than 12 months after the balance sheet date.

Deferred taxation	An estimate of a tax liability payable at some estimated future date, resulting from timing differences in the taxation and accounting treatment of certain items of income and expenditure.
Depreciation	An estimate of the proportion of the cost of a tangible fixed asset which has been consumed (whether through use, obsolescence or the passage of time) during the accounting period.
Discounted cash flow	Technique for assessing the present value of future income and payments (cash flow) which takes into account the time value of money.
Distribution	The amount distributed to shareholders out of the profits of the company, usually in the form of a cash dividend.
Dividend yield	The relationship between the amount of dividend per share and the market share price of listed companies.
Dole-Pickle bill	United States legislation by which cross-border leasing was effectively abolished for that country.
Double-dip lease	A lease that takes advantage of tax and funding incentives from two sources, usually situated in two different countries.
Double entry	A system of bookkeeping whereby the amount of each transaction the business enters into is recorded in two places according to the manner in which the transaction increases or decreases any one or more of the business's assets, liabilities, capital, revenue, or expenses.
Dry lease	The lease of an aircraft without the crew.
Earnings per share	The amount of profit (after tax, but before any extraordinary items) attributable to shareholders divided by the number of Ordinary shares in issue.
Economic Value Added	Return over and above a company's average cost of capital (WACC) multiplied by market adjusted capital employed (Equity Value Added considers only equity capital).

Enterprise Value (EV)	The market value of both the equity and quoted debt securities, plus any other debt (both long and short-term) less cash, deposits and short-term loans to others, plus the present value of operating lease contracts.
Equity	A form of financing which provides a share in the ownership of an entity and on which dividends are paid out of the profits earned by the entity concerned.
Equity participation	Where the lessor or one of the group of lessors participates in a leveraged lease. Equity participants hold trust certificates to provide evidence of their beneficial interest as owners under the owner trust.
Exceptional item	Income or expenditure that, although arising from the ordinary course of business, is of such unusual size or incidence that it needs to be disclosed separately.
Expense	A cost incurred, or a proportion of a cost, the benefit of which is wholly used up in the earning of the revenue for a particular accounting period.
Export credit	A long-term sales financing with a non-payment guarantee and (optionally) interest rate support from the government of the manufacturer's country.
Extraordinary item	Any significant amount of income or expenditure arising from events outside the ordinary activities of the business and which, because of its unusual nature, needs to be separately disclosed.
Finance lease	A lease where ownership and the associated benefits and risks, are transferred to the lessee at the end of the lease period. Rentals are net to the lessor. Taxes, insurance, maintenance are the responsibility of the lessor. Rentals over the life of the lease are sufficient to cover the cost of the equipment plus a return on investment.
First loss deficiency guarantee	A guarantee given by the manufacturer on the continued value of the product.
Fixed asset	Assets held for use by the business rather than for sale.

Fixed cost	A cost that does not necessarily vary with changes in the scale of operations, *e.g.*, rent.
Forward contract	An agreement between two parties to exchange a certain underlying asset for a specified price, called the forward or exercise price, at a specified future date.
Futures contract	Similar to a forward contract, but can be traded on an exchange, which regulates the market in terms of contract specification, policing margin payments and providing a clearing house.
Gearing (Debt/Equity Ratio)	The ratio of debt to equity, usually expressed as the proportion which long-term borrowings bear to shareholders' funds.
Going concern concept	The assumption that the business will continue in operation for the foreseeable future, *i.e.*, that there is no intention to curtail or significantly reduce the scale of operations.
Goodwill	Any surplus consideration paid over and above the value of net tangible assets acquired.
Gross profit	The difference between sales and the cost of goods sold.
Group	A number of companies operating under the same controlling ownership.
Historic cost convention	The convention by which assets are valued on the basis of the original cost of acquiring or producing them.
Holding company	A company that controls another company as a result of owning more than 50 per cent of its equity share capital.
Institutional investors	Investors such as banks, insurance companies, trust funds, pension funds, foundations, educational institutions, *etc.*
Interest cover	The relationship between the amount of interest payable during a period and the amount of profit (before interest and before tax).
Internal rate of return (IRR)	The discount rate that equates a project's future net cash flows with the initial investment (or, alternatively, results in a zero net present value).

Japanese leveraged lease	A type of lease originated in Japan in 1986 by which cross-border leasing of commercial aircraft is financed through Japanese funds (equity is provided by blind pool of investors and non-recourse debt is provided by Japanese financial institutions).
LASU	Large Aircraft Sector Understanding: An agreement negotiated through OECD by the countries of the European Community and the USA in 1985, covering export sales of aircraft and helicopters, and ruling cash down payments, credit terms and fixation of interest rates.
Lease	A contract between a lessor and lessee for the right to use an asset. The ownership of the asset is retained by the lessor, but the right to use it is given to the lessee for an agreed period of time in return for a series of rentals paid by the lessee to the lessor.
Lease term	The non-cancellable period for which the lessee has contracted to lease the asset.
Lessee	The user of the equipment which is being leased.
Lessor	The owner of the equipment which is being leased.
Leveraged lease	A lease in which at least three parties are involved: a lessee, a lessor and a provider of long-term debt. The debt is a significant part of the transaction, generally without recourse to the lessor.
Liability	An amount owed.
LIBOR	London Inter-bank Offered Rate; and is usually the rate offered for either 3 month or 6 month US dollars.
Liquidity	A term used to describe the cash resources of a business and its ability to meet is short-term obligations.
Listed investments	Investments the market price for which is quoted on a recognised Stock Exchange.
Long lease	A lease with an unexpired term in excess of 50 years.

Long-term liability	An amount payable more than 12 months after the balance sheet date.
Materiality	A subjective judgement of the extent to which any amount is significant in the context of the financial position of a business as described in the balance sheet or its reported profit or loss.
Minimum lease payments	The payments over the lease term that the lessee is or can be required to make, together with any amounts guaranteed by the lessee (or related party), to the extent that it is likely that these payments will be made.
Minority interest	That part of a group's net assets owned by shareholders other than the holding company.
Net assets	The net amount of total assets less total liabilities.
Net book value	Amount at which an asset could be sold in its existing condition at the balance sheet date, after deducting any costs to be incurred in disposing of it.
Net present value (NPV)	The discounted value of future net revenues, benefits, cash flows or rental streams, allowing for the time value of money.
Nominal value	The face value of a share or other security.
Non – (or limited) recourse	Lenders places a high degree of reliance on the project, and their rights to the borrower's assets are limited.
Over-the-Counter (OTC)	The OTC market is a network of securities dealers or brokers and not an exchange. These firms make the market by posting buy and sell offers on a bulletin board. Issuers of securities traded in the OTC market do not have to comply with SEC or other exchange rules.
Operating lease	A lease where the lessor retains ownership, and the associated risks and property advantages, of the asset at the end of the lease period, which may be quite short.
Option	The right, but not obligation, to buy a specified quantity of an underlying asset at a specified price, called the strike or exercise price.
Overhead	An expense that cannot be attributed to any specific part of the company's operations.

Post balance sheet event	Any event occurring after the balance sheet date, but before the accounts are issued, which is sufficiently significant to be either reflected or noted in the accounts.
Prepayment	The part of a cost which is carried forward as an asset in the balance sheet to be recognised as an expense in the ensuing period(s) in which the benefit will be derived from it.
Price/earnings ratio	The relationship between the latest reported earnings per share and the market price per share.
Profit	The difference between the revenues earned in the period and the costs incurred in earning them. A number of alternative definitions are possible according to whether the figure is struck before or after tax, extraordinary items, distributions, *etc.*
Profit and loss account	A statement summarising the revenues earned and the costs incurred in earning them during an accounting period.
Project finance	Financing where the lender looks to the project's cash flow to repay the debt and pay interest, and to the project's assets for security.
Provision	The amount written off in the current year's profit and loss account in respect of any known or estimated loss or liability.
Prudence concept	The philosophy which says that when measuring profit provision should be made for all known or expected losses and liabilities, but that revenue should only be recognised if it is realised in the form of cash or near-cash.
Purchase option	Option to purchase the asset; bargain purchase option is an option to purchase the asset at below market value.
Put option	An option to sell an asset to another party at a set price at a particular future date.
Quick ratio	The relationship between those current assets readily convertible into cash (usually current assets less stock) and current liabilities.
Related company	A company in which the investing company holds a substantial (generally not less than 20 per cent) and long-term interest and over which it exercises significant influence.

Repossession	The act of recovering the leased asset from the company and country where it is leased.
Repossession insurance	Insurance against the inability to recover leased equipment in the event of a default (for example, non-return of an aircraft by a foreign government or inability of the lender to de-register the aircraft.)
Reserves	The accumulated amount of profit less losses, and any other surpluses, generated by the company since its incorporation and retained in it.
Residual value of an asset	Cost of an asset less any part of the cost that has been depreciated or amortised or treated as an expense or loss. (Also, the value of the leased equipment at the conclusion of the lease term.)
Revenue	Money received from selling the product of the business.
Sale-leaseback	A transaction which involves the sale of equipment by the owner and the subsequent lease of the same equipment back to the seller.
Samurai lease	Japanese-sourced lease designed to fund foreign assets in order to help to reduce the Japanese balance of payments surplus.
Sensitivity analysis	A part of financial or economic appraisal that tests the effect of various forecasting assumptions on the net present value or internal rate of return.
Share capital	Stated in the balance sheet at its nominal value and (if fully paid, and subject to any share premium) representing the amount of money introduced into the company by its shareholders at the time the shares were issued.
Shareholders' 'fund'	A measure of the shareholders' total interest in the company, represented by the total of share capital plus reserves.
Share premium	The surplus over and above nominal value received in consideration for the issue of shares.
Sub-lease	A transaction in which the leased equipment is re-leased by the original lessee to a third party, while the lease agreement between the two original parties remains in effect.

Subsidiary company	Any company in which the investing company has an interest of more than 50 per cent in the voting share capital, or otherwise is a member of it and controls the composition of its board of directors.
Syndicated loan	A loan made available by a group of banks in predefined proportions under the same credit facility.
Tax credit	The amount of tax deducted at source (at the basic rate of income tax) by a company from any dividend payment.
Timing difference	An adjustment to accounting profit in order to arrive at taxable profit which arises from the difference between the accounting and taxation treatment of certain items of income and expenditure.
Total Shareholder Return	Combination of share price performance and dividends paid over a defined period (TSR)
Turnover	Revenue from sales.
Useful life	The period of time during which an asset will have economic value and be usable. Useful life is sometimes called the economic life of the asset.
Variable cost	A cost that increases or decreases in line with changes in the level of activity.
Walkaway lease	A lease which allows the possibility for the lessee to return equipment to the manufacturer providing a short notice is given without having to make penalty payments.
Wet lease	The lease of an aircraft with crew and other back-up.
Working capital	Current assets less current liabilities, representing the amount a business needs to invest – and which is continually circulating – in order to finance its stock, debtors and work-in-progress.
Work-in-progress	Goods (or services) in the course of production (or provision) at the balance sheet date.

Sources: How to Understand and Use Company Accounts by Roy Warren; Aircraft Financing edited by Simon Hall; Guidelines for Infrastructure Development through Build-Operate-Transfer Projects; and the author

Index